HUMANITY'S BIGGEST SECRETS

Drago De Silver

ISBN: 978-0-9575495-0-0

DEDICATION

To those who wish to open their minds.

To those who have dedicated their hearts and minds
to uncover and reveal the truth.

To those who have died in the fight for truth.

For those who believe the world is not all it seems.

The Truth will set you free.

As Ignorance dies...Wisdom will arise and survive.

ABOUT THE AUTHOR

Drago De Silver obtained Bachelor's and Master's degrees from leading UK universities. He has worked in industry and travelled extensively over the globe. Since 2005 he has been fascinated with history and topics beyond the public eye. Years of research and questioning mainstream concepts have led him on the journey to write this book, to enlighten those who wish to be enlightened.

Dependent on the reader's reception of this book, he intends to continue his research to deliver weird and wonderful mystical books. This time they will be based on hidden dimensions, ancient magic, witchcraft and the possibility of a civilisation existing within the depth of the ocean floor

You look but you don't see
You hear but you don't listen.

To question is not to be disruptive.
To question is to understand the truth.

Drago De Silver

CONTENTS

INTRODUCTION

What is reality? What do you think you know? How do you know what you think you know is true? Because everyone else believes it, it must be true? Well, at one point in time, everyone 'knew' the Earth was the centre of the universe...everyone 'knew' the Earth was flat. So does that make it so? Have you seen the Earth as flat? But have you seen the Earth as round... for yourself? If not, how do you 'know' it is round? I don't expect you to demand to go to Space to see it for yourself, but it is important to be inquisitive and to keep an open mind about what is true as opposed to what you're told. Is the accepted reality a false reality? Close your eyes, take a deep breath and ask yourself: how does my intuition answer this question?

In this book, I will present a variety of topics which will give you a clear indication of the secrets of humanity. Our subconscious seems to be partially aware of these secrets. Are you one of those people who believe in the saying 'seeing is believing'? If so, I ask you:

1) When you switch on the radio, can you see the radio waves?
2) When you connect to the Internet wirelessly, can you see the Wi-Fi signals?
3) When you turn on the microwave, can you see the micro-waves heating the food?
4) During an X-ray, can you see the X-rays penetrating your body?

The answer is no.

You must, therefore, accept that there are things around you which you cannot see. A little study on the electromagnetic spectrum can aid your understanding, but simply put, our eyes can only see a tiny percentage of what is really around us. We see less than one percent of reality. Some believe the Universe to be a single infinite entity, in which many worlds and realities reside, which we can neither see nor hear. In research you may wish to conduct, you will find that the Universe seems to be infinite. You will also find there are billions of planets out there in Space and we reside on just one tiny planet. It is believed there are times when realities collide, bonding together. For example, the bonding of the physical world and the spiritual world, giving rise to entities such as ghosts. One need only study the Ouija board to discover this, although I strongly advise against this.

The aim of this book is to encourage you to ask questions about your accepted version of reality. Why is this important? Well, do you want to live life in ignorance? And how do you expect to get far in life without asking the basics such as What? Why? When? Who? How?

Do you remember the 1960's rock band which became the most commercially successful act in the history of popular music, known as The Beatles? One of the group's members, John Lennon, wrote a song called Imagine. I urge you to listen carefully to this great song. Take note of the mention of there being no Heaven, Hell, countries or religion.

1) Have you ever wondered where the terms Heaven and Hell originated? If you're now directing your thinking to a specific religion, was this the first religion to refer to Heaven and Hell? And have these definitions changed over time? What is their origin? I have noticed the term 'heavens' to be synonymous with Space.

2) No countries? Has anyone heard of Pangaea? The continents were once joined together as one enormous continent! The word Pangaea in Greek means 'all the Earth'. What separated these is said to be a drift by the sea – a theory called Continental Drift, put forward by Abraham Ortelius (Cartographer and Geographer) in 1596, and developed further by Alfred Wegener (Polar Researcher, Geophysicist and Meteorologist) in 1912.

No religion? Well, what is religion? What is considered to be the first civilisation on Earth? Did they have a religion? What was the Ancient Egyptian's name for religion? You may find the answer difficult to find. Why? Because there was no word for religion.

This book will introduce some topics which are considered to be alternative. These include things which are not part of mainstream education. Ask yourself why? I hope this book helps you to start thinking critically and researching issues on your own. Whilst reading, take on-board what you wish. If there are found to be any errors, then I apologise for these in advance.

Whatever an individual's role in society, do not be too quick to judge them, in a positive or a negative light. Everyone has the ability to think for themselves, and this is what everyone ought to do.

Finally, I hope reading this book opens your mind to alternative thinking, and therefore helps you to develop your attitude and mind-set in a positive way. Look at more angles in situations. Start to question things. To question is not to be disruptive; to question is to begin to understand the truth.

Hemos sido Tratados como borregos.

John Lennon – Imagine

PART 1
THE HUMAN POTENTIAL

ABILITY

This book is filled with weird and wonderful topics. I want to start with us – Humans. Without knowing the human potential, can you really know how far your own abilities can go? Do you truly know what men and women have succeeded at in the past, and what men and women can succeed at in the future? In my opinion, a greater human potential = a greater human imagination = a greater consideration of possibilities.

For example, without the imagination of Thomas Edison, would we have the lightbulb? Without the imagination of Nikola Tesla, would we have the radio? Imagine what you can create and how you can positively change the world if you understand your human potential.

You are intelligent. You are capable of such extraordinary things. Who do you admire? Martin Luther King? Gandhi? JFK? Michael Jackson? Well, they were human just like you. Do not describe yourself as 'normal'; describe yourself as unique. I believe we all have a gift. These people found theirs, and you can also find yours. It takes time, patience and experimentation. If you live your life in a bubble, finding yourself bored every day, then change things! Otherwise, you will remain in this bubble. Will you be happy in life?

The following words spring to mind, from two unique individuals, just like you. The world famous scientist, Albert Einstein, told us: "Insanity is doing the same thing over and over again and expecting different results." The world famous martial artist and actor, Bruce Lee, said: "There are no limits." You may be asking what place all of this has in this book. My purpose for including the above is to remind you that you as a human being are very special. Do not underestimate the importance of human activity, both past and present.

CRITICAL THINKING

Regarding the past, remember Winston Churchill's saying "history is written by the victors". I believe that life was once a balance of good and evil, and it should still be to this day. I also believe that those considered to be 'good' had no need for invading other lands, stripping others of their resources or carrying weapons of attack. I believe the 'bad' were the opposite, and therefore killed the 'good' and took over and manipulated ancient teachings. This is my belief. But, if this is true, then wouldn't that mean that history as we know it has been manipulated and written by those with 'bad' intentions – those who do not want us to know the truth? If this is the case, then why hide it from us?

If it is our history, then we are entitled to know its beginnings. History has lessons to teach us about first encounters between civilisations. The less advanced civilisation is either enslaved or exterminated. As an example, just research the Inca Empire and Francisco Pizarro Gonzalez, a Spanish conquistador. Another example is the encounter between Christopher Columbus and the indigenous peoples of the Americas.

Of the present day, ask yourself: are you aware of what really goes on around you? How do you obtain this information? How do you know this information is not filtered? Why would it be filtered? What is there to hide?

There are two famous quotations with which you may be familiar:

"History repeats itself" – Karl Marx, German Philosopher.

"If history repeats itself, and the unexpected always happens, how incapable must Man be of learning from experience?" – George Bernard Shaw, Irish Dramatist & Socialist.

Considering these, now ask yourself:

- If we don't learn from our past, how can we develop ourselves and therefore avoid repeating mistakes?
- If we don't learn from our past mistakes, how can we become successful? And how can we then help our children to be successful?
- If we don't know our history, how do we know what we're truly capable of? What was proved to be possible then? And what can be possible now?

It is my view that history is, therefore, crucial to the development of human potential. Can a healthier lifestyle create a better you? Of course it can. You don't have to be a scientist to know or to prove this. For the body, trust a mirror. For the mind, trust your intuition.

I have heard among many other things, that the pineal gland can develop our human potential. I have heard that we use a tiny fraction of our brain. How true is this? For example, if we only use around 5% of our brain, what about the remaining 95%? Is it junk? If you believe in God, which many of us do, then why would God fill the remaining portion of our heads with useless parts? Isn't the brain supposed to be one of the most important organs of our body? If we used this 95% then how powerful could we become? Aristotle, Greek Philosopher and Polymath said "Of all animals, man has the largest brain in proportion to his size." This is something for you to ponder.

Today, we have something powerful at the tips of our fingers, which no one had in the past, and which can bring immense knowledge to us in a matter of seconds! Aside from books, we have the Internet. I strongly believe the Internet will change in time. The Internet of the future may not contain such a vast array of information. Life is short, and time is of the essence, so use it wisely.

In a park, I once saw a parent ask his son where God is. The son pointed to the sky. I thought to myself, "Isn't that where extra-terrestrials are supposed to come from?"

In contrast to the above, I have heard that God is omnipresent. He is "everywhere". Consciousness/energy is also everywhere isn't it? I have seen this concept somewhere before...in the movie *Star Wars* – the power of The Force. If there is a God – in terms of an all-powerful being – and God is righteous, then why do innocent people get killed? And why does God allow wars to commence?

"The important thing is not to stop questioning. Curiosity has its own reason for existing" – Albert Einstein, Theoretical Physicist.

Porque" God is not righteous. Este dios es un enfermito sadista y sociopata que se goza y nutre del sufrimiento de nosotros los pendejos terricolas.

Humanity's Biggest Secrets

PART 2
THE FUTURISTIC PAST

DARWIN'S THEORY OF EVOLUTION

Mankind came out of the Dark Ages and the Middle Ages, reached the Age of Enlightenment, experienced the Industrial Revolution, and entered into an era of advanced technology: the era of genetic engineering, the era of space flight. Yet, according to Charles Darwin, we came from apes, didn't we?

We will now take a journey to unravel the meaning behind the title of this chapter, The Futuristic Past.

"Truth is stranger than fiction"
– Mark Twain, American Author and Humourist.

I'm sure everyone has heard of Charles Darwin. He was the 19th Century Naturalist who famously wrote *On the Origin of Species*. In this book he proposed his theory of Evolution. Much of the general public had been taught that his theory was indeed fact. Darwin's theory of evolution explains how different species have evolved from simple life forms over time. It says that from over 3 billion years ago, the first bacteria (prokaryotes) evolved into another form, and another, which eventually evolved into fish, dinosaurs... to hominids, Neanderthals, and finally to us, Homo sapiens.

So, Darwin says that we came from chimpanzees and gorillas. Interesting. Until Darwin, many scientists were in agreement with the biblical account that animals produce after their own kind. But as the evolution theory was given more authority, scientists became under pressure to prove Darwin's hypothesis and explain how life-forms could possibly have changed from one form into another.

We are told that the way evolution proceeds is through damage due to some outside influence such as cosmic rays, which cause a cell to make mistakes, called mutations. Gradually one organism is supposed to have changed into another organism all the way from a single cell, to invertebrates like clams or starfish, and then the vertebrate fishes, the reptile, birds, mammals and finally man. So according to Darwin, here we are now, humans, the product of billions of mistakes. How does this make you feel, being called a mistake? Does God make/create mistakes?

Scientists know that the genetic code prevents one life-form from changing into another kind. So they speculate that mutations or damages to the DNA must be responsible for the evolutionary process. They believe this in spite of the observable evidence that no new species has ever resulted from a mutation. Geneticist, Dr. Lane P. Lester Ph.D.: "Mutations are almost always harmful. They can bring about small adjustments in a particular species, but no way are they able to change one kind of creature into another."

If evolution has really occurred, we ought to able to see the evidence in the fossil record (the sum total of current palaeontological knowledge). This is the record of the past. However, from careful analysis of the fossil record, there are no recorded instances of one type of animal ever changing into another. We ought to see cats and dogs, and their transitional forms of 'cogs' and 'dats'. There should be no complete division of a cat from a dog. Again, no transitional forms of species can be found. Since Darwin's time, evolutionists have searched for fossil evidence to support the idea that life forms have evolved. Was Darwin's theory simply speculation without invaluable fossil proof of transitional forms?

In collaboration with evolutionists, oil companies have drilled wells throughout the world, examining layers of the Earth to depths in excess of 5 miles. Of the millions of fossils unearthed, not one sample of a transitional form has been discovered. Over the years, the research of geology and archaeology have also failed to produce the evidence that supports the claims of evolution.

The best example of a transitional form that evolutionists usually give is of Archaeopteryx. This is supposedly the missing link between reptiles and birds. Evolutionists have misdated and misidentified this extinct bird. Another bird has since been found which has been dated to be 75 million years older than an Archaeopteryx. Therefore, Archaeopteryx cannot be the ancestor of the birds. According to Evolutionists, reptiles are supposed to have converted their scales into feathers. A scale of a reptile is nothing but a fold in the skin. How could a fold in the skin ever have been turned into the intricate design of a feather? Nothing has ever been found to be intermediate between the fold in the reptile's skin and the feather of a bird.

Because no fossil record exists to confirm evolutionary assumptions, questionable artwork is relied upon and exhibited as fact. Misleading artistic interpretations depict fish magically growing legs and changing into amphibians.

Let us now focus on man. Again, man is supposed to have developed from ape-like creatures. The more I've learnt about Palaeontology, the more I believe that Evolution is based on faith alone. To aid evolutionary concepts, artistic depictions have gone beyond ethical boundaries. Despite having no foundation for the ape-to-man theory, scientists and artists continue to deceive the public with life-like but imaginary illustrations. These artists vainly entertain natural progressions of apes to humans, and assume their hair colour, skin tones and facial expressions, from no more than a tooth, a piece of bone or even no evidence at all.

Dr. Donald Johanson, Director of the Institute of Human Origins in Arizona, U.S, discovered the three-and-a-half foot tall Lucy in 1974. Lucy looks like a chimpanzee, and yet there is an alleged ape-to-man missing link. Johanson said that although it is an ape-like creature, it walked upright. Well today, the Bonobo chimpanzee wanders around in the African rainforest, walking upright virtually all the time. So Johanson's statement of walking upright doesn't prove anything. In fact, the only features of Lucy that hint at an erect posture are the knee and hip joints. Using computer analysis, Dr. Charles Oxnard concluded that Johanson's claims for the hip are unfounded, and it must be pointed out that the knee was not even found with Lucy. The knee joint was found over a mile away and 200 feet deeper than the other bones!

Johanson says that the human family and ape family diverged and went on their own individual evolutionary trajectories. He also says that he doesn't know precisely what the common ancestor was, but it resembled something like Ramapithecus.

However, Ramapithecus was formed out of nothing but a fragment of a jaw and several teeth. Additionally, for many years, Ramapithecus was held up as our ape-like ancestor. Dr. Pilbeam who at Harvard and Yale University, and as Curator of Paleoanthropology at the Peabody Museum of Archaeology and Ethnology, had found around 40 of these Ramapithecus, some fairly complete, said that they are not on the direct line to becoming man at all. They are more like an orangutan. Yet Evolutionists continue to believe that Ramapithecus is an ape-man link.

Another so-called missing link, Java Man (Homo erectus), was devised by Eugene Dubois, when he found an ape-like skull fragment fifty-feet from a human leg bone. However, just before he died, Dubois confessed that he also found two human skulls at the same location. Java Man is still accepted by Evolutionists today and it is presented to the public as a true missing link between ape and man.

Let us look at another of these supposed missing links, Piltdown Man. In this case, a human skull had been created with the jaw of an orangutan with filed teeth. This was done to make the jaw look somewhat human. The whole case of Piltdown Man was a complete hoax.

Neanderthal man was originally found in the Neanderthal valley in Germany. These creatures virtually look modern, but some of them had a stooped and brutish appearance. Upon X-ray examination of the bones, it was discovered they had rickets (defective bone growth), which typically results from a lack of vitamin D or calcium and from insufficient exposure to sunlight. Neanderthals were reclassified from being a separate species, to Homo sapiens – the same as modern man.

Another missing link was called Nebraska Man. Nebraska Man, consisted of nothing but a single tooth. Yet around the single tooth, artistic pictures were drawn of an ape-like creature that had evolved into man. It turned out later that this tooth was actually the tooth of an extinct pig.

It is my belief that Man has always been man. Scientific evidence shows this, and this is consistent with the account of creation presented in the book of Genesis. I find it difficult to believe that ancient civilisations such as Egypt, the construction of the Pyramids, invention of calendars, mathematics and music were a result of the evolution of an ape. How many apes in the past few hundred years have been able to do this? So, if the theory of Evolution is not correct, where could we have come from?

In light of the information given and insufficient evidence of Evolution, if you were asked to draw a family tree for man, would you be inclined to draw a huge question mark? Well, there is another theory to man's beginnings, with arguably more evidence. Are you ready?

ANCIENT ASTRONAUT THEORY

Thanks to the science of Archaeology, experts now know that the first great civilisation emerged almost 6,000 years ago. Hence, this civilisation is older than the Greeks, older than the Mayans, older than the Incas. The people of this society were called Sumerians – the 'black-headed ones' – after their land Sumer. Sumer, translated as 'Land of the civilised kings' was located in southern Mesopotamia, which is modern day Iraq. This land is commonly referred to by historians and archaeologists as The Cradle of Civilisation. The heartland of Sumer is located between the rivers Tigris and Euphrates. Babylonia emerged from Sumer.

The Sumerians were one of the first cultures to build cities with streets, cobblestones and a sewage system. They also invented the first known writing system by using cuneiform script on clay tablets. In the 19th Century, archaeologists exploring the ancient ruins of Nineveh (modern-day Mosul, Iraq) discovered a whopping 22,000 of these clay tablets! When they were later translated, the text described many stories similar to those found in the Judeo-Christian Bible.

In modern day Iraq, a text was discovered in 1849 by the British Archaeologist Austen Henry Layard, named the Babylonian legend of Enuma Elish. The text tells of how humans were created by an extra-terrestrial race, known as the Anunnaki.

Differing immensely from Darwin's theory of Evolution, this is referred to as the Ancient Astronaut Theory.

These Anunnaki are described in ancient Sumer texts as descending from the sky. The term Anunnaki means 'those who from the heavens came'. It says that these beings descended in flying vehicles from the sky, and there are descriptions as well as depictions of the Anunnaki in statues and carvings. They can be seen to look like modern day space travellers with strange suits, and some of them wore wrist-watches, boots, helmets, and above all, wings. They were described or depicted as floating above some 'regular people'.

Space travellers? From another planet? Wearing watches thousands of years ago? Are you thinking 'are you serious?' Let me point something out. What is our place, on planet Earth, in the universe? Dr. Melvin Calvin, of the Chemistry Department at University of Berkeley, has said that there are at least 100,000,000 planets in the visible universe, which are like Earth, meaning they're habitable. Has anyone heard of Kepler-22b? So, what is the likelihood that we are not alone in the Universe? And since our species is relatively new, is it not possible that life has surpassed our human intelligence on even some of these 100,000,000 planets?

For generations, biblical scholars either ignored biblical references of ancient kingdoms or categorised these as legend or lore. Through the study of historical relics and the translation of ancient languages, many biblical researchers now believe that the previously questioned Old Testament references are indeed historically authentic accounts of flourishing, advanced cultures.

Many stories that exist in Genesis, such as the story of the flood, and of Adam and Eve, come from the ancient Sumerians. If you study the Genesis document which says that God made Adam from clay, and took Eve from Adam's rib, you discover that it's an abridged version of a much more complicated document that comes from Babylonia and Sumer. These ancient texts give a complicated story of powerful non-human, god-like beings, actually engineering man, making us for specific purposes.

The ancient texts of Sumer, Egypt and India predate the Bible by thousands of years. The *Bible* was originally written in Hebrew.

In 1976, Zecharia Sitchin, an Azerbaijani-born American author, published his own translations of the Sumerian clay texts in a series of books called The Earth Chronicles. According to Sitchin, the clay tablets describe an alien race known as the Anunnaki, who came to Earth to mine for gold and take it back to their home planet, Nibiru, because they needed gold for their atmosphere, as the gold content in their atmosphere was depleting.

I am someone who is fond of watching and analysing movies. Considering the above information – an extraterrestrial race coming to Earth for resources, it makes me think of *War of the Worlds* (2005), Skyline (2010) and *Cowboys & Aliens* (2011). All of these movies involve invading aliens collecting resources from Earth. Is there a message in such movies or are they simply entertainment?

According to Sumerian text and Sitchin, the 'Adamu' were the first modern humans, created by the Anunnaki around 450,000 years ago. This creation was derived by mixing their own DNA with the DNA of the species on the earth at that time – pre-historic man, the Neanderthals. Through genetic engineering, the Anunnaki created Homo sapiens, modern-day human beings.

Could alien genetic manipulation be the actual missing link of Charles Darwin's theory between ape and man?

Swiss author, Erich Anton Paul von Daniken, says that the Anunnaki took one cell from one of our ancestors and changed the cell by an artificial mutation, thus changing the DNA.

alien genetic manipulation

Zecharia Sitchin has conducted vast investigations into ancient cultures and written many books. One such investigation took him to a 6,000 year old temple in an excavated area of the ancient city Erech (Sumerian 'Uruk'), in Mesopotamia. Until its discovery, only around 150 years ago, Erech was only known through passages in the *Bible*. The temple is dedicated to a female goddess named Inanna, 'Queen of the Sky', also referred to in later times as Ishtar. A statue of her at the temple shows her divinity, marked by a pair of horns. She held a jar containing the water of life, and she was surrounded by a symbol which some refer to as entwined snakes.

This was the symbol of science at that period, 6,000 years ago. Some find the symbol to be a precursor of the Egyptian Ankh, which was the symbol of life and creation. Doesn't the entwined snake symbol remind you of the symbol still used today to indicate medicine, healing, DNA? The caduceus of Hermes? For the Sumerians, this was the symbol for genetic manipulation of DNA.

The idea that in our Solar System there was a race of intelligent beings far older than us can certainly force us to re-think many questions, including the origin of humans, and therefore Darwin's theory of Evolution.

If I told you that officials from NASA believe in the Ancient Astronaut Theory, would it be more plausible?:

- Josef F. Blumrich (1913–2002) was Chief of the Systems Layout Branch of NASA, and a sceptic of the theory until he read the story of Ezekial, a Hebrew prophet born in 622 BC (Jerusalem) who died in 570 BC (Babylon). Ezekial describes encounters with spaceships! This inspired Blumrich to write his 1974 book, *The Spaceships of Ezekial*, using his technical acumen of Aeronautics to explain the events which occurred.

- Maurice Chatelain was Chief of NASA Communications Systems. He is one of NASA's officials who helped put man on the moon and who conceived and designed the Apollo space craft. He confirmed that Neil Armstrong had reported seeing two UFOs on the rim of a crater. Chatelain believes that some UFOs may come from our own Solar System, specifically from Saturn's Moon, Titan.

Saturn is very interesting, and I have written much about it in the final section of this book. Chatelain, along with Blumrich, wrote a superb book in 1978,

Our Ancestors Came From Outer Space – A NASA Expert Confirms Mankind's Extraterrestrial Origins. If the Ancient Astronaut Theory is complete nonsense, then why are such highly reputable individuals from NASA supporting it? Chatelain wrote: "The astronauts were not limited to equipment troubles. They saw things during their missions that could not be discussed with anybody outside NASA. It is very difficult to obtain any specific information from NASA, which still exercises a very strict control over any disclosure of these events. It seems that all Apollo and Gemini flights were followed, both at a distance and sometimes quite closely, by space vehicles of extraterrestrial origin-flying saucers, or UFO's (unidentified flying objects), if you want to call them by that name. Every time it occurred, the astronauts informed Mission Control, who then ordered absolute silence. I think that Walter Shirra aboard Mercury 8 was the first of the astronauts to use the code name 'Santa Claus' to indicate the presence of flying saucers next to his space capsule. However, his announcements were barely noticed by the general public. It was a little different when James Lovell on board the Apollo 8 command module came out from behind the dark side of the moon and said for everybody to hear: "We have been informed that Santa Claus does exist!" Even though this happened on Christmas Day 1968, many people sensed a hidden meaning in those words that were not difficult to decipher."

Chatelain then went on to say how the astronauts had photographed various UFOs and when the first moon landing of Apollo 11 was made on the Sea of Tranquillity, two UFOs hovered over Neil Armstrong and Edwin 'Buzz' Aldrin, who took photos of them, which appeared in the June 1975 issue of Modern People magazine.

There was even some talk that the Apollo 13 mission carried a nuclear device aboard that could be set off to make measurements of the infrastructure of the moon and whose detonations would show on the charts of several recording seismographs placed in different locations. The unexplained explosion of an oxygen tank in the service module of Apollo 13 on its flight to the moon, according to rumours, was caused deliberately by a UFO that was following the capsule to prevent the detonation of the atomic charge that could possibly have destroyed or endangered some moon base established by extraterrestrials.

It was also said that during their flights our astronauts frequently felt as if some external force were trying to take over their minds. They experienced strange sensations and visions. What seems almost certain is that some of the astronauts did have psychological problems and changes of personality after their missions in space. Some turned deeply religious, some seemed to develop mental trouble – facts that of course could be ascribed to pure coincidences without particular significance.

The experiments in telepathy carried out in space by some astronauts have been discussed and even published. Special symbol cards of geometric figures were used to transmit thoughts from the participant in orbit around the moon to the correspondent on the surface of the earth. Most of these experiments were successful, much more so than similar telepathic experiments conducted on Earth, which generally had a lower score.

One astronaut who conducted much research concerning telepathy and the paranormal, is Apollo 14 Astronaut, and retired Captain in the U.S. Navy, Edgar Dean Mitchell.

Then there is the case of astronaut Gordon Cooper that arouses curiosity for more than one reason. He was the pilot of Mercury 9 in 1963 and of Gemini 5 in 1965, and he was unquestionably one of our most skilled space pilots, yet he never flew an Apollo. Gordon Cooper, now manufacturing skydiving parachutes after having quit the space programme, has never told anybody outside NASA what he saw in space. But there are those who think NASA may have removed him from the Apollo flights because he had seen too much. It is also curious that this man, who is not only an astronaut but is also a scientist, has now become a firm believer in extraterrestrial life and civilisations and is convinced that space visitors to earth have been around for a long time, from the most distant past up to this very day. Not long ago, Gordon Cooper participated in an archaeological expedition to South America that discovered the remnants of a very old and very advanced civilisation dating back more than five thousand years. Pottery, sculptures, and hieroglyphs very similar to Egyptian artefacts of the same period, were discovered, confirming once more the theory that Egyptian and American cultures had a common origin. It is quite natural for a famous astronaut to be interested in ancient astronauts but one may still wonder whether Cooper did not acquire his sudden interest in extraterrestrial civilisations by seeing for himself in space things that he did not have the right to tell us about.

ORIGINS QUESTIONED

Could we be the product of genetic engineering? Does anyone remember Dolly the sheep of Scotland? She was the first cloned mammal. After Dolly, animals have been cloned around the world, including mice, cows, monkeys and pigs. So if animal and mammal cloning has been conducted, would human genetic engineering be impossible?

Returning to film, some good movies in my opinion are *Blade Runner* (1982), *Gattaca* (1997), *The Sixth Day* (2000), *The Island* (2005) and even the recent movie *Prometheus* (2012). These all just happen to revolve around the issue of genetic engineering. If such an issue is so absurd, why are such multi-million pound movies being produced? Again, perhaps there is a message to be taken from these rather than seeing them as pure entertainment?

Back to the Adamu, was this Adamu species solely created for slave labour, to mine gold for the Anunnaki? This is what Sitchin believes.

Referring to the biblical texts of Adam and Eve; they may have been two individuals at the start of time; they may have been the first of the genetically created human beings. Adam is Hebrew for 'Man'. Adamu is what the Sumerians referred to as 'First Man', the Anunnaki slaves.

An interesting quotation from the writer and researcher into anomalous phenomena, Charles Fort: "The Earth is a farm. We are someone else's property."

So do the Sumerian tablets actually describe an alien race conducting mining operations on a global scale?

Thousands of miles away from Sumer, in South Africa, ancient gold mines have recently been discovered. According to scientists, some excavations date back around 150,000 years. How do we know that these excavations weren't conducted by humans?

In many languages in Africa, the native word for Star means 'Bringer of knowledge or enlightenment'. Some African cultures believe that extra-terrestrial beings have been visiting Earth for tens of thousands of years. For example, Zulu legends speak of a time when visitors from the stars came to excavate gold and other natural resources. The mines were worked by artificially produced flesh and blood slaves, created by the first people.

I must also add something here which was discovered on the Internet via YouTube – an interesting video regarding Michael Jackson. Please see my

28

website www.DragoDeSilver.com to watch the video, as it may be deleted from YouTube at any moment. The video appears to be taken from a conference with Michael Jackson around 2009. He says: "They manipulate our history books. The history books are lying. You need to know that. You must know that." I am yet to come across a school history book containing information regarding ancient astronauts. Is this what Michael Jackson was talking about? Or was he referring to another theory? What Michael meant here, I will leave you to interpret. Although he was neither a scientist nor an archaeologist, I am sure there are many people who will argue that being perhaps the most famous pop star for decades, and doing what he did, over many years, perhaps he made friends with very powerful people who knew certain things.

If the Ancient Astronaut Theory is the correct version of events, what does this suggest about out future? If alien visitors have been to Earth before, why not return? Or did they all even leave the Earth?

And what would be the general reaction of the public if the Ancient Astronaut Theory was true? It will strengthen the general concept that our history of religions in the world needs to be revisited. What do we make of history now? And what are we supposed to be doing with this history now? What is our reason for existence? This is something for you to think about.

Did past scriptures contain questionable information about man's origins, which are still available to the masses today, yet hidden? Over the past hundreds and thousands of years, scriptures have been re-written over and over again, to the point where the original messages may have been lost due to mistranslation. I do wonder why exactly scriptures are re-written in the first place. To understand the basic effect of mistranslation, consider the game Chinese Whispers. I will now give you some examples of reported mistranslations in modern scriptures. You can research the validity of this and think about the implications for yourself.

The *Bible* has been translated into over 2,000 languages. And in case you think the *Bible* originates from Christianity, this is far from the truth. The *Bible* is Hebrew in origin. It was then translated into Aramaic and then into Greek. Hebrew and Aramaic are both Semitic in nature, as is Akkadian. Akkadian stems from Sumer – one of the oldest civilisations we know of.

What are the chances of the original *Bible* remaining intact up to the present day? Have you ever wondered why the King James Bible is referred to as the 'Authorised Version'? Simply using common sense, an authorised version of something means that some of the original has been removed. There is information being hidden from you. But why? Are you ready for the examples of reported mistranslations?

First of all, know this... investigations have concluded that Hebrews were Henotheistic. This means they believed and worshipped one god from many gods! For some reason after a long period, Henotheism was replaced with Monotheism, the belief in the existence of one god.

Note: I wonder which god this is from the many gods of Henotheism? A righteous god was chosen from the group, right? Although we have wars and the killings of innocent people around the world. If a righteous god was chosen, then something over time has gone drastically wrong, perhaps caused by an outside force.

The evidence of Henotheism, and that we were genetically engineered, will be demonstrated through the following examples. The *Companion Bible* will be used because as well as providing the scriptures, it provides very interesting footnotes:

- Genesis 1 and 2: "In the beginning God created the Heavens and the earth. And the earth was without form and void."

Now, an example of the Hebrews being Henotheistic is in the book of Psalms. Psalms is a book from the Hebrew Bible. Psalms 82 says: "God standeth in the congregation of the mighty; he judgeth among the gods." The footnotes say "God, in Hebrew – Elohim. He standeth officially in the congregation of the mighty = the GOD'S. The word God, is Elohim. God is standing officially, representing himself, the god of the Hebrews, in a congregation of the mighty." This means there is more than one god:

- Genesis 1.26 says: "And God said, Let Us make man in Our image after Our likeness." *murando of ser humano, yo tra pregunto, c que' clase de dio es ese?*

Let's break this sentence down. Firstly, what is not being said is that God is creating a new creature called Man. Here, God (Elohim, being plural), hence the gods, are saying, "Let Us make man in Our image after Our likeness". What is being said is that someone has come here on Earth, who we refer to as Elohim in Hebrew, the Gods, and they are saying upon looking at the indigenous creatures that we today call Hominids, "come let Us make man in Our image after Our likeness". So there seems to be some kind of a genetic experiment with the first human creatures on Earth. The footnotes say that 'image' means 'likeness'. The likeness of the Elohim, the gods. The image and likeness is physical, not moral. We look like them. They do not look like us. In pictures, we see that God is depicted as a Man.

- In Genesis 3.22: *"And the Lord God said, Behold, the man is become as one of us; to know good and evil."*

Here, the gods are talking to each other after they have made this new creation, taking the Neanderthal or ancient hominids and procreating with the females, they created a new race – us. Their creation looked like them and thought like them, knowing good and evil.

In Genesis 11 is the story of the building of the Tower of Babel and how God came down from the heavens to see what the people were doing:

- Genesis 11.6 says: "And the Lord said, Behold, the people is one, and they have all one language; and this they begin to do; and now nothing will be restrained from them, which they have imagined to do."

- Genesis 11.7 says: "Go to, let us go down, and there confound their language, that they may not understand one another's speech."

Here, it seems the gods who have created us are saying, "My goodness, look at what we have created. We have created this creature that is now out of control. It is smart, clever and wise. It is doing creative things. Let us go down and see what they're doing."

In the *Bible* we have heard that Adam and Eve were created by God. Where exactly was the creature 'Adam', or man, formed? In the first book of the Old Testament Bible, does it not say "God created man in the Garden of Eden?" NO! In Genesis 2.8, it says: "And the Lord God planted a garden eastward in Eden; and there He put the man whom He had formed." It doesn't say He formed man there, it says that's where He put the result of the experiment, into a place the ancient people called the garden of Eden.

Later on we begin to see that this garden of Eden is talked about in all of the ancient scriptures, not as a garden as we would perceive it, but it was a protected area; the area which was cordoned off by the gods so that the other remaining ancient hominid creatures (or Neanderthals) could not access the area where the experiment was taking place. The experiment was the cross-breeding of animals with humans and gods. The area of the experiment was called the Garden of Eden.

It is interesting that the footnote says formed – "As a potter." In Isaiah 64, we read: "But now, O Lord, Thou art our Father; we are the clay, and Thou our Potter; and we all are the work of Thy hand." The Bible in the Hebrew tradition is giving us the idea that we are moulded, like a potter would mould a new creation. So God is presented to us as the potter.

In ancient Egypt, the God Khnum formed man, and God was known as the potter. This is where it seems the Hebrews got the concept of God being the potter, the designer of the human creature.

Note: Are human-beings an experiment or a creation of a higher life form which in Hebrew we call Elohim, or Gods? If so, what is the purpose of the experiment? Is this what alien-abductions are about – to see if we have evolved or are mutating? How long is the experiment planned to run? Are we being watched? I am reminded of The Observers from the Fringe television series.

Regarding the creation of man, the Quran says, in the 13th verse of chapter 49 (Surat Al-Hujurat): "O mankind! We created you." Again, it is not 'I', but 'We'.

In the Bible book of Genesis, there is the story of the Flood of Noah's day. God seeks to wipe out all of mankind by the great deluge. After the flood is over, Noah, his wife and their three sons and their wives (only eight people) are left alive on the Earth. After the flood is over and all of mankind has been destroyed, God then says to Noah, in Genesis 9.1: "And God blessed Noah and his sons, and said unto them, Be fruitful and multiply, and replenish the earth."

Now, what is meant by RE-plenish the Earth? Obviously, if there were people on the Earth and God decided to destroy them, and God wanted to have people on the Earth again, then obviously you have to re-plenish the Earth. Re means to do it again. I wonder why the population was destroyed, and would a righteous God allow people to die? ← no! Solamente un hijo de P.

32

Part 2: The Futuristic Past

So, we have Adam and Eve being created by God. And after the flood, Noah is told by God to replenish the Earth. But back in Genesis Chapter 1 when God is creating Adam and Eve, the first human pair, God says the same thing to them! In Genesis 1.28, regarding Adam and Eve, God says: "And God blessed them and God said unto them, Be fruitful, and multiply, and replenish the earth." Does this mean that Adam and Eve are not the first human couple?

Again, Genesis 1 and 2: "In the beginning God created the Heavens and the earth. And the earth was without form and void." Surely logic alone will tell you that there is something wrong here. God doesn't create something that has no form and is void, and yet it's supposed to be a creation. So there must be a mistranslation here.

The footnotes clarify the statement "the earth was without form and void." In Hebrew, it is "tohu va bohu". The word "was" = became, and "without form" = waste, and "void" = desolation. So, God created the Earth, and then it became a waste and a desolation.

In Jeremiah 4.23, the Hebrew term "tohu va bohu" arises again. We are told that Jeremiah is given a vision by God of the world as it was before man was created. It says: "I beheld the earth, and lo, it was without form, and void". In Jeremiah 4.25–26: "I beheld, and lo, there was no man, and all the birds of the heavens were fled. I beheld, and, lo, the fruitful place was a wilderness, and all the cities thereof were broken down." Jeremiah is saying, 'I beheld the earth when there was no man, and it was a beautiful paradise, and then it became a waste and a desolation'.

Adam and Eve were a re-creation, and were told to do it AGAIN. This implied that the Earth has had many ancient civilisations that have been destroyed, maybe by atomic warfare, maybe by other-world technology that has destroyed life on the Earth. The movie *Knowing* (2009) is very interesting indeed, and relates to re-creation.

In Genesis 4, there is an interesting story about Adam and Eve's first two sons, Cain and Abel. Cain kills his brother Abel. Genesis 4.8 says: "And Cain said to Abel his brother "Let us go into the field" and it came to pass, when they were in the field, that Cain rose up against Abel his brother, and slew him."

So, we have four people in the garden, the protected area. We have the male and female, Adam and Eve, who are told to re-do/replenish the Earth again. At the start of replenishing the Earth, they have two sons, Cain and Abel. Cain kills his brother. Now we have only three people.

However, in Genesis 4, there is a very interesting scripture. When God(s) find out that Cain has killed his brother, in Genesis 4.13–16 it says: "And Cain said unto the Lord, My punishment is greater than I can bear. Behold thou hast driven me out this day from the face of the earth, and from thy face shall I be hid; and I shall be a fugitive and a vagabond in the earth; and it shall come to pass that everyone that findeth me shall slay me. And the Lord said unto him, Therefore whoever slayeth Cain, vengeance shall be taken on him sevenfold. And the Lord set a mark upon Cain lest any finding him should kill him. And Cain went out from the presence of the Lord, and dwelt in the land of Nod, on the east of Eden."

The point here is that Cain is afraid to be sent out of the garden, or the protected area, because he says that everyone out there that will find him will kill him. He thinks there is somebody out there. God says Adam and Eve are the first couple, and yet Cain is afraid that somebody will get him if he goes out there and he has God believe him because God said he will put a mark on Cain so nobody will kill him. ¿en qué quedamos?

Who were these other people that Cain was concerned about? Pre-Adamic creatures. Who exactly were these? I talk about them later. But I will say the following for now: If Pre-Adamic creatures were unthinking animals, why would Cain have been so scared to be amongst them? Surely Elohim, being a god, could have protected him, right? Unless, the Pre-Adamic creatures were:

1) Just as intelligent as man;
2) Roaming in large numbers;
3) Enemies of man;
4) Much more inclined to be evil than good – because who simply tortures and kills a person?

Is it these Pre-Adamic ancient civilisations, with their intelligence (and therefore high technology), whose remains we are finding as pyramids around the world and even in the ocean?

Note: Are you aware of the pyramids in Bosnia? They are larger than those in Egypt! Discussed later is a pyramid in the ocean near Japan.

STAR WARS

This section is not about the movie. Or is it, in some way? Many people not only simply pay attention to, but also obsess over, glamorous movie stars, sport stars and pop stars.

If I told you of a galactic federation of planets existing in our past (perhaps also in the present?), populated by and ruled by extra-terrestrials, would you call me crazy? What if I told you that it is said that some of the world's top movie stars, among others, actually believe this, and pay many thousands of pounds to join a belief system called Scientology (founded by L. Ron Hubbard)?

What are the *Star Wars* movies about? Various species of extra-terrestrials, robotic droids, space travel, use of sophisticated technology, a galactic republic/empire, and The Force – something which to me seems akin to consciousness. Do you remember the television series *Battlestar Galactica*? Wasn't this somewhat similar to *Star Wars*?

How about the many decades of films and series of *Star Trek*? Again including various species of extra-terrestrials, space travel, use of sophisticated technology, a galactic federation and various empires. How about the 2009 TV series *V*? This involved a species of extra-terrestrials coming to Earth via space travel and the use of sophisticated technology (such as Blue Energy), amongst other things. Do you remember the Bliss? Wouldn't you consider that to be mind control through consciousness?

This book was not intended to be detailed with various movies and television series, but I cannot help but mention those which relate to the book's content. Have you ever asked yourself 'what is the purpose of a movie?' Yes it can be a break from the norm, a relaxing time to laugh, cry and raise adrenalin levels. But again, do you ever wonder if there is there a message to be received?

Here is another interesting quotation from Charles Fort in his book *The Book of the Damned*: "I think we're property. I should say we belong to something: That once upon a time, this earth was No-man's Land, that other worlds explored and colonized here, and fought among themselves for possession, but that now it's owned by something: That something owns this earth – all others warned off. Pigs, geese, cattle. First find out they are owned. Then find out the whyness of it. I suspect that...we're useful...something now has a legal right to us, by force, or by having paid out analogues of beads for us to former, more primitive, owners of us – all others warned off – that all this has been known, perhaps for ages, to certain ones upon this earth, a cult or order, members of which function like bellwethers to the rest of us, or as superior slaves or overseers, directing us in accordance with instructions received – from Somewhere else – in our mysterious usefulness."

The movie *War of the Worlds* (1953, 2005): Extra-terrestrials journey to Earth in an apparent lightning storm. These aliens travel down directly to the ground, powering up gigantic extra-terrestrial tripod-looking machines, which collect and kill humans all over Earth.

The point I am trying to make here is that surely the extra-terrestrial tripods were already here before humans? Hidden, buried deep within the ground. Otherwise, don't you think certain people/entities would have known of their existence? Such as oil and gas companies building pipelines, electricity companies, water companies, underground rail companies? Is this a movie with a message? Perhaps you can ask the director of the 2005 version, Steven Spielberg, for his honest answer.

Additionally, the movie *The Day The Earth Stood Still* (1951, 2008): A sphere acting as a kind of spacecraft arrives in New York City, on board is a human-alien (Keenu Reeves, as Klaatu) and a giant powerful robot. I will not describe the entire movie – you can watch it for yourselves. However, the reason I mention it now is because of certain a scene (from roughly 30 mins and 20 secs into the movie) between Klaatu and the United States Secretary of Defence (Kathy Bates, as Regina Jackson):

Regina: "Do you represent a civilisation?"
Klaatu: "I represent a group of civilisations."
Regina: "Where is this group of civilisations?"
Klaatu: "All around you."
Regina: "What is your purpose in coming here?"
Klaatu: "There is a gathering of world leaders not far from here. I will explain my purpose to them."
Regina: "...Why have you come to our planet?"
Klaatu: "Your planet?"
Regina: "Yes, this is our planet"
Klaatu: "No. It is not."

bell-wether — a male sheep, usually wearing a bell that leads the flock.
a leader of a sheeplike crowd.

Part 2: The Futuristic Past

Again, are movies just entertainment, or do they contain a message? I think you should be contacting the directors of these kinds of movies for an explanation. If they just say, 'it's only to entertain' and they believe 'science-fiction' movies attract a lot of sales, ask yourself, why are we so attracted to this particular genre? Do we subconsciously know something about the past and these movies actually open our subconscious memory bank?

. I will now raise a separate issue. On Earth, things are created by nature or by us, its inhabitants, and things are destroyed by nature or its inhabitants. In my opinion, unfortunately its inhabitants do a lot more of the destroying through wars, murders and economics. (You should all be asking yourselves 'What really is nature?'). If creation and destruction are conducted on Earth by nature and its inhabitants, why can't creation and destruction be conducted in Space by nature...and its inhabitants? And with Space, I am not referring to us humans as its only inhabitants. Read on.

Do you know that the Earth will most likely be destroyed? This is a fact. Mercury and Venus will also most likely be destroyed. This will happen 'naturally' due to our Sun. As you know, the Sun is our closest star. A star, like a human, is born, grows AND dies. A star's sequence is: Protostar to Fusion ignition – Main Sequence, to a Red Giant/Supergiant and then to a White Dwarf/Black Hole.

If you think this won't or can't happen: "The first evidence of a planet's destruction by its aging star has been discovered by an international team of astronomers. The evidence indicates that the missing planet was devoured as the star began expanding into a "red giant" – the stellar equivalent of advanced age." *ScienceDaily*, August 20th, 2012 So, here is an example of creation and destruction in Space by natural means. Now what about its inhabitants?

Remember what I said in the Introduction: *At one point in time, everyone 'knew' the Earth was the centre of the universe...everyone 'knew' the Earth was flat.* I wonder how many scientists, religious groups, those with authority, and the general public, 'knew' this to be true. Imagine what we will know tomorrow.

Consider the following paragraphs carefully. How great would your life be if you were confined to living inside your house for the rest of your life? Would you be content in living your entire life only in your bedrooms, bathroom, living room and dining room? Your only view of anything of the

ese hubiera sido mi destino si yo no me hubiera casado.

37

outside-world would obviously only be by looking through your windows.

By living in your house, you wouldn't know of the Earth's size, mass, any cities, oceans, transportation methods, animals, plants, museums, different rocks, soils, scents, tastes, etc. You would not feel and fully experience the sunshine, rain or the wind. You would not have the opportunity to speak to people of different cultures, religions, colours, hobbies and interests.

For those of us who are technologically advanced in our homes, and for those of us with the equipment, we could decide to build and install a camera, microphone and other sensors onto a small radio-controlled aeroplane. We could not operate it for long because the battery would die and the plane would be out-of-range. It could travel perhaps 50 metres outside of your house. With its camera, microphone and sensors, would it give us a whole new understanding of the Earth? Would we have reached a new frontier? And for those of us who built these planes, shouldn't we tell everybody of all the photos, videos and sounds the plane recorded? What is at risk if we do? What can we do with this information?

As much as you may love your home, I think you would soon deem yourself to be living in some kind of prison. You may go insane. I ask you, isn't the Earth very similar to your home? Isolated? Step outside of your home and look upwards. What do you see? Depending on the time of day and weather, you could see a clear blue sky with light from a beautiful Sun, or, the night sky with beautiful shining stars.

Imagine what we could see, feel, touch, taste, and hear, if we could 'step outside' of Earth. I'm positive you would all say that a 50-metre range aeroplane to understand the entire Earth is absolutely pathetic. I completely agree with you. On the same note, I would say that a satellite or probe travelling billions of miles to understand the entirety of Space is also pathetic.

Voyager 1 has been considered to be the farthest man-made object from Earth, travelling 122 AU. AU stands for Astronomical Unit, and 1 AU equals just over 92,955,807 miles. Therefore 122 AU gives us a distance of: 11,340,608,454 miles (Eleven billion, three hundred and forty million, six hundred and eight thousand, four hundred and fifty four miles).

Considering the scenario with the house and radio-controlled aeroplane, see Figure 1: Vehicle Measurements below and subsequent information to gain some 'enlightenment' concerning how much we really know about our Solar System.

Vehicle	Distance of Vehicle (miles)	Estimated Distance of (miles)	Ratio Travelled %	Level of understanding in relation to ratio
Aeroplane	0.0310685 (1 metre equals 0.00062137 miles. Multiply this by 50).	Earth: 7,926.98	0.00039193362	Pathetic
Space probe	11,340,608454	Solar System: 1,360,873,014, 480,000	0.0008333333	Is there much difference with the aeroplane?!

Figure 1: Vehicle Measurements

Is that really our understanding of our Solar System? 0.0008333333% ? IT GETS WORSE! Carefully consider the following, in relation to the 0.0008333333 result above: This space probe is only measured here in relation to our Solar System! To truly understand how insignificant our highly technologically-advanced space probe is in relation to our true understanding of what is beyond Earth:

- Our Solar System is located within the Milky Way galaxy;
- This Milky Way galaxy is said to be around 100,000 light years in diameter = 100,000 x 5,865,696,000,000 miles (1 Light Year), resulting in 5,865,696,000,000,000,000 miles;
- The closest galaxy to the Milky Way is said to be the Canis Major Dwarf galaxy, which is 30,000 light years (175,970,880,000,000 miles) away from the Solar System;
- There are at least 100 billion galaxies in the Universe;
- Research has stated that the size of the Universe is infinite. So can't the number of galaxies be infinite? *of course!*

You don't need a scientist or astronomer to tell you what these figures mean. These mean that the possibility, knowledge and opportunities for 'weird and wonderful things' out there for us to experience, is ENDLESS! And we know nothing about them. This also means, KEEP AN OPEN MIND.

This chapter, The Futuristic Past, will delve into ancient technologically advanced civilisations and cosmic battles. However, I will begin by introducing some fascinating modern-day astronomical events.

Ronald Reagan was an American actor before he became the 33rd Governor of California in 1967–75. After this, he became the 40th President of the United States, from 1981–89. This President was the first, in a speech, to talk about... a potential alien invasion! Not once, but on at least two occasions! On December 4th, 1985 at Fallston High School in Maryland, United States, speaking about his first summit with the Soviet Union Prime Minister Mikhail Gorbachev in Geneva, President Reagan said: "When you stop to think, we're all God's children wherever we live in the world, I couldn't help but say to him, just think how easy his task and mine might be in these meetings that we held, if suddenly there was a threat to this world, from some other species, from another planet outside in the universe. We'd forget all the little local differences that we have between our countries, and we would find out once and for all, that we really are all human beings here on this earth together. Well, I don't suppose we can wait for an alien race to come down and threaten us, but I think that between us, we can bring about that realisation."

On February 17th, 1987, in the Grand Kremlin Palace, Moscow, Mikhail Gorbachev confirmed the conversation in Geneva during a speech to the Central Committee of the Soviet Communist Party. On page 7a of the *Soviet Life Supplement*, it reports that Gorvachev said: "At our meeting in Geneva, the U.S. President said that if the earth faced an invasion by extraterrestrials, the United States and the Soviet Union would join forces to repel such an invasion. I shall not dispute the hypothesis, though I think it's early yet to worry about such an intrusion..."

Have you noticed that Gorbachev did not say that Reagan's comments were absurd or unfounded? He accepted them as fact, and said that it will happen, but not yet!

On September 21st, 1987 at the General Assembly of the United Nations, President Reagan said to the world nation's: "In our obsession with antagonisms of the moment, we often forget how much unites all the members of humanity. Perhaps we need some outside, universal threat to make us recognise this common bond. I occasionally think how quickly our differences worldwide would vanish if we were facing an alien threat from outside this world. And yet, I ask, is not an alien force ALREADY among us?"

Note that Gorbachev was the Prime Minister of the massive Soviet Union, and he was powerful enough and credible enough to discuss such sensitive, world-changing issues with the United States President. If Gorbachev had no integrity, would he have been Prime Minister? And would the U.S. President be discussing such things with him?

QUESTION: How did Gorbachev know not to worry about an intrusion YET?

If country A is preparing to fight country B, and A knows that they can take one year to develop their offensive weapons and strategy, then doesn't that mean that A has knowledge from somewhere, from infiltrators/insiders and surveillance, that B has not planned to mount an attack within that year?

QUESTION: If an alien force is already among us, why are we not told the details? As we live on this planet, do we not have the right to know and prepare ourselves and our families?

QUESTION: What makes them think that aliens have the agenda to attack us? Why not make peace with us and share knowledge? How do they know (or say they know) of the aliens being a threat?

QUESTION: Is there another explanation for how Gorbachev knew that an alien attack was not coming yet? Continue reading, and I will let you draw your own conclusion.

President Reagan established some very interesting programmes during his time at the White House. One of these was the multi-billion dollar 'Star Wars' programme. The concept behind this was to develop a 'defensive' weapon system to detect the launch of a Soviet nuclear missile and disable/destroy it before it would re-enter Earth's atmosphere and hit its target. However, it is believed that the Star Wars Programme was not intended to protect the United States against the Soviet's nuclear missiles, but to protect the Earth from an 'alien invasion'.

Are you not convinced about the Star Wars Programme being intended for something aside from the Soviet Union? Remember that after 69 years the Soviet Union collapsed, in 1991. The Guardian, Friday, 12th February,

2010 reported: "The U.S. this week achieved a goal that has eluded it since Ronald Reagan's Star Wars programme by knocking out a ballistic missile using a high-powered laser beam mounted on a plane. The successful test was carried out yesterday in California, the US Missile Defence Agency (MDA) said, making real what had previously been confined to the realms of science fiction." Now that the Soviet Union no longer exists, what is left of the Star Wars Programme?

You need to be aware of one of the most famous names in the space industry, Mr Werner von Braun, a German-American Rocket Scientist, Space Architect and Aerospace Engineer. He and his colleagues were recruited by the U.S. to work on a missile programme. He later became one of the founders of the U.S. NASA programme. Braun aided the development of the Saturn V rocket used on Apollo space missions. A source from NASA, Robin Williams, has described Braun as "Without doubt, the greatest rocket scientist in history." Would you describe Braun as a genius? What were his intentions? Now, read on.

Before Braun was employed by the United States, he was an SS officer, vital to Nazi Germany's rocket development programme, and responsible for the design of the V-2 combat rocket which continuously bombed London, England, during the Second World War. I ask you again: what were his intentions?

Now I shall introduce you to someone within the aerospace 'circle', Dr. Carol Rosin. She is an awarding winning educator, leading Aerospace Executive, Space and Missile Defence Consultant, and a former spokesperson for Werner von Braun. She has said: "The strategy that Werner Von Braun taught me was that first the Russians are going to be considered the enemy... Then terrorists would be identified, and that was soon to follow... Then we were going to identify third-world country 'crazies'. We now call them Nations of Concern. But he said that would be the third enemy who we would build space-based weapons. The next enemy was asteroids. Now, at this point he kind of chuckled the first time he said it. Asteroids-against asteroids we are going to build space-based weapons. And the funniest one of all was what he called aliens, extraterrestrials."

In our Solar System, we have the Sun, with four 'inner planets' called the terrestrial planets (Mercury, Venus, Earth and Mars), and four considerably larger 'outer planets' called the gas giants (Jupiter, Saturn, Uranus and

Neptune). These are the inner and outer planets of what, exactly? The Asteroid Belt, full of asteroids and small planets. Doesn't the Asteroid Belt seem inconsistent to you compared with the rest of the Solar System? It is said that the Asteroid Belt is where asteroids come from, and the Kuiper Belt and Oort cloud are where comets come from. I ask you, where do the Asteroid Belt, Kuiper Belt and Oort cloud come from? I shall introduce you to an astronomical law named Titius-Bode law, also known simply as Bode's law. It is named after the 18th Century German Astronomer, Johann Daniel Titius, and the later German astronomer Johann Elert Bode. This law was established by these astronomers because they noticed that the distance of the planets' orbits from the Sun followed a mathematical pattern. From this pattern, they concluded that some planets were in fact 'missing'! Before jumping to the conclusion that this is ludicrous, let me tell you that this law correctly predicted and found the planets Uranus in 1871 and Ceres (the largest object in the Asteroid Belt) in 1801. The original version of the Law/Formula is $a = (n + 4) / 10$ where a in the formula is the average distance of the planet from the Sun, and the result is in Astronomical Units (1 Astronomical Unit equals 92,955,807 miles) and n in the formula makes up the sequence of 0, 3, 6, 12, 24, 48 and so on. A new value n is double the previous number.

The table on page 43 shows the distances of the planets from the Sun in the Solar System. The distances shown are those calculated from Titius Bode's law (TBL), with 'real' distances. From 1801 to the 1860s, Ceres was considered to be a planet. From 1930 to 2006, Pluto was also considered to be a planet. However, they are now both classified as dwarf planets.

The difference between TBL and the Real Distance seems to be very large. However, if Neptune is skipped, the TBL of 38.8 is very close to Pluto's Real Distance of 39.44, therefore giving an error of only 1.62%. Is this law incorrect or did something 'irregular' occur with the planet Neptune? Keep in mind that Pluto is not classified as a planet anymore.

There was a significant problem with Ceres – in the region of the Asteroid Belt. Ceres was so tiny compared to the other planets in our Solar System that it couldn't even be considered a moon. The realisation of this issue came when another tiny so-called planet was discovered in 1801 by German astronomer Heinrich Wilhelm Matthaus Olbers, roughly the same orbital distance from the Sun. It was given the name Pallas.

Planet	n	TBL (AU)	Real Distance (AU)	% Error TBL vs Real
Mercury	0	0.4	0.39	2.56
Venus	3	0.7	0.72	2.78
Earth	6	1	1	0.00
Mars	12	1.6	1.52	5.26
Ceres*	24	2.8	2.77	1.08
Jupiter	48	5.2	5.2	0
Saturn	96	10	9.54	4.82
Uranus	192	19.6	19.2	2.08
Neptune	384	38.8	30.06	29.08
Pluto*	768	77.2	39.44	95.75

Figure 2: Planet Comparison

Olbers then established a theory behind this irregularity, that the two 'planets' Ceres and Pallas were actually remnants of a larger planet, larger than Saturn, which exploded (now known as the Exploded Planet Hypothesis of Dr. Tom Van Flandern). He predicted that more of these so-called planets including irregular-shaped objects, would be discovered in the same or a very similar orbit around the Sun.

Note: Since the discovery of more asteroids after 1845 in the vicinity of the same orbital distance from the Sun, Pallas and Ceres have been re-classified as asteroids.

44

French mathematician and astronomer, Joseph Louis Lagrange, agreed with Olbers and went on to say that the unusual elongated orbits of comets in that region were the by-products of an explosion.

In 1972, the Canadian astronomer Michael William Ovenden, played a big role in astronomy by:

- Developing upon the Titius-Bode Law, not only predicting the distance of the orbiting planets, but also their satellites/moons;
- Agreeing with Lagrange and Olber (Exploded Planet Hypothesis);
- Concluding and predicting that between Mars and Jupiter, there was in fact a planet...which is now the Asteroid Belt! This planet was colossal in size, larger than all the planets put together!

The Asteroid belt was once a giant planet? If you found a pile of rubble on a street full of buildings, wouldn't there be a likelihood that it was once a building too? To knock down a building would require bulldozers and a wrecking ball swung by a crane. What would be needed to 'knock down' a planet of this size? Immense energy! Could the explosion have shifted the planets' orbits into an adjusted trajectory? Given the energy required to demolish a planet of this magnitude, I would say it is possible. Therefore, the Titius-Bode Law could be 100% accurate. But this poses some difficult questions in the Exploded Planet Hypothesis, such as how could such enormous power be amassed? And how did this explosive power 'target' this planet? Was it internal to the planet, or external?

The Exploded Planet Hypothesis does, however, explain the unusual occurrences of meteorites. What is a meteorite? It is an object that falls from space into Earth's atmosphere, surviving impact and ranging in size. You can find the term meteorite to include the word 'natural' in its definition – a 'natural object'. However, I will not use that word here. Why? What is meant by 'natural' when relating to outer space? If natural means 'naturally formed in space – in its current state as a meteorite', then I will that say I have never believed this. However, if natural means 'naturally formed in space', then I am more inclined to believe this. I believe that meteorites are remnants of something larger. This larger object could have been formed naturally in space, and therefore in this instance, I believe meteorites to be remnants of something larger that have fallen from space.

45

One such meteorite, named Williamette, made from iron and nickel, was discovered in Oregon, U.S.A. It is the sixth largest meteorite in the world, thus far.

There are known to be meteorites with unusual features, such as those that melted a long time ago from a heat blast, badly charred, with evidence of being formed in high-temperatures and pressures, containing diamonds, etc. Diamonds are formed at high temperatures and pressures, at depths of 87–120 miles in the Earth's mantle. Carbon-related minerals provide the carbon source, and the growth occurs over a period of 1 billion to 3.3 billion years. Diamonds are brought close to the Earth's surface through volcanic eruptions by magma, which eventually cools to form igneous rocks. Therefore, as diamonds are said to be found in meteorites from outer space, can this not mean they were formed at a high temperature and pressure at such great depths in another planet's mantle? The carbon-related minerals have grown over billions of years, and after a potential planetary explosion, the diamonds were spewed out from the magma in the planet, and the igneous rock formed from the magma's cooling and solidification whilst being flung through space towards the Earth?

Some of Neptune's moons lie within the Roche limit. The Roche limit, also known as the Roche radius, is the distance within which a celestial body, typically held together by its own gravity, will eventually disintegrate from a second celestial body's tidal force – which exceeds the first celestial body's own gravity. Inside a celestial body's Roche limit, the orbiting (first) body will disintegrate and spread itself, forming rings around the second body. Outside the Roche limit, the remaining material of the celestial body will combine together to form one large mass.

It is strange that four of Neptune's moons (from 13 known moons), are orbiting within Neptune's Roche limit. Inside the limit, Neptune's gravitational pull is so strong that no material could have amassed into such large objects, in this case moons. This means the moons must have been captured or dragged within the Roche limit by tidal forces on the planet's surface. Neptune's largest moon is directed backwards and inclined, suggesting the moon is actually a captured Kuiper Belt ice body similar to Pluto and its largest moon, Charon.

The Kuiper Belt, also known as the Edgeworth-Kuiper Belt, lies within the Solar System, but beyond all the planets. It extends from Neptune's orbit (30

AU) to 50 AU from the Sun. It is similar to the asteroid belt, however, rather than being made up of mainly rock and metal, the Kuiper Belt is mainly composed of frozen volatiles, such as ammonia, methane and water. The asteroid belt contains rocks and metals. The Kuiper Belt contains water, ammonia and methane. We encounter meteorites with diamonds, and these are all components of a planet. With the addition of anomalies in celestial body alignments, doesn't the Exploded Planet Theory seem a plausible theory?

In an article by Maggie McKee, *New Scientist* magazine (May 22nd, 2005), it was reported that Neptune may have captured Triton from a planet with twice Earth's mass, early in the Solar System's history, as it collided with that planet. In 2005, some astronomers proposed that Uranus and Neptune had formed much closer to the Sun before migrating outwards and swapping places in the process.

In 2010, David Shiga reported in *New Scientist* magazine (March 22nd, 2010) that enough material may have been left to form a planet with two Earth-masses that may have had Triton as a satellite. Triton, which is larger than Pluto, moves through its orbit in the opposite direction of Neptune, suggesting the satellite didn't form with Neptune, but was later captured by it. This would explain Neptune's excess heat and Triton's strangely inclined orbit.

The Exploded Planet Hypothesis was used by Olbers to explain the existence of asteroids. Nowadays, many people don't even know or care for the multiple asteroids in existence in outer space. However, Lagrange found the theory to explain the origin of comets (celestial objects made of a nucleus of ice and dust, forming a tail of gas and dust particles when near the Sun).

It is believed that comets originate from two destinations – some coming from the Kuiper Belt (taking under 200 years to complete an orbit around the Sun), but most being from the Oort cloud (taking over 200 years to complete an orbit around the Sun).

The Oort cloud is a supposed cloud, 50,000 AU or 1 light year from the Sun, containing over a trillion comets, surrounding the Sun. It is believed the comets that make up the Oort cloud were thrown out of the inner Solar System by Jupiter and Saturn.

The comets therefore originated in the inner Solar System, formed from one giant mass. Wouldn't a giant mass of this size be termed a 'planet'?

y ¿quien y cómo cuentan todo esos trillones

And I don't see how a planet (Saturn and/or Jupiter) can throw out another planet. Does this happen today? No!

Consider a street full of buildings. One, two or even ten buildings do not and cannot just throw another building. But what if an explosion occurred from within a building, i.e. from a bomb, could this 'throw' the building into millions of smashed bricks and blocks, over the entire street? Of course! Now instead of an inside-explosion, how about some kind of explosive impact external to the building, i.e. a giant wrecking ball? Can the building be 'thrown' into millions of smashed bricks and blocks over the street? Yes! Remember, the explosion – bomb or wrecking ball, will not throw every brick or block into one direction, but in all directions, and a small remnant of the building will remain in the same region.

Considering the common sense scenario outlined above, why can't the comets from the Oort cloud have originally formed one giant planet in the inner Solar System (in the same orbit as the Asteroid Belt), and the planet somehow exploded internally or because of an outside force? Does the Exploded Planet Hypothesis still seem too crazy to believe?

From our scenario, remembering that some bricks would have remained, and now considering the effect of the Roche limit, could the Asteroid Belt be the remains left behind at the place of explosion/impact?

Dr. Flandern believed that this explosion/impact must have occurred recently (in astronomical terms), otherwise something like a passing star or galactic tide would have diminished the Oort cloud.

An interesting individual of the 20th Century (1874–1932) was an American writer and researcher into anomalous phenomena, Charles Fort. In his book, Book of the Damned, he mentions many mysterious things such as frozen fish, frogs and a variety of materials falling from the sky, including huge, oversized flint arrowheads and axes – evidence for the existence of giants. Could these have come from remains of an exploded planet?

Another strange aspect of the Solar System which relates to the Exploded Planet Hypothesis refers to Earth's moon – the various mascons. A mascon (mass concentration) is a region on the moon's crust (or planet) which contains a large/noticeable positive gravitational anomaly. This anomaly is in the form of an excessive distribution of mass on or beneath the moon's surface. NASA scientists discovered that as the Lunar Orbiter Spacecraft (launched in 1966–67) passed over certain areas (now known as mascons), the stronger gravity field caused the craft to dip slightly and increase in speed.

The moon's mascons remain a mystery but scientists generally agree that they are the result of impacts. Are the mascons impacts from an exploded planet? Some of the known mascons on Earth's moon are: Imbrium, Crisium and Serenitatis. Note the Latin translations for the moon mascons – Imbrium (Latin for 'Sea of Showers', and Crisium (Latin for 'Sea of Crises'). When I saw an image of the moon with Imbrium, it reminded me of the image of the Death Star, in the final *Star Wars* movie.

Something else which I find of great interest. In March 2009, NASA launched a space observatory named Kepler, in order to discover Earth-like planets orbiting other stars. Around 200 AU from our Solar System, Kepler made the first detection of a planet orbiting two stars. This planet, Keplar 16-b, orbits two of the150,000 stars that the spacecraft has been monitoring between the constellations Cygnus and Lyra. Kepler detected the planet through what is known as a planetary transit – an event where the brightness of a star dims as a result of a planet crossing in front of it. Planets orbiting double stars have been a favourite for sci-fi writers for a long time. The most famous of these is from the 1977 *Star Wars* movie, *A New Hope*, which showed a double-sunset viewed from the fictional planet Tatooine.

Until NASA'S discovery in 2009, astronomers generally did not know that such planets systems could exist. Now, because of Kepler 16-b, astronomers have confirmed that the double-sunset seen by Luke Skywalker is possible. It has been reported that the planet Kepler 16-b, is cold, gaseous and around the size of Saturn. The stars are both smaller than the Sun, and about 2 billion years younger than our Solar System. They orbit each other and so take turns to eclipse each other.

I wonder just how much of the *Star Wars* movies are not science-fiction, but actually science-fact. Perhaps astronomers should be asking the creator of the *Star Wars* movies, George Lucas, about space? He evidently knew about twin star systems over 30 years before astronomers and scientists!

However, if the Exploded Planet Hypothesis is correct (and I am certainly leading towards this conclusion), then this additional planet, being larger than Saturn, may have been bright enough to see in the daytime, like a sun. Again, I'm thinking of that *Star Wars* scene of the two suns, but in our own

Solar System. I also believe the exploded planet to have been more water-based than land-based. This is because asteroids and comets are said to have a large water content. And as I have already discussed, asteroids and comets are originally from the exploded planet.

Astronomers have been arguing for decades over how Earth got its water. In 2011, an international team of astronomers used the European Space Agency's Herschel Space Observatory to study Comet Hartley 2. On October 5th, 2011, the results were published in the international journal *Nature*. The astronomers discovered the comet to contain ocean-like water!

In addition to the above, there is vast evidence which shows Mars was mysteriously flooded with water during its past. Extensive regions on Mars's surface are eroded with channel markings. Drainage patterns are found where water travelled downhill over large open areas and ground water has seeped to the surface. Scientists have concluded the flooding to be a recent development, and water may still be present. The water on the surface of Mars could have originated from its neighbouring planet, the exploded planet.

Dr. Flandern speculates the exploded planet to be populated with intelligent human-like life, with skeletal structures much larger than ours. Charles Fort reported huge oversized flint arrowheads and axes – fit for giants. In Dr. Flandern's original formulation, he proposed the planet's explosion to have occurred around 3,200,000 years ago. However, this caused problems as the astronomical evidence and the actual geophysical evidence seems to be the same, with the exception of the date. Dr. Flandern, in his book, *Dark Matter, Missing Planets, and New Comets*, said: "Such a major explosion should leave evidence all over the Solar System, and apparently has. Yet in the geological record on Earth, there is little to support the hypothesis of a major explosion specifically at 3.2 million years ago. There is evidence for the onset of a series of ice ages about then, after a long span of tropical climate. And the origin of man dates to around then. But one would have expected a global layer of carbon deposits, enrichment in the element iridium, shocked quartz from impacts, multiple impact craters, micro-tektites and micro-diamond formation, enhanced volcanism, atmospheric and ocean changes, a single global fire, mass extinction of species, and many other dramatic changes. Such things are seen in several places in the geological record, but not nearly 3 million years ago according to the presently adopted geochronology. Strikingly, all those features are seen together at the Cretaceous-Tertiary (K/T) boundary, dated at 65 million years ago, when the dinosaurs and many other species became extinct."

So, 65,000,000 years seemed plausible for a planet to explode, but not 32,000,000 years. Therefore, to explain Earth's geological record, Dr. Flandern argued for the possibility of multiple planetary explosions, at different dates. Is it possible, however, that Dr. Flandern was correct with his original date of 3,200,000 years? In my view, to explain the absence of geological debris on Earth, the Earth could have been at its farthest distance from the exploded planet, the moon in orbit between the planet and Earth, with Mars somewhat in the path of the exploded planet – therefore protecting Earth.

Dr. Flandern revised his Exploded Planet Hypothesis, by considering that there may have been at least two planets in orbit between Mars and Jupiter, which exploded in different periods. This revised hypothesis causes an issue with the Titius-Bode Law, because now instead of looking for one missing planet, the search is on for two planets in the same orbit. The Law predicted one planet. Dr. Flandern now had both Mars and a smaller planet (called 'C'), as satellites of Planet A. From an explosion, these three objects evolved into a double-planetary system. He says that C exploded over 3,200,000 years ago, which left Mars with craters, a flood of water and increased volcanic activity. The problem with this theory of Dr. Flandern's is that it is very rare for a planet to explode, and now we are left with two explosions.

Are you thinking "So what if there was another planet or two in our Solar System, what is the big deal?" Pluto was recently discovered and that didn't seem to be 'mysterious'. So, what is so special about an exploded planet(s)? Considering the above, I can think of two reasons why the exploded planet(s) should be fully investigated, and why we should be determined to know about it/them: (1) The planet's way of life and (2) The explosion.

These can be broken down into:

- Life the planet(s) contained, which was very powerful
- Way of life, which was likely to be sophisticated and technologically advanced
- How the planet exploded
- Was the explosion due to an outside force? Why was the planet destroyed? And by whom/what?

Cydonia is a region on Mars that contains the "Face on Mars".

The answers to the above will reveal an incredible amount that could change our way of life on Earth, forever. Is this why the exploded planet is not even mentioned in the mainstream, and why we are not encouraged to question its significance?

Aside from the flooding of Mars which I have already mentioned, an explosion (from planet A or C) could have severely affected Mar's magnetic pole alignment. The explosion would have plummeted debris, amongst other things, into the planet. Additionally, Mars would most likely have been stripped of its life, water and atmosphere. In addition to the exploded planet, I believe Mars contained intelligent life. This is due to the following: Face on Mars: In 1975, a pair of American space probes named Voyager 1 and Voyager 2 were sent to Mars and imaged this stunning feature. Cydonia is a region on Mars which has attracted both scientific and popular interest. Cydonia contains the Face on Mars, which is over 1 mile long, over 1 mile wide and 400 metres high! It is located between the Arandas Crater and Bamberg Crater. Richard Hoagland (a former NASA Advisor, Science Advisor to Walter Cronkite and CBS News, and Space Museum Curator), believes the face to be an artificially created humanoid face, as do many others.

Interestingly, the 2000 movie directed by Brian De Palma, *Mission to Mars*, contained the Face on Mars. I advise you to watch it. The ending shows an alien demonstrating to the astronauts what happened to Mars. Mars is depicted as being covered with water and struck by some sort of object (from Planet A's explosion?). In the film, the Martians evacuated their world in spacecrafts, except for one, which went to Earth and deposited a sample of DNA into an ocean which at the time contained no life. This DNA evolved into fish and land mammals. Note, humans were shown on-screen, but they were not shown transforming from land mammals into apes and then into humans.

Also in *Mission to Mars*, the last Martian spacecraft leaves the Face on Mars in order reach the same destination as the other spacecrafts. One of the astronauts chooses to remain onboard for this adventure and to learn about these Martians, hence developing his mind, wisdom and perhaps spirituality. The interesting point to be made, is that this last remaining spacecraft breaks through the Face in the exact region of where the pineal gland/third-eye is located. Is there a message here? The pineal gland is discussed later in detail.

Note: In the 2012 movie directed by Ridley Scott, *Prometheus*, the very first minute shows a spacecraft of an advanced humanoid race on Earth. One of the aliens, called an Engineer, drinks a dark liquid, causing its body to disintegrate and fall into a waterfall. The event seems to be a ritual sacrifice. The point is that we see this alien's DNA break down and recombine (mixing of alien DNA and Earth substance) to form life on Earth.

Both movies convey the same message. Are they simply entertainment? You can contact the directors for their honest answer.

Have you properly looked at the official image/poster for the 1982 movie, directed by Steven Spielberg, *E.T. the Extra-Terrestrial?* Compare it with the stunning Sistine Chapel ceiling, painted by Michelangelo (the famous Italian Renaissance Sculptor, Painter, Architect, Poet and Engineer) between 1508 and 1512. In the movie poster, showing the image of outer space, E.T.'s finger is touching a human child's finger, and the Earth is directly beneath this action. Doesn't this resemble God touching Man (The Creation of Adam painting) on the Sistine Chapel ceiling? Again, it is a painting called, The Creation of Man. Don't you think Spielberg is sending you a message here? Remember the epigraph:

You look but you don't see,
You hear but you don't listen
To question is not to be disruptive.
To question is to understand the truth.

This is now out of scope with the Face on Mars, but I believe these comparisons are important to make. And as I have touched on the Sistine Chapel, I will continue. Steganography is the art and science of writing hidden messages in such a way that only the sender and intended recipient know what the message is. Steganography was widely used in art. Michelangelo, like Leonardo Da Vinci, was a very bright individual. I am sure both knew exactly what they were painting.

Note: In the Sistine Chapel, have you looked closely at the postures of God, Adam and their fingers? God is not on the land, (is he in Space?), he is really stretching out to touch Adam. With God's angels (colleagues), it seems they are doing one of two things; either they are helping to stabilise God so he doesn't fall, or they are trying to prevent him from touching Adam. Now,

(all of the above)

(Dios se está apuntando de un ángel)
Adán como que no tiene mucho interés de
tocar el dedo de "dios".

how can God 'fall'? Isn't he omnipotent? Notice that the angels' bodies are leaning away from him, or trying to pull him away. If they were encouraging God to 'meet with' Adam, surely they would be leaning towards God. And why would they need to stabilise God from falling? He is supposed to be all-powerful. Unless the implication is that he would be at risk if he did fall, and is therefore a hint at his mortality.

In the movie *E.T. the Extra-Terrestrial*, you remember how the boy loved the alien, and became emotionally attached to it? Perhaps this is shown in the movie poster with both the alien and young human's fingers pointed towards each other. However, in the Sistine Chapel, it is quite clear that Adam is leaning away from God. He does not stand, or even sit upright to make it easier for God to touch him. Adam is not embracing God. Adam's finger is not stretched out at all. And look at his posture. Does he seem eager to be touched by God?

One last thing to note is the giant red craft which God and the angels are in. I thought both could fly? Again, I thought God was omnipotent? The object is obviously not a cloud. Clouds are not red, and the sky itself is blue – it is a nice bright day. Could it be some sort of spacecraft? Does this sound a bit far-fetched? I advise you to look over my questions again regarding the Sistine Chapel and try to answer them, and come up with your own questions.

Why is the Sistine Chapel important? Because it is supposed to show the creation of man. If you think Michelangelo a fool, then let me tell you that he was considered the greatest living artist in his lifetime, and is nowadays considered to be one of the greatest of all time. And I highly doubt a fool would be permitted to paint in the best-known chapel in the Apolostolic Palace, the official residence of the Pope in the Vatican City.

- Fort: A three-walled enclosure in Cydonia. Maybe it is the foundation of a unique pyramid that was never completed? I use the word 'unique' deliberately because pyramids on Earth are four-sided.
- Cliff and Pyramid: East of the Face, is a nearly two-mile-long cliff. To the east of the cliff is a very large crater with a tetrahedron/three-sided pyramid on its edges. As the cliff and pyramid are not damaged from the crater (from a meteorite), this means they were built after the crater was formed.

- Tholus: A hill or mound in Cydonia, which strangely has a spiral ramp encircling it like a pathway to the top. As Richard Hoagland points out, if a vertical line is drawn along the cliff, to the top of Tholus, and another line drawn from the top of Tholus to the tetrahedron on the crater's edge, the angle formed is 19.5 degrees. This angle is found many times throughout Cydonia.
- D & M: An enormous five-sided pyramid! A pentagon-based pyramid, located to the south-west of the Face.
- Other pyramids: A group of large pyramids to the West of the Face, in a location named 'The City' or 'City Square'.
- Further structures: More interesting anomalies exist in regions aside from Cydonia. In Utopia, which is half-way around Mars from Cydonia, there are two features which are situated in straight lines, called 'Runway' and 'Bow-tie'.
- Xenon 129: Haven't you wondered why Mars is red? It has a very thin atmosphere for a planet of its size. Gamma ray spectrometry taken over the past few years has shown spiking radiation from Xenon-129. An increase is also seen on Earth after a nuclear reaction or nuclear meltdown has occurred, such as Chernobyl, Ukraine in 1986 and Fukushima, Japan, in 2011.

The nuclear explosion filled the Martian atmosphere with radio isotopes (Xenon-129). The radioactivity explains why the planet is red. So what was its colour before the nuclear explosion? What colour would Earth be if its atmosphere was filled with Xenon-129 isotopes?

I have heard that nuclear explosions can occur naturally. I ask you, have you ever heard of a nuclear explosion occurring on Earth by itself? The explosions which occurred on Earth stemmed from within nuclear facilities, i.e. Chernobyl and Fukushima. These facilities did not build themselves; they were created by hundreds or thousands of people ranging from builders, specialists and scientists to management teams.

So how did the explosion occur? I refer you again to Planet A and the scenario of a street full of buildings. If one building (one planet) collided with another, would both buildings consume themselves? No. All the bricks would not just disappear. Many would be reduced to rubble. Would the buildings be destroyed? In their original form, yes, but not completely. Could one knock the other off its base? Yes, and both buildings would end up in different positions. Can a building suddenly explode on its own? No, unless it is fitted with detonators, or a highly explosive flammable already contained in the building suddenly explodes. But something or someone has to cause this material to explode. There must be a spark.

Note: A building cannot and does not just decide one day to collide into another building. And a building cannot explode by itself. There has to be a catalyst. Could the nuclear explosion have occurred on Mars itself? Or was the destruction of Mars caused by the explosion of Planet A? Or some other outside force? And if it was impact from Planet A, what caused A to explode? Dr. Flandern implies that the exploded planets may have been blown up deliberately in an act of war by intelligent beings. This is what I believe, and this is what ancient scriptures support.

An outside force, such as intelligent beings, would need to be in possession of highly sophisticated engineering ability, knowledge of quantum mechanics, nuclear physics, and much more.

To explode an entire planet would require a colossal amount of energy. I am again reminded of the Death Star from the *Star Wars* movie. What kind of physics could be involved in the creation of weapons, enough to explode an entire planet?

I will now introduce you to Hannes Olof Gosta Alfven, (1908–1995). Alfven was a genius. He was a Swedish Electrical Engineer, Plasma Physicist and he won the Nobel Prize in Physics in 1970 for his work on Magnetohydrodynamics (also known as magneto fluid dynamics or hydromagnetics). Alfven presumed that electrical plasma filaments exist in very large inter-galactic electrical currents. The existence of such intensity of energy leads to the theory that planetary scarring and searing is possible. And if planetary scarring and searing is possible, so is it possible that a planet may be blown up.

For those who do not know, plasma is considered to be the fourth state of matter, aside from solids, liquids and gases. Plasma contains many electrically charged particles, and plasmas are estimated to make up over 99% of the visible universe.

What is a filament? A filament is a long thin structure of galaxies, which can span up to 500,000,000 Megaparsecs in length. A parsec is a unit of length used in astronomy. One parsec is around 3.26 light-years, thus 19.2

trillion miles. A megaparsec is a million parsecs. Therefore, to say a filament is enormous is an understatement!

The following quotation is included to introduce the concept of space being full of electricity. Published in *The New Astronomy* in 1948: "Nearly everything we know about the celestial universe has come from applying principles we have learned in terrestrial physics: Newton's law of motion, our studies of the spectrum of light, our explorations of the nucleus of the atom and other major discoveries in our physics laboratories have contributed to our enlightenment about the stars – their motions, their chemical composition, their temperatures and their source of energy."

"Yet there is one great branch of physics which up to now has now told us little or nothing about astronomy. That branch is electricity. It is rather astonishing that this phenomenon, which has been so exhaustively studied on the earth, has been of so little help in the celestial sphere. Electricity has illuminated our cities but has shed no light on stellar phenomena; it has linked the earth with a dense net of communications but has given no information about the universe around us."

"Certainly we have seen plenty of evidence of electrical phenomena out in space. Within the last few decades we have discovered several important electrical effects in the heavens; strong stellar magnet fields could only be caused by large electric currents, radio waves emanating from the sun and from many star systems, and the energetic cosmic rays, which are electrically charged particles accelerated to tremendous speeds."

"These phenomena, however, are still very mysterious. We have no idea how electric currents may be generated and transmitted in the stars or in space. Although we know a great deal about electricity, almost everything we know is based on its behaviour in wires. We generate electricity by moving copper wires in a magnetic field, and we can transport, broadcast and use electrical energy only by means of wires. Any electrical engineer, asked what he could do without using metal wires at all, would certainly say nothing."

"But there are no wires in the stars. They consist entirely of hot gases. While physicists have given much study to the behaviour of electric current in gases, we know of no means by which gases can generate electricity. Hence the electrical phenomena in stars present us with a completely new problem."

"We cannot bring the stars into our laboratories. But we can investigate electrical behaviour in a medium roughly comparable to the gaseous body of a star and under comparable conditions. We know that there are magnetic fields in stars. We also know that very hot incandescent gases, which make up a star, are good electrical conductors. In the interior of a star the gases are under such great pressure that they may be much denser than ordinary liquids. Since we cannot work with gases under such pressure in a laboratory, the closest we can come is to use a liquid. Of the common liquids, mercury is the only one which is a good conductor of electricity."

"We have recently conducted some simple experiments with mercury in a magnetic field and observed several very curious and striking results.

"Everyone is acquainted with the 'mercurial' behaviour of mercury. If you tap the side of a vessel containing a pool of mercury, the surface quakes and ripples as if it were alive: We found that when we placed such a pool in a strong magnetic field of 10,000 gauss, its behavior instantly changed. It did not respond to jarring of the vessel; its surface stiffened, so-to-speak. The magnetic field gave a curious kind of viscosity to the mercury. This was illustrated dramatically when we dipped the two ends of a bent metal wire into the liquid and moved them through it. Ordinarily an object dragged through mercury moves as easily as through any liquid. But when the magnetic field was applied, the wire pulled the mercury with it, producing a big surge in the pool. It was like moving a stick through honey or syrup.

This behaviour is easily explained. The wire and the surface of the mercury between its ends form an electricity-conducting circuit. When the wire is moved across the magnetic field, it creates an electric current. Since an electric current always produces a magnetic field, the new current creates a second magnetic field. This interacts with the one we have already applied to the pool of mercury, just as two magnets attract or repel each other. The force between the two magnetic fields opposes the motion which is producing the current. As a result the wire sticks to the mercury as if it were a very viscous liquid."

"Let us now consider another experiment that disclosed a more remarkable and illuminating phenomenon. We fill a small tank with mercury. The tank has a movable bottom which can be rotated back and forth like the agitator in a washing machine. In the absence of a magnetic field, the slow oscillation of this agitator, stirring the mercury at the bottom of the tank, will not disturb the surface of the mercury at the top of the tank; the mercury molecules slide past one another so that the motion dies out before it proceeds very far up the tank. A mirror floating on the surface, with a beam of light shined on it to show any slight movement, stays perfectly still. When a strong vertical magnetic field is applied to the tank, however, the motion at the bottom is quickly communicated to the top."

What we have created here is a new kind of wave, which was predicted theoretically about ten years ago but was actually produced for the first time in this experiment. The wave is the result of a coupling between magnetic and hydrodynamic forces. When the mercury at the bottom moves in the magnetic field, it generates electric currents. These currents, with their attendant magnetic fields, produce mechanical motion in the mercury immediately above, which in turn creates new currents that act on the next layer. Thus the movement is communicated up through the whole body of the liquid. This rising wave of motion is called a magnetohydrodynamic wave. It has three characteristics: it produces (1) mechanical motion, (2) a magnetic field, and (3) an electric field.

What has all this to do with the stars? It is possible to show that our mercury model reproduces many of the essential properties of stellar matter. To be sure, the magnetic fields in the stars are very much weaker than the 10,000 gauss of our experiment (the sun's general field is estimated at between 1 and 25 gauss). But our theory tells us that if we made the vessel larger, we could produce the magnetohydrodynamic effects with a smaller magnetic field; the magnetic force required would decline in proportion to the increase in size of the vessel. Hence in a star, which is, say, 10 billion times as large as our experimental vessel, the magnetic field need be only one 10-billionth of the laboratory field. The stars' fields are much stronger than this.

"The results of our experiments lead to an entirely new way of looking at the behaviour of stellar matter. It has always been assumed that the movement of gases in stars obeys the laws of hydrodynamics, as they apply to ordinary liquids and gases. But if a magnetic field drastically changes the properties of the dense stellar gases as it does in the mercury model, then they must behave very differently from ordinary fluids. Let us see whether the curious behaviour of mercury in a magnetic field can shed any light on some of the great mysteries in astronomy."

"Consider sunspots. Few astronomical phenomena have been more thoroughly studied. We have charted their paths across the sun's surface, discovered their cycle of activity and their effects on solar radiation, analyzed their light and learned from the splitting of their spectral lines (the so-called Zeeman effect) that they have strong magnetic fields. But what sunspots are, how they originate, how they can produce magnetic fields – that seems more difficult to explain. It was once thought that sunspots were great eddies in the solar atmosphere, similar to cyclones on the earth. The motions of gas in sunspots, however, are not at all like those of the air in cyclones."

The pieces of the puzzle begin to fall into place if we think of the mercury model. We can assume that the energetic nuclear reactions in the interior of the sun cause violent motions of the matter there. This would correspond to the stirring of the mercury at the bottom of the vessel. In the sun's general magnetic field, whose lines of force apparently run from the centre of the sun out to the surface, these motions would generate magnetohydrodynamic waves that would travel to the surface. The waves would account for the strong magnetic fields associated with sunspots."

"As we have seen, magnetohydrodynamic waves also generate an electric field. This may well account for some of the other phenomena observed on the sun's surface. The very high voltages generated by the waves may discharge into the sun's atmosphere, very much as a discharge tube in the laboratory produces corona discharges into the air. Such discharges would explain the solar prominences. The marvellous motion pictures of solar prominences taken at Pic du Midi in the Pyrenees and at the High Altitude Observatory near Climax, Col., give a vivid impression that they are electrical discharges."

"The sun's emission of radio noise, another great mystery, would also be accounted for by this method of generating electricity. As radio listeners know too well, all sorts of electric currents – in transmission lines, household appliances and so on – produce radio noise. The large electric currents generated in stars by magnetohydrodynamic forces would give rise to radio waves and broadcast them into space."

"Finally, the magnetohydrodynamic process seems to offer a plausible explanation for the great energy of the cosmic rays. How these particles are driven to their fantastic energies, sometimes as high as a million billion electron volts, is one of the prime puzzles of astronomy. No known (or even unknown) nuclear reaction could account for the firing of particles with such energies; even the complete annihilation of a proton would not yield more than a billion electron volts."

"But if we suppose that the cosmic-ray particles are driven by electric and magnetic fields in space, in the same way as we accelerate particles in our big laboratory accelerators, it is easy to see how they could reach very high energies indeed. We know that interstellar space is not absolutely void. Although the matter in it is very thin, certainly not more than an average of one atom per cubic centimetre, in the vastness of the universe it adds up to an enormous amount of material. In at least some regions the interstellar matter is ionized, so that it is a good electrical conductor. Furthermore, there are good arguments for assuming that a weak magnetic field (some millions of a gauss) pervades all of space. It is likely, therefore, that magnetohydrodynamic waves roam ceaselessly through space, generating weak but very extensive electric fields, especially near the stars. If so, we can picture charged atomic nuclei being propelled across electrified space, gathering speed as they go and crashing into the earth's atmosphere with energies far beyond any that could ever be generated within any star or planet."

Now let us return to Alfven presuming that electrical plasma filaments exist in very large inter-galactic electrical currents, thus making planetary scarring, searing and more, possible.

Dr. Flandern has suggested that there is evidence of a large electrical discharge in our Solar System, from Lunar and Martian sinuous rilles. A rille is used to describe a long and narrow depression in the lunar or martian surface which resembles a channel. A sinuous rille meanders in a curved path, and is commonly thought to be the remains of a collapsed lava tube or extinct lava flow. It is said to usually begin at an extinct volcano. However, NASA has said that the origin of sinuous rilles remains controversial. An example of a rille on Mars is the huge Mamers Vallis. It is a long canyon with a length of over 600 miles, average width of 15 miles and a depth of 1200 metres.

An example of a sinuous rille on the Moon is Hadley Rille. This is a valley, just under 1 mile wide and over 300 metres deep. This was a primary site of exploration for the Apollo 15 mission, because puzzles remain with the rille. Dr. Flandern said: "Mars displays evidence that there was enough water for a brief period to produce flowing rivers and channels, although that would be impossible today. Sinuous rilles on the Moon and Mars are almost certainly water-carved features, and relatively recent as well, judging from the lack of overlying craters. The assumption that they must be from lava flows is inconsistent in some cases, since the rilles don't slope away from potential lava sources, and neither lava nor any other candidate substance is known to carve sinuous features."

Some rilles indicate that water isn't their origin, but massive electrostatic discharges instead. This planetary scarring means there is a type of physics which could be engineered to create a weapon, powerful enough to blow up a planet. We shall now delve into the realm of plasma.

PLASMA WEAPONRY

Plasma physics is known to have a strong influence on astrophysical phenomena. The majority of matter in the universe is in the form of plasma, and plasma is a good conductor of electricity. Alfven was sure that plasma played an important role in the universe. He was confident that electromagnetic forces are much more important than gravity when referring to interplanetary (between and amongst planets) and interstellar (between and amongst stars) charged particles.

Electromagnetism describes the relationship between electricity and magnetism (the physical phenomenon produced by the motion of electric charge, resulting in attracting or repelling forces between objects). Electricity and magnetism depend on each other, because a changing electric field creates a magnetic field, and a changing magnetic field creates an electric field. During Alfven's experiments with plasma, he noticed that the filaments he saw in aurora displays were actually being produced in his laboratory.

Kristian Olaf Birkeland (1867–1917), a Norwegian scientist, was the first person to explain the nature of Aurora Borealis (Northern Lights). He believed that solar wind, generated in space caused the aurora. The mainstream view contradicted this by arguing that currents cannot cross a vacuum (space that is empty of matter), and therefore currents had to be generated by Earth. Alfven supported Birkeland's theory, which was proved to be correct when a probe was sent into space.

Solar wind is a stream of charged particles (made up of electrons and protons) released from the upper atmosphere of the Sun. The stream of particles varies in speed and temperature, and the stream can escape the Sun's gravity because of the particles' high kinetic energy and the high temperature of the Sun's corona (a type of plasma atmosphere of the Sun, extending millions of miles into space. A corona can be easily seen during a solar eclipse). The solar wind creates the heliosphere, a bubble of charged particles in the space surrounding the entire Solar System. The solar wind strikes the Earth, warming it, and controls the weather, giving energy for life to exist.

Other phenomena from the solar wind include the aurora. The aurora is a beautiful display of lights in the sky, most commonly at the Earth's north and south poles, therefore referred to as the Southern (Antarctic) Lights or Northern (Arctic) Lights. The bombardment of solar electrons on the Earth's two main gases (oxygen and nitrogen), create the aurora high in the atmosphere.

Eric J. Lerner, an independent plasma researcher and science writer, authored *The Big Bang Never Happened* (1991), which supports Alfven's theory of the Big Bang. Regarding Alfven's plasma experiments, Lerner explained: "Whenever a piece of vacuum equipment started to misbehave, there they were. They were there too, in photographs of solar prominences and of the distant Veil and Orion nebulas.... Many investigators had analysed the laboratory filaments before, so Alfven knew what they were: tiny electromagnetic vortices that snake through a plasma, carrying electrical currents. The vortices are produced by a phenomenon known as the 'pinch effect'. A straight thread of electrical current flowing through a plasma produces a cylindrical magnetic field, which attracts other currents flowing in the same direction. Thus the tiny current threads tend to 'pinch' together, drawing the plasma with them... The converging threads twine into a plasma rope, much as water converging toward a drain generates a swirling vortex, or air rushes together in a tornado. The filaments are plasma whirlwinds."

This important phenomenon implies: "Magnetic fields and currents can concentrate matter and energy far faster and more effectively than can gravity. The magnetic force of a plasma thread increases with the velocity of the plasma. This leads to a feedback effect: as threads are pulled into the vortex, they move faster, which increases the force on the threads of current and pulls them still faster into the filament. In addition, a contracting mass tends to spin faster... This generates a centrifugal force which fights the contraction. Magnetic filaments can carry away this excess spin, or angular momentum, allowing further contraction, while gravity cannot."

According to Alfven's theory: "A galaxy, spinning in the magnetic fields of intergalactic space, generates electricity, as any conductor does when it moves through a magnetic field...The huge electrical current produced by the galaxy flows in great filamentary spirals toward the centre of the galaxy, where it turns and flows out along the spin axis. This galactic current then short-circuits, driving a vast amount of energy into the galactic core. The galaxy 'blows a fuse': powerful electrical fields are created in the nucleus which accelerate intense jets of electrons and ions out along the axis (of spin)."

Alfven discovered another plasma phenomenon, that energy can be released suddenly and explosively: "By forming the filamentary structures observed on the smallest and largest scales, matter and energy can be compressed in space. But it is clear that energy can be compressed in time as well – the universe is filled with sudden, explosive releases of energy. One example that Alfven was familiar with is the solar flare, the sudden release of energy on the sun's surface, which generates the streams of particles that produce magnetic storms on earth...Understanding the explosive release of energy was the key to the dynamics of the cosmos."

Lerner's interest in plasma cosmology led him to investigate controlled fusion research, and to Winston Bostick, an American physicist who discovered plasmoids, plasma focus and plasma vortex phenomena.

Fusion is a form of nuclear energy which is created when light-weight atoms join together. Fusion is the process at the core in every star, for example, the Sun. Atoms are constantly moving. The hotter they are, the faster they move. Our Sun's core temperature reaches a whopping 15 million degrees Celsius. At this temperature, hydrogen atoms are colliding at extremely high speeds. The natural electrostatic repulsion that exists between the positive charges of their nuclei is overcome, and the atoms join/fuse. The fusion of two light hydrogen atoms (H-H) produces a heavier element, helium atom.

However, the mass of this resulting helium atom is not the complete total of the two initial atoms, because some mass is lost but a great amount of energy is gained. This is described by Einstein's formula: $E=mc2$, where the small amount of mass lost (m), multiplied by the square of the speed of light (c2), giving the large figure (E), which is the amount of energy created by a fusion reaction. It has been said that every second, our Sun turns 600 million tonnes of hydrogen into helium, thus releasing a massive amount of energy. What we see as light and warmth is the result of a fusion reaction – hydrogen nuclei colliding, joining heavier helium atoms, thus releasing an enormous amount of energy.

Bostick's research focused on a fusion device called the plasma focus. This is a machine which creates, by electromagnetic acceleration and compression, short plasma that is so hot and dense that it can cause nuclear fusion and emit X-rays. This electromagnetic compression is called a 'pinch'.

The plasma focus is similar to a plasma gun which forces plasma in the form of a plasmoid, without pinching it. A plasmoid is a consistent structure of plasma and magnetic fields. A plasma focus can increase the power density of its emissions by a factor of ten thousand trillion over that of the incoming energy – comparable to the ratio of a quasar to a galaxy.

Plasma weapons have been used in sci-fi movies for decades. In the movies, it is a type of ray-gun which fires a stream, bolt, pulse or toroid of plasma. The device causes serious burns and often the immediate death of living creatures, and melts and evaporates other materials. A handful of movies in which such devices appear are; *Iron Man 1 and 2* (Tony Stark's plasma cannon): *Star Trek* (Various spacecraft and hand-held weapons): Star Wars (Blasters and light-sabers): *Terminator 2* (At the start of the movie, the human-resistance and terminators use plasma rifles): *Terminator 3* (The villain, T-X, reconfigures its right forearm into a plasma cannon): *Transformers* (Multiple characters use plasma weapons). How fictional are these weapons in movies? Today, we have:

- Plasma focus machine (already discussed)
- Plasma torches, used for cutting metal and concrete, by projecting very short-distance plasma streams
- Microscopic, short plasma bursts from Nd: YAG (Neodymium-doped yttrium aluminium garnet) lasers, used in medicine, especially ophthalmology
- Shiva Star, a high-powered pulsed-power device located at the Air Force Research Laboratory on the Kirtland Air Force Base in New Mexico. It was said to be used for the Strategic Defence Initiative, and is now being used for magnetized target fusion. I have found some sources stating

that the device was designed to produce a ground-based plasma weapon, capable of firing plasma bullets at incoming ballistic missile warheads. The device's fast capacitor bank is said to store 10 million joules of energy before suddenly releasing it.

The misuse of a plasma focus device allows a variety of phenomenon to be accessed, from anti-gravity and thermonuclear fusion (the same explosive energy as the hydrogen bomb) to deadly radiation. If such energy could be manipulated, it could amass such immense power to be used on a planetary-scale. Has something already been created by mankind, for destructive means? Unfortunately, yes – the atomic bomb.

Dr. Julius Robert Oppenheimer (1904–1967), an American physicist, Professor of Physics and 'Father of the Atomic Bomb' for his role in the Manhattan Project. This was a research and development programme by the United States, the United Kingdom and Canada, during the Second World War (1939–1945). In the aftermath of the atomic bomb, Dr. Oppenheimer commented: "We knew the world would not be the same. Few people laughed, few people cried, most people were silent. I remembered the line from the Hindu scripture, the Bhagavad-Gita. Vishnu is trying to persuade the Prince that he should do his duty, and to impress him, takes on his multi-armed form, and says: "Now I am become death, the destroyer of worlds." I suppose we all thought that, one way or another."

Two nuclear weapons were used in the Second World War by the United States. One was detonated over Hiroshima, and the other detonated over Nagasaki, both in Japan. Over 200,000 Japanese people, mostly civilians, were reportedly killed. It is now estimated that there are over 19,000 nuclear warheads around the world (as of 2012).

Research indicates, as Oppenheimer's comment does, that knowledge of occult texts was known amongst the scientists involved in this 'line of work'. They may have been investigating ancient myths and legends of the gods and their wars to extract data which could further the cause of building such powerful and deadly weapons. Germany, especially including Nazi Germany, carried out deep research in the ancient Vedic culture of India, as well as Mesopotamia (Sumer, Babylon, Akkadia and Assyria). These texts may have been behind the motivation to create such weapons.

THE SUBCONSCIOUS MIND

Still related to plasma physics, powerful weaponry and ancient history, I want for the moment to bring something else to your attention... the subconscious mind. I have often wondered, why is it that so many of us are attracted to science fiction movies and comic books? We watch or read about things that seem to be so strange, impossible and vastly different to our current way of life, and yet we are so intrigued by them. Why? As I have briefly mentioned already, I believe this is because of our subconscious mind. The conscious mind is responsible for logic, calculations and other day-to-day actions such as lifting, running and cycling. The subconscious mind is much more interesting. This stores all of your previous life experiences (supposedly), beliefs, memories, skills and every image you've ever seen. The subconscious also controls aspects of your life such as breathing.

Sigmund Freud, the famous Austrian Neurologist who became known as the Father of Psychoanalysis, regarded the mind as being like an iceberg, where the largest part is hidden beneath the water, hence, beneath the conscious.

Carl G. Jung said "When a man is fifty years old, only one part of his being has existed for half a century. The other part, which lives in his psyche, may be millions of years old..." Jung's comment implies that the spirit or soul of man is eternal.

How else could a person's subconscious be aware of events in the distant past? The body is finite, a vehicle only lasting for a maximum of roughly one hundred years. The soul lives in multiple bodies, thus experiencing many lifetimes, resulting in the notion of past life experiences. This, I believe.

In his 1989 book *Memories, Dreams, Reflections*, Prof. Carl Jung says: "Somewhere deep in the background I always knew that I was two persons. One was the son of my parents... The other was grown up – old in fact – sceptical, mistrustful, remote from the world of men, but close to nature... and above all, close to the night, to dreams, and to whatever 'God' worked directly in him... anyone who entered was transformed and suddenly overpowered by a vision of the whole cosmos... Here lived the 'Other' who knew God as a hidden, personal, and at the same time, supra-personal secret... The play and counterplay between personalities No.1 and No.2... is played out in every individual... No.2 has been of prime importance, and I have always tried to make room for anything that wanted to come to me from within. When I was 'there', where I was no longer alone, I was outside time; I belonged to the centuries; and He who then gave answer was He who had always been."

In his book, _The Power of Silence_, Carlos Castaneda wrote: "Don Juan commented that inside every human being was a gigantic, dark lake of silent knowledge which each of us could intuit... Two obviously separate parts were within my being. One was extremely old, at ease, indifferent. It was heavy, dark, and connected to everything else... The other part was light, new, fluffy, agitated. It was alone, on the surface, vulnerable. That was the part with which I looked at the world. "

Could movies (or television series) such as _Star Wars, Star Trek, Lord of the Rings, Harry Potter, Thor and The Avengers_ actually contain some real event(s) which did occur in our past and our subconscious mind knows this? And is this why we are attracted to them?

- _Star Wars_ (1977–present): As mentioned earlier, this contains multiple species of extra-terrestrials, robotic droids, space travel, use of sophisticated technology, a galactic republic/empire, and The Force – something which seems to me to be similar to consciousness. I have already discussed unexplained anomalies with the Moon, Mars, Saturn and ancient civilisations.
- _Star Trek_ (1966-present): Same as above.
- _Thor and The Avengers_ (2011 and 2012): These contain sophisticated technology/weapons, space travel, magic and gods from Nordic mythology. These will be discussed in more detail later.
- _Harry Potter_ (1997–2011) _Harry Potter_ contains magic. Yes, ladies and gentlemen, magic is real and I'm sure your subconscious knows it. There are various types of magic, such as Ceremonial magic, Divinatory magic, Black magic, White magic. If you still don't believe it, then why were up to 60,000 witches executed between the 15th and18th Centuries? Have you heard of the 'witchcraft trials'? If magic did not exist then why was legislation introduced in England, Scotland, Wales and Ireland, such as the Witchcraft Act of 1735?

Note: White magic and Black magic are both simply magic, but the name is dependent on the user's intentions. White is used for good intentions, and Black is used for bad intentions. Isn't this similar to The Force from

Star Wars? Can't the Dark Side of the Force be considered Black magic? It uses negative energy/consciousness or bad intentions. Additionally, it is argued that not all those executed in the witchcraft trials were actually witches, but innocent women accused of being witches.

Harry Potter, as with *Lord of the Ring*s (described below) contains many magical creatures. Some of the creatures here are the same as those in *Lord of the Rings*: Centaurs, dragons, fairies, giants, gnomes, imps, kelpies, leprechauns, mer-people, pixies, salamanders, trolls and unicorns. Did they all exist? If you are still sceptical about *Harry Potter* being associated with ancient history, I will tell you that the werewolf in the *Harry Potter* books, named Fenrir, refers directly to Nordic mythology. Fenrir is the son of Loki, the (often wicked) son of the giant Laufey.

Lord of the Rings (1937–2003) also contains magic, so the above applies. However, in addition to this, Sauron's ring of terrible power has inscriptions on it, translated as: "One ring to rule them all, one ring to find them, one ring to bring them all and in the darkness bind them." However, prior to translation, exactly what language is the inscription in? Is it a make-believe language? No. Research has shown that the language is the witchcraft language of runes. Norse mythology tells us that the god Odin brought the runes to humans. After being used for two thousand years in northern Europe and Scandinavia, the runes were brought to the British Isles by Viking and Saxon invaders.

Another aspect of *Lord of the Rings* is the inhabitation of the land by hobbits, elves, wizards, dwarves and goblins. Dwarfs are prominent in Teutonic and Scandinavian legend. They are beings that dwell in mountains and in the Earth, associated with wisdom, mining and crafting. Elves are supernatural beings in Germanic mythology and folklore. Elves were first declared to exist in Old English and Old Norse texts, and are prominent in traditional British and Scandinavian folklore. In early modern folklore, they became associated with the fairies of Romance culture. Goblins are legendary evil or mischievous creatures, also possessing magical abilities.

Could such mythological entities have existed? To indicate the potential likelihood, I'll refer to a Sylph. A sylph is a mythological creature in the Western tradition. Sylphs appear as angels and spirit fairies, and they are often attached to a specific location such as a tree, river, plant or mountain. These are said to be described as human in form; others are like animals or half-human and half-animal; some are helpful, some evil. They are said to be invisible to humans, except to those with the gift of clairvoyance. Do you not believe in invisible things? How about ghosts? Or God?

Manly Palmer Hall (1901–1990), a Canadian-born author and mystic, produced the famous work *The Secret Teachings of All Ages*, whilst in his twenties. He has been widely recognised as a leading scholar in religion, mythology, mysticism and the occult. Carl Jung (the famous Swiss Psychologist and Psychiatrist who founded Analytical Psychology), when writing Psychology and Alchemy, actually borrowed material from Hall's private collection.

Regarding Sylphs, in *The Secret Teaching of All Ages*, Hall says: "The sylphs sometimes assume human form, but apparently for only short periods of time. Their size varies, but in the majority of cases they are no larger than human beings and often considerably smaller. It is said that the sylphs have accepted human beings into their communities and have permitted them to live there for a considerable period; in fact, Paracelsus wrote of such an incident, but of course it could not have occurred while the human stranger was in his physical body.

By some, the Muses of the Greeks are believed to have been sylphs, for these spirits are said to gather around the mind of the dreamer, the poet, and the artist, and inspire him with their intimate knowledge of the beauties and workings of Nature. To the sylphs were given the eastern corner of creation. Their temperament is mirthful, changeable, and eccentric. The peculiar qualities common to men of genius are supposedly the result of the cooperation of sylphs, whose aid also brings with it the sylphic inconsistency. The sylphs labor with the gases of the human body and indirectly with the nervous system, where their inconsistency is again apparent. They have no fixed domicile, but wander about from place to place – elemental nomads, invisible but ever-present powers in the intelligent activity of the universe."

The movie *The Golden Compass* (2007) also contains magic. Like many movies, this should be watched and analysed closely for messages. I have included this movie because there is something I find fascinating about it – the Dust. To me this seems extremely similar to The Force in *Star Wars*, where the Dust is similar to the positive side of consciousness and free will. This movie revolves around the Dust, and the Magisterium's suppression of it. I do wonder why the sequel to this movie has not been made. Upon watching this great movie, doesn't the Magisterium remind you of a certain entity? And coincidently (although I do not believe in coincidences), where does the word Magisterium come from? According to Wikipedia *"The Magisterium is the teaching authority of the Church."*.

THE TESSERACT AND NORDIC MYTHOLOGY

There is a specific object I wish to discuss because it has been the focal-point in multiple movies and it is linked with ancient mythology. Aspects of this ancient mythology are still used today, and everybody in the western world uses words from this ancient mythology everyday and yet hardly anyone consciously realises! I will inform you of these words in a minute. The object is the Cosmic Cube, also known as the Tesseract, Hypercube or Tetracube. A tesseract is a four-dimensional representation of a cube. A square is 2D, a cube is 3D, and a tesseract is 4D. Each point in the tesseract coordinates to a line which builds the 4D cube. This 4D cube is one of the most well-known 4D objects.

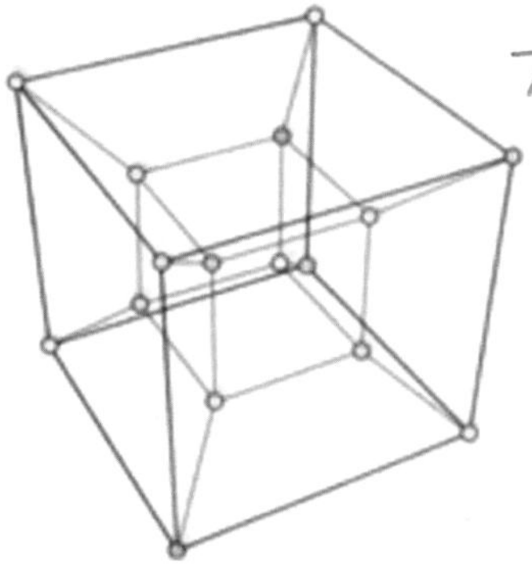

square - 2D
cube - 3D
Tesseract - 4D

The Cosmic Cube

Figure 3: Tesseract, Hypercube or Tetracube

In film, the tesseract continuously appears as an object of unspeakably intense power. Its energy is so powerful that it can create life or destroy it, depending on who is in possession of it and how its power is wielded. It can disintegrate humans and other objects simply by touch. It can even destroy an entire planet – sounds like a plasma weapon to me! It has been depicted in movies:

Day of week	Swedish	Danish/ Norwegian	German	Dutch	Origin
Monday	Mandag	Mandag	Montag	Maandag	Day of the moon
Tuesday	Tisdag	Mandag	Montag	Dinsdag	Day of Tyr God of law and son of Odin
Wednesday	Onsdag	Mandag	Montag	Woensdag	Day of Odin (Woden or Wotan)
Thursday	Torsdag	Mandag	Montag	Dondersdag	Day of Thor/Donar or Thunder (sun of odin)
Friday	Fredag	Mandag	Montag	Vrijdag	Day of Frejya or Frigg (wife of odin)
Saturday	Lordag	Mandag	Montag	Zaterdag	Day of Saturn/bath/ Sabbath
Sunday	Sondag	Sondag	Sonntag	Zondag	Day of the Sun

Figure 4: Modern influence of Nordic Mythology

- *Transformers* (2007-2011): The cube, said to be of unknown origin, is named the AllSpark, the object which created the robotic race. The Decepticons wish to obtain it to build an army by giving life to machines on Earth so they can take over the planet.
- *Thor* (2011): The cube seems to be 'The Casket', and it's a source of great power. It is believed to be of Asgardian origin, and is briefly shown in the movie. One of the actors, Erik Selvig reads a book on Norse mythology showing an illustration of Odin carrying the cube in his hand.
- *Captain America*: The First Avenger (2011): The tesseract somehow came to Earth from Odin's artefact chamber. It is found by a Nazi German SS officer, in a Viking church in Norway. The officer (Johan Schmidt) harnesses the tesseract's power to use as a weapon against the world. The tesseract falls into the Arctic ocean, which is then discovered by Howard Stark, the father of Tony Stark (Iron Man), and founder of a counter-terrorism and intelligence agency named S.H.I.E.L.D (Strategic Homeland Intervention Enforcement and Logistics).
- *Iron Man 2* (2010): While Tony Stark is briefly going through his father's research papers, a drawing of the tesseract appears. This tesseract is used to create the super energy behind the Iron Man technology.
- *The Avengers* (2012): Loki comes into contact with an alien race of the Chitauri and masters, Thanos and his servant named The Other. Loki promises to retrieve the Tesseract for them from Earth. In the movie, the Tesseract acts as a transportation device, manipulating space and time.

These listed movies all contain the Tesseract, which had belonged to the Nordic gods. What I would like to know is if Nordic gods are simply myths that are told to children, and hence the Tesseract also be a myth, then why is it that Nordic gods have left numerous traces in modern vocabulary and elements in western life, which we use today? See the table on page 72. From the millions of possible names which could be given to the days of the week, I wonder why four of them are dedicated to Nordic mythology and the remaining three are dedicated to the Moon, Saturn and the Sun? The term extra-terrestrial means 'not originating from Earth'. The Moon and Saturn, as discussed in Part 3 of this book, seem to be extra-terrestrial. The Nordic god Odin, his wife Frigg and their son's Thor and Tyr, are not of this Earth, and therefore they are extra-terrestrials. Why has the authority of this entire planet officially named the days of the week after extra-terrestrials? Aren't we told by them that extra-terrestrials don't exist? Billions of us on Earth mention the days of the week constantly, or we dedicate certain days of the week to certain activities. Isn't this some kind of Extra-terrestrial worship which we are unknowingly conducting on a daily basis? And before the above names were the official names for the days of the week, they were named after planets, and the term 'days of the week' was 'Theon hemerai', which translated as 'Days of the Gods' in Greek. So, in essence, the days of the week are the same as today, and therefore Days of the Extra-terrestrials?

CELESTIAL CATASTROPHES AND ANCIENT MYTHOLOGIES

A lightning storm can be quite a terrifying event for us. However, we have some understanding of why they occur. Did the ancient's understand? The common theory is that in ancient times, lightning was a terrifying event, and the ancients created myths which personified cosmic events, such as lightning. For example, Norse mythology refers to the god Thor, the god of thunder, whose weapon was the thunderbolt. His hammer represented lightning.

A comparison of ancient cultures reveals multiple global images of lightning, and these are in no way as subtle as the lightning we experience today. Ancient cultures would carve or engrave petroglyphs/images into rock of what they saw. Dr. Anthony L. Peratt, an American physicist with an interest in the fields of plasma physics, nuclear fusion and nuclear weapons, pointed out that ancient petroglyphs (dated to be thousands of years old) had an uncanny resemblance to plasma discharges/geometries created in laboratories. These discharges resembled the following petroglyphs:

- The Squatter Man (found worldwide)
- Stacked Torus, from an American Indian site in Arizona
- The Divine Thunderbolt of the Sumerian god Ninurta
- Greek depictions of Zeus' thunderbolts

Note: In the image of Ninurta wielding Thunderbolts, Ninurta is actually wearing something on his wrist which looks very much like a wrist-watch.

How powerful were these lightning bolts in ancient times? Well, there is evidence of planetary-sized discharges in our Solar System. Mars and the Moon have be victims of major electrostatic discharges, scarring their surface. As stated earlier, rilles on the Moon and Mars indicate that water isn't their origin, but massive electrostatic discharges instead. Jupiter's moon Europa also shows signs of large electrostatic discharging. These major discharges show that our Solar System was much more electrically active than the present day.

The following will describe that the ancients somehow mysteriously knew more specific information about the huge discharges occurring in space. When the planet Mars was photographed by the space probe, Mariner 4, in 1965, it revealed a giant hemispheric scar, up to five hundred miles across and four hundred miles deep! This is called Valles Marineris.

Many ancient cultures had a recurring theme in their myths, of a hero, a warrior struck down by a lightning weapon and left scarred on the body. The earliest astronomical archetype/symbol of the warrior-hero was, specifically, the planet Mars. For example in Greek mythology when Ares, the planet Mars was wounded in battle, he roared with the shout of a thousand warriors and rushed to Zeus to display the deep scar. In Hindu mythology Indra, the god of lightning, has a scar on his head, and a thunderbolt is said to have scarred the ten-headed king of the demons, Ravena.

These ancient myths corresponding to the scar on the planet Mars creates a problem. How did someone or something actually observe the electrical discharge from Earth and record the event in petroglyphs? How did someone or something record the exact shape of plasma discharges? There are three possible answers:

1. Ancient humans did actually somehow observe and accurately record what was seen, in myths and petroglyphs
2. Someone or something else observed these events in outer space, and gave the knowledge to the ancient humans, who in turn recorded the findings and created the mythologies
3. The ancient humans actually possessed and conducted plasma experiments just like we have done in modern laboratory experiments. However, they personified their observations by creating myths, petroglyphs and mythological symbols. However, if they had such technology, surely they would have no need to record the results by carving symbols into rock; they should have had sophisticated technology for recording the results.

Aside from these, another problem arises. As already stated, the petraglyphs are thousands of years old, but the Exploded Planet Hypothesis occurred millions of years ago. And were all mythological references to gods and their wars simply metaphors for an exploded planet? If so, why did the ancients not create the petraglyphs of circular orbs? Why did the ancients give the gods arms, legs, faces, beards... and a wrist-watch, in the case of the Sumerian Nunerta.

Also, the symbols carved into the rock were such accurate depictions of electrical plasma discharges. How was this possible? And why give the gods the technology, i.e. Thor's hammer, for displays of power, but also personalities and the motivation to use them? Unless, the ancients are actually describing real events in real war(s).

Immanuel Velikovsky, a Russian-Jewish psychiatrist and independent scholar, published many controversial books, one of which was the 1950 U.S. best seller, *Worlds in Collision*. His books used comparative mythology and ancient literary sources to argue that in ancient times, the Earth had suffered catastrophic close-contact with other planets. This refers to Catastrophism – the theory that the Earth suffered sudden geological changes, caused by global and violent events (such as Noah's flood), instead of gradual evolutionary processes (weathering, erosion, transport, deposition).

It has been recognised that a pattern exists between ancient myths and celestial cosmic catastrophes – which had disastrous consequences for Earth's life, climate, geography, topography, and even its own celestial mechanics. Before discussing the celestial bodies, I wish to draw a comparison between myths and deities from different civilisations. Here are some myths which parallel each other, from different civilisations:

- **The Flood:** A flood is sent by a deity or deities to destroy civilisation, to punish their actions. Most of these myths contain a hero who tries to ensure rebirth. This myth arises in Mesopotamia literature, the Hebrew Bible, Aztec, Hindu and Greek mythologies.
- **Creative sacrifice**: Cultures, especially those that grow crops, have stories about divine figures whose death creates an essential part of reality. This myth arises in Chinese mythology as Pangu, Vedic mythology as Purusha and the Norse mythology as Ymir.

Nike - disa de la Victoria

Part 2: The Futuristic Past

Domain	Deity: Roman	Deity: Greek	Deity: Egyptian	Deity: Sumerian
King of the Gods	Jupiter	Zeus	Osiris	Erech
Queen of the Gods	Juno	Hera	Isis	Ninhursag
God of the Sea	Neptune	Poseidon	Yam	Ninhursag
Goddess of Victory	Victorai	Nike	nekht	-
Messenger of Gods	Mercury	Hermes	Toth	Isimud
Sun God	Sol	Helios	Ra	Marduk
God of Love	Cupid	Eros	Bes	-
Goddess of Love	Venus	Aphrodite	Hathor	Inanna, Ishtar
Light	Phoebus, Apollo	Apollo	Horus	Nusku, Aos
War	Mars	Ares	Anhur	Ningirsu, Inanna, Ishtar
Virgin, Moon	Diana	Artemis	Khonsu	Nanna, Aa, Anunit, Mah, Sin
Wisdom	Minerva	Athena	Thoth	Enki, Ab, Ea
Underworld	Pluto	Hades	Osiris	Nergal, Zu, Ishtar, Satan
Crops	Ceres	Demeter	Osiris	Enlil, Emesh
Woods and Pastures	Faunus	Pan	-	-
Fire	Vulcan	Hephaestus	Sekhmet	Nergal, Gabil, Gibil, Nusku, Shamash
Wine	Bacchus	Dionysus	Sesmu	Geshtinanna

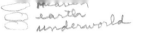

- **Dying god**: Many myths feature the resurrection of a god, such as the Mesopotamian god Tammuz, Egyptian god Osiris, Greek gods Adonis and Dionysus.
- **Axis mundi**: Multiple myths mention a place (Axis mundi) located at the centre of the world that acts as a point of contact between levels of the universe. The axis mundi is often marked by a mythical object. Myths describe a great tree or pillar joining heaven, earth and the underworld. A cosmic tree, whose branches reach heaven and whose roots meet hell, is featured in Vedic India, ancient Germanic and ancient Chinese mythologies.
- **Titanomachy**: Many cultures have a group of younger or more civilised gods who attempt to conquer the older gods, who represent chaos. In Greek mythology, the Olympians overpower the older Titans. In Babylonian mythology, the Enuma Elis depicts Marduk triumphing over Tiamat, the chaos monster. In Hindu mythology, the Devas (gods) battle with the Asuras (demons). In Celtic mythology, the Celtic gods of life and light battle with the ancient gods of death and darkness.

On page 77 I have included a table comparing deities. What is a myth? It is a sacred story, showing a religious or idealised experience, involving supernatural characters, and endorsed by rulers or priests. These myths have been told to ancient civilisations for many years on Earth. What are the chances that every civilisation mentioned above actually had the exact same event occur during their era? None. As the myths were virtually identical, what about the deities? Considering the table on page 77, don't they seem virtually identical?

Were the Sumerians told that their deities existed as actual living-breathing people? Were the Greeks told that their deities existed as actual living-breathing people? Was it the same with the Egyptians? If any of the people disbelieved in deities and the myths in their civilisation, were they charged with heresy and blasphemy, tortured and killed? Didn't this happen in the much more recent past? And why were the ancient civilisations told these myths? To keep them in fear and under control? And if what they had been told were actually lies, then:

- Why did the rulers or priests endorse such lies?

- What did they have to gain?
- What was the truth?
- What were the repercussions of knowing the truth, for both the rulers/priests and the masses?

Were the myths true? If so, they originated from the very first civilisation on Earth. Therefore all subsequent civilisations were in some way copying the original 'set' of deities and myths. If so, what was the original civilisation on Earth? Do we know of a civilisation older than Sumer, ancient China and the Indus Valley (which all seem to have co-existed during the same period)? What is the true source of these myths and deities? Or were told by the myth-makers as stories, but were received by non-human intelligent beings who observed the mythical events and passed them down to humanity. Remember, a myth is endorsed by priests. It can therefore be concluded that priests create the myths. Thus, the priests were in contact with these extra-terrestrials, received the information from them, and passed it down to humanity.

Referring to the first point above, haven't you wondered from which civilisation the submerged stone structures off Yonaguni Jima could be from? If you are unaware of the recent discovery at this location in Japan, an ancient city has been found which includes a large stone step-pyramid. Masaaki Kimura, a marine geologist, estimated the city to be 5,000 years old, and submerged by an earthquake. Could this be older than Sumer, ancient China and the Indus Valley?

Before I now summarise Velikovsky's views of the celestial cosmic catastrophes which occurred, I'll mention that his ideas written in *Worlds in Collision* were criticised and rejected by the mainstream academia. Perhaps not every piece of information was correct, but some of it was. It should be known that this book was an instant New York Times bestseller for eleven weeks, while being in the top ten for twenty-seven weeks. The point is, why did so many people purchase it? Did they subconsciously know that something in the mainstream didn't seem quite right and this book could reveal it? I believe so.

I am not saying that the mainstream opinion is always wrong, but it was the mainstream who said the Earth was flat, and it was the mainstream who said the Earth was the centre of the universe. And it is mainstream opinion that says humans are the only intelligent life. Yet, as this book shows, there is ample evidence of this being wrong. In the book's preface, Velikovsky writes: "Worlds in Collision is a book of wars in the celestial sphere that took place in historical times. In these wars the planet earth participated too...The historical cosmological story of this book is based on the evidence of historical texts of many peoples around the globe, on classical literature, on epics of northern races, on sacred books of the peoples of the Orient and Occident, on traditions and folklore of primitive peoples, on old astronomical inscriptions and charts, on archaeological finds, and also on geological and paleontological material"

Velikovsky suggests that around the 15th Century BC, a large comet came within very close proximity to the Earth and changed the planet's orbit and axis, thereby causing major catastrophes – mentioned in the early mythologies and religions around the world.

Alan F. Alford, a British writer and speaker on ancient religion, mythology and Egyptology, says in his book, *The Atlantis Secret*: "In this book, I present not only a complete decoding of the lost continent of Atlantis, but also a complete decoding of ancient Greek religion in its entirety. I am able to decode the myths of the Olympian gods and their associated mystery cults; I am able to decode the myth of the golden age and the fall of man; I am able to decode the scientific cosmogonies of Thales, Anaximander, Heraclitus, Anaxagoras, Empedocles and Philolaos; I am able to decode the 'soul origin' of Orpheus, Pythagoras, Parmenides, Socrates and Plato; and I am able to decode Plato's Theory of Forms, his account of creation by the Demiourgos, and his story of Atlantis. Behind all these ideas there lies a single secret of stunning simplicity – the age old myth of exploded planet."

So, Alford evidently appears to support Van Flanden's theory of the Exploded Planet Hypothesis. Alford is saying that behind the Greeks' mysterious philosophies and rituals is an abundance of metaphors and stories which stem from an exploded planet. Alford's views are not restricted to the Greeks: "The religions of the ancient Near East are best described as 'exploded planet cults.'" Alford says:

- The exploded planet was invisible by nature, thus explaining the ancients' worship of visible substitutes – meteorites, statues, fertility-gods, weather-gods, Sun, Moon and stars.

- The worship of the gods in anthropomorphic form was an entirely predictable offshoot of the exploded planet cult.
- The exploded planet cult was as profound, involving the death of a living planet and the rebirth of life on another planet – the Earth. There is no need to suppose any deeper, hidden meaning to the ancient myths.

According to Alford, when ancient mythological scriptures or clay tablets tell of wars of the gods, they are actually collisions of celestial bodies. Divine arrows, stones, missiles and lightning bolts of the gods could be metaphors for electrical discharges.

God is said to be from heaven. A meteorite or asteroid is said to be remnants of an exploded planet. They have a heavenly aspect as they fell from heaven, and they have an earthly aspect and they fell to the earth's surface. Therefore, the children of the gods are meteors and asteroids which crashed on Earth.

Important Note. I do not agree with every view expressed by Velikovsky and Alford in their books. Those I do not agree with have not been included here. And although it is being said that common ancient myths and deities are actually derived from celestial events, this does not change the fact that our past was arguably highly sophisticated, as well as perhaps significantly influenced by extra-terrestrials. The significance of extra-terrestrials is too great to put everything not-of-Earth down to an exploded planet.

I feel it is important to reiterate: Were the myths true? If so, they either:

- Originated from the very first civilisation on Earth. Therefore all the subsequent civilisations were somewhat copying the original 'set' of deities and myths. If so, what was the original civilisation on Earth? Do we know of an older civilisation than Sumer, ancient China and the Indus Valley (which all seem to have co-existed during the same period)? What is the true source of these myths and deities?
- Were told by the myth-makers as stories, but received by non-human intelligent beings who observed the mythical events and passed them down to humanity. Remember that a myth is endorsed by priests, and it can, therefore, be concluded that priests create the myths. Thus, the priests were in contact with these extra-terrestrials, received the information from them, and passed it down to humanity.

Something for you to think about...In every civilisation you can think of, whether you have read about them in books, or watched them in films, why have the priests seemed to be the most important figures on Earth? How did they receive their power of influence? And how exactly did they retain it?

It is my belief that regarding the myths being true - the second point above is accurate. There is a 'set' of gods with bloodlines, a record of interplanetary war with resulting catastrophes, and astronomical, quantum-mechanical, spiritual and esoteric knowledge, passed down to the high priests by intellectual beings.

HUMAN PHOBIAS

If violent cosmic events occurred in our historical past, why doesn't the human race remember them? And have you ever wondered where our phobias come from? Why are some of us scared of spiders, heights, closed spaces? Do you not find this strange? Several hundred phobias have been identified. The reason for these phobias:

- Some may be triggered by a traumatic event occurring in a person's life
- Some are linked to physiological problems caused by how one is raised
- Phobias can be genetic!

Again, I have included the words of Carl G. Jung: "When a man is fifty years old, only one part of his being has existed for half a century. The other part, which lives in his psyche, may be millions of years old..."

So can't the psychological trauma from the catastrophe have been engraved in our subconscious and manifested itself as our phobia? From Velikovsky's book, *Worlds in Collision*: "It is an established fact in the learning about the human mind that the most terrifying events of childhood (in some cases even of manhood) are often forgotten, their memory blotted out from consciousness and displaced into the unconscious strata of the mind, where they continue to live and to express themselves in bizarre forms of fear. Occasionally they may be converted into symptoms of compulsion neuroses and even contribute to the splitting of the personality."

"One of the most terrifying events in the past of mankind was the conflagration of the world, accompanied by awful apparitions in the sky, quaking of the earth, vomiting of lava by thousands of volcanoes, melting of the ground, boiling of the sea, submersion of continents, a primeval chaos bombarded by flying hot stones, the roaring of the cleft earth, and the loud hissing of tornadoes of cinders."

"There occurred more than one world conflagration; the most horrible one was in the days of the Exodus. In hundreds of passages in their Bible, the Hebrews described what happened. Returning from the Babylonian exile in the sixth and fifth centuries before this era, the Hebrews did not cease to learn and repeat the traditions, but they lost sight of the fearful reality of what they learned. Apparently, the post-Exile generations looked upon all these descriptions as the poetical utterances of religious literature."

"The Talmudists in the beginning of this era disputed whether a deluge of fire, prophesied in old traditions, would take place or not; those who denied that it might come, based their argument on the divine promise found in the Book of Genesis, that the Deluge would not be repeated; those who argued to the contrary, reasoning that though the deluge of water would not recur, there might come a deluge of fire, were attacked for construing too narrowly the promise of the Lord."

"Both sides overlooked the most prominent part of their traditions: the history of the Exodus and all the passages about the cosmic catastrophe, endlessly repeated in Exodus, Numbers, and the Prophets, and in the rest of the Scriptures."

"The Egyptians in the sixth pre-Christian century knew about the catastrophes that overwhelmed other countries. Plato narrates the story which Solon heard in Egypt about the world destroyed in deluges and conflagrations: "You remember but one deluge, though many catastrophes had occurred previously."

"The Egyptian priests who said this and who maintained that their land was spared on these occasions, forgot what happened to Egypt. When, in the Ptolemaic age, the priest Manetho starts his story of the invasion of the Hyksos by acknowledging his ignorance of the cause and nature of the blast of heavenly displeasure that befell his land, it becomes apparent that the knowledge which was possibly alive in Egypt in the days when Solon and Pythagoras visited there, had already sunk into oblivion in the Ptolemaic age. Only some hazy tradition about a conflagration of the world was repeated, without knowing when or how it occurred."

"The Egyptian priest, described by Plato as conversing with Solon, supposed that the memory of the catastrophes of fire and flood had been lost because literate men perished in them, together with all the achievements of their culture, and these upheavals "escaped your notice because for many generations the survivors died with no power to express themselves in writing".

"A similar argument is found in Philo the Alexandrian, who wrote in the first century of this era: "By reason of the constant and repeated destructions of water and fire, the later generations did not receive from the former the memory of the order and sequence of events." Although Philo knew about the repeated destructions of the world by water and fire, it did not occur to him that a catastrophe of conflagration was described in the Book of Exodus. Nor did he think that anything of this sort took place in the days of Joshua or even of Isaiah. He thought that the Book of Genesis comprised the story of "how fire and water wrought great destruction of what is on the earth", and that the destruction by fire, about which he knew from the teachings of the Greek philosophers, was identical with the destruction of Sodom and Gomorrah."

"The memory of the cataclysms was erased, not because of lack of written traditions, but because of some characteristic process that later caused entire nations, together with their literate men, to read into these traditions allegories or metaphors where actually cosmic disturbances were clearly described."

"It is a psychological phenomenon in the life of individuals as well as whole nations that the most terrifying events of the past may be forgotten or displaced into the subconscious mind."

"As if obliterated are impressions that should be unforgettable. To uncover their vestiges and their distorted equivalents in the physical life of peoples is a task not unlike that of overcoming amnesia in a single person."

TIAMAT AND GIANTS

Let me summarise what has already been said about the exploded planet:

- The additional planet was roughly the size of Saturn, and it may have been bright enough to see in the daytime, like our Sun.
- The exploded planet would have been more water-based than land-

based. This is because asteroids and comets are said to contain a large content of water. And as discussed, asteroids and comets are originally from the exploded planet.

- The water on the surface of Mars could have originated from its neighbouring planet, the exploded planet.
- In Charles Fort's book, Book of the Damned, he mentions many mysterious things such as frozen fish, frogs and a variety of materials falling from the sky, including huge oversized flint arrowheads and axes – evidence for the existence of giants.
- Dr. Flandern speculates the exploded planet to be populated with intelligent human-like life, with skeletal structures much larger than ours.

The name of the exploded planet is said to be Tiamat.

Earlier in this book, it had been discussed that humans were genetically engineered by extra-terrestrials, called gods (Elohim).

In Genesis 6.1–2: "And it came to pass, when men began to multiply on the face of the earth, and daughters were born unto them. That the sons of God saw the daughters of men that they were fair; and they took them wives of all which they chose."

Now relating back to what was said earlier in this section. Who were these other people that Cain was concerned about? Pre-Adamic creatures. Who exactly were these? If Pre-Adamic creatures were dumb silly animals, why would Cain have been so scared to be amongst them? Surely Elohim, being a god could have protected him? Unless the Pre-Adamic creatures were:

- Just as intellectual as man;
- Roaming in large numbers;
- Enemies of man;
- Much more inclined to be evil than good – because who simply tortures and kills a person? Unless that someone is a stone-cold killer who doesn't show empathy and doesn't listen to reason.

In all of the ancient scriptures of the world which we know of, not just the Bible, but also in the Bhagavad Gita, Vedas, Upanishads and others in the ancient east, there is mention of the fact that there has been on this earth alien life-forms cohabiting with us and having a sexual connection with humans.

Thousands of years ago, even hundreds of years ago, the earth was a different place. Yes man was here, but if aliens were cross-breeding with humans, the offspring obviously won't be typical children. As Cain pointed out, there were also creatures of great stature that caused horror and death. These included giants – also referred to as Nephilim in Hebrew.

The scriptures say in Genesis 6.4: "There were giants in the earth in those days; and also after that, when the sons of God came in unto the daughters of men, and they bare children to them, the same became mighty men which were of old, men of renown." Deuteronomy 2.20, 3.11–13, Joshua 17.15 and others show that giants existed on the earth before the deluge and afterwards in the land of Canaan. Considering this and what was said by Charles Fort, why can't it be said that as well as giants already roaming the earth, the remains of the exploded Tiamat including waters, giants and their bones, also came onto the earth?

Before reading this book, you probably thought of giants as the stuff of fairytales. But now you have read evidence of giants, and evidence of them being the offspring of the gods having sexual intercourse with humans, so why can't off-world giants and their remains have come to Earth from Tiamat? Note: The offspring from the sons of the gods turned out to be more than mere giants, but this will be discussed in detail in my next book. For now I will say that ancient literature and artwork is full of examples of creatures which are half-breeds. Hercules, Gilgamesh and Achilles were part man and part god, weren't they? How could this have happened unless they were genetically manipulated?

There is evidence of this genetic engineering in the Book of Jasher. Chapter 4.18 says: "And their judges and rulers went to the daughters of men and took their wives by force from their husbands according to their choice, and the sons of men in those days took from the cattle of the earth, the beasts of the field and the fowls of the air, and taught the mixture of animals one of species with the other, in order therewith to provoke the Lord."

I wish to point out that if sons of god were producing offspring such as giants, and there was mass genetic engineering going on, couldn't this be how dwarfs, fairies, goblins, and elves came into being? They exist in *Lord of the Rings* and *Harry Potter*, but there is also an abundance of genetically engineered and half-beings in the movie (and series by C.S Lewis), *The Chronicles of Narnia: The Lion, the Witch and the Wardrobe* (2005).

Should Fantasy movies which we watch today actually be called History movies? Have you seen the film *The Cabin in the Woods* (2011)? This is a fantastic movie, and as I have said throughout this book, there are messages in movies! I believe it is well worth explaining the story to you here.

The movie is based on the actions of 5 individuals: Dana, Marty, Holden, Curt and Jules – all of whom are unknowlingly manipulated by a team of technicians/employees. You should ask yourselves, employees of what kind of 'company'? In the last scene, The Director of 'the company' appears. To the two surviving individuals, Dana and Marty, the Director explains the facility and their purpose. Dana and Marty are part of a ritual sacrifice (I will not go into this concept, but I'll say that the Mayan's and others were well versed in it). The Director is acted by Sigourney Weaver. She is well-known worldwide for her roles in the *Alien* movies. The Director says the ritual is older than anything known to man and that even she and her peers aren't sure of everything, but the ritual is conducted worldwide to appease The Dark Gods who once ruled the Earth.

Now you understand why I have included this movie. The Director says that the (very horrifying) monsters Dana and Marty have seen are nothing compared to the Dark Gods. Dana and Marty realise they are standing over a pit which leads to where the old Gods are sleeping. The Director explains that the ritual is meant to keep them dormant, and it must have specific guidelines (as rituals do). She says that the order of killings of the (originally) five individuals doesn't matter as long as Dana is the last one left, because she is the Virgin, and it is up to the Gods whether they want to kill Dana. Why keep a virgin for last? If the sacrifice is not completed, the Dark Gods will come above the surface and destroy mankind.

Remember how in *War of the Worlds* (2005), the extra-terrestrial machines are already below the Earth's surface? Meaning they were here before mankind?

The Director says Marty must die to save the world. Marty says that if a bloodthirsty ritual needs to be performed (the killing of innocents) to save mankind, then maybe mankind isn't worth saving. I think he has a point. The Director is killed by something, and she falls into the pit where the Dark Gods reside. As Marty and Dana both survive, the ritual is not performed, and therefore according to the Director, the end of mankind is imminent. The ground shakes and cracks open, and a giant hand smashes through the surface and slams down on the ground. It is the hand of the first of the old Gods, climbing to the surface.

This scene reminds me of the movie *Wrath of the Titans* (2012), which revolves around the re-awakening of the Titans' ferocious leader Kronos (which is the name for the planet Saturn), who resides in the abyss of Tartarus, a dungeon deep within the Earth.

Can you see:

- How clear these patterns are?
- Movies contain messages?
- Fantasy, could actually be History! And again, our subconscious knows this which is why we are attracted to such films.
- The Director in the movie (Sigourney Weaver), the head of the technicians who are controlling the actions of the five individuals, is actually a Priest. The five individuals represent the public, the technicians are the guards and second in-charge of the human world, and the Director/Priest gives the orders to the guards. Note The Director is not a queen. Kings and queens are not known to be in direct contact with the gods, but priests are. And, I strongly believe that priests (high priests) were always higher in rank than nobility.

In movies you may have seen that it is the priest who interacts with the gods and then relays their orders to the 'henchmen'. See, for example, the movie *300* (2006). By the way, *300* also shows Oracles giving messages to the priests. The movie *Minority Report* (2002) also contains Oracles. Why? Because oracles were actually real in ancient times. But I will save this matter for my next book.

Now, back to giants. How tall were they? Well, you only need to switch on your television or check on the Internet to see how tall Andre The Giant, The Great Kali and The Big Show, were/are in Wrestling entertainment.

However, there are reports of giants being much larger. Giants' bones have been excavated and results have shown that they ranged from around 7 feet tall to a whopping 36 feet tall! They had teeth the size of an adult's fist. And up to six fingers, six toes and double rows of teeth! It is obvious now why Cain was so scared (however, I don't feel for him because he should not have killed his brother!). It seems the giants were also enemies of men – another factor explaining why Cain was so scared of being sent out of Eden, the protected area.

So, it seems that whatever stories you have heard as a child about kind gentle giants, were a lie. Unless perhaps there are a few – considered 'wimps' and therefore treated as outcasts. Here I refer you to *The BFG* by Roald Dahl.

How much do we humans care whether we step on an ant, or if we hit an animal on the road? Why shouldn't this apply to giants with humans? Why should they treat us any different to ants? In the story Jack and the Beanstalk, what are we told the giant says:

"Fee, fi, fo, fum,
I smell the blood of an Englishman;
Be he alive, or be he dead,
I'll grind his bones to make my bread!"

Stephen Quayle has written "There is also reason to think that some of those bones of giants, which did survive to be discovered, have been hidden from public view. That is to say, these proofs that giants existed have been collected...The question then is why would museums choose to hide giants away behind closed doors and in locked cabinets to be seen only by a very select few? Could there be a conspiracy?"

I ask you reader, how can an accountant hide a company's figures from the tax man, and not get into trouble with the company owner? Unless the accountant is the actual owner of the company. So, who actually owns the museums around the world? A council? Well, who is the head of those councils? And do they answer to someone higher up the chain? Who is at the top?

Have you heard that Hitler wanted to create a super race of people? A Master race called the Aryans? Who were the Master race in history? Not humans! Humans were inferior to the giants and other offspring of the gods. As evil as Hitler was, he knew about ancient history, probably much more than most of us know. I wonder where he came into possession of such information? Yes he took things by force, but, surely he was also handed information and taught its correct meaning? Who would have had more power (to possess such information) over such a powerful leader like Hitler?

Wikipedia defines master race as "a concept in Nazi ideology in which the Nordic race, a branch of what in late-19th and early-20th century taxonomy was called the Aryan race, represented an ideal and 'pure race'. In Nazi ideology this 'Nordic' race was the purest example of the original racial stock of those who were then called the Proto-Aryans, whom the Nazis believed to have prehistorically dwelt on the Northern German Plain and to have ultimately originated from the lost continent of Atlantis. The Nazis declared that the Nordics, nowadays referred to as the Germanic peoples, were the true Aryans because they were less racially mixed with 'non-native' Indo-European peoples than other people of what were then called the Aryan peoples (now generally called the Indo-European peoples), such as the Slavic peoples, the Romance peoples and the Indo-Iranian peoples. Based on this claim that the 'Nordic' peoples were superior to all other races, the Nazis believed they were entitled to world domination. The concept is known as Nordicism.

It has been said that the Nazis searched for the genetic material of giants in order to re-create the ancient gods. I wonder if any of the Nazis are still alive to this day to corroborate this. Have the remains of any giants been found? Yes! And I believe you should keep the following comments of Stephen Quayle in mind: "Archaeologists often discover these large bones in graves. But these are usually dismissed as being the bones of 'mastodons' – a premise that's hard to justify given the fact that the creatures are often buried in human graves wearing armour along with a shield and massive sword."

- In the 1950s, Euphrates Valley in south-east Turkey, a 14–16 feet tall skeleton was found in tombs, containing the remains of giants
- In the ancient sources from Historia Augusta (Roman biography collection of Roman Emperors) to Herodian, they say that the Roman Emperor, Maximinus Thrax (also known as Maximinus I) from 235–238 AD, was 8 foot 6 inches tall.
- It is said in Samuel Chapter 17 of the Hebrew Bible, that Goliath (11th Century BC) of Gath (one of the five cities of the Philistines) was 9 feet 9 inches tall.
- King Og, Amorite King of Bashan, who along with his army was killed by Moses in the Battle of Edrei, was at least 12–18 feet tall. And 'Og'

translates as 'Gigantic' in Hebrew. He is spoken of in Deuteronomy 3.11.

- In 1577 AD, a skeleton of 19 feet and 6 inches was found under an overturned oak tree in the Canton of Lucerne, Switzerland.
- In 1456 AD, a 23-foot skeleton was found beside a river in Valence, France.
- In 1613 AD, a 25-foot skeleton was found near the castle of Chaumont in France.
- In 200-600 BC, two separate 36-foot skeletons were discovered by Carthaginians.

There are multiple legends around the world which associate the creation of life with wars, catastrophes and giants, for example, the Inca legend of Viracocha. Viracocha is the creator god in Inca mythology. Viracocha created the universe, sun, moon, stars, and civilisation. Before man roamed the Earth (Pre-Adamic), other worlds existed containing creatures such as ferocious giants. Their actions displeased him so they were destroyed by fire. Another world was created, with a similar outcome and this was destroyed by the flood.

In myths of the Arikara (a group of Native Americans in North Dakota) and Caddo (south-eastern Native American) people, floods destroy evil giants, thus making the world safer for the existence of humans. Several Indian mythologies in Mexico and America tell of cycles of destruction, where an entire world was destroyed by fire, flood, ice, wind or other disasters. The Aztecs believed the first creation ended with a flood. In Mayan mythology, a flood wipes out the wooden people created by the gods, in an early attempt to create humans.

References relating to creation and destruction before the creation of Heaven (outer space), Earth and humans are clues about when ancient war and planetary destruction occurred. Regarding creation, flood and destruction accounts, there are astounding parallels between the accounts of the Babylonians (Enuma Elish) and the Okanagans (Samah-tumi-whoo-lah). I will first include a description of Enuma Elish, the creation account dating back to at least 1700 BC:

Before heaven and earth were formed, there were two vast bodies of water. The male freshwater ocean was called Apsu, and the female saltwater ocean was called Tiamat. Through the fusion of their waters, successive generations of gods came into being. As in the Bible's Genesis Chapter 1, water is the primeval element, but here it is identified with the gods, who have unmistakable gender.

Younger gods were created through sexual union. These younger, noisy gods disturbed the tranquillity of Apsu, so Apsu devised a plan to destroy them. The wisest younger god, Ea, found out about Apsu's plan, and killed Apsu. To avenge her husband, Tiamat decided to get rid of the younger gods with the help of her guard Kingu.

When the younger gods heard about this, they found a champion in the god Marduk. He agreed to defend them only if they would make him king. After they tested his powers, they enthroned him.

When Marduk and Tiamat met on the field of battle, Tiamat opened her enormous mouth as if to swallow Marduk and plunge him into the deep. Marduk responded by casting one of the winds into her body, expanding her like a balloon. He then took his bow and shot an arrow into her belly, thus splitting her in half. Marduk cut her in two pieces like a clam, and from her dead body, he made the heavens. The clamshell of heaven became a barrier or firmament. Marduk also fixed the constellations in the heavens. They, along with the moon, established the course of day and night, and the seasons.

Marduk then created a plan to relieve the menial and dull work of the gods. They were tired of labouring to meet their daily needs. So, Marduk created humanity from the blood of Kingu, and they were to be the servants of the gods.

In appreciation for their deliverance, the gods built Marduk a palace in Babylon, called Esagila, meaning 'house with its head in heaven'. This is where Marduk sat on his throne.

Now, from Stephen Quayle's book, *Genesis 6 Giants: Master Builders of Prehistoric and Ancient Civilisations.* Here is the Okanagan myth of their lost island of origin, Samah-tumi-whoo-lah: "Long, long ago, when the sun was younger and no bigger than a star, there was an island far off in the middle of the ocean. It was called Samah-tumi-whoo-lah, meaning 'White Man's Island'. On it lived a race of giants – white giants. Their ruler was a tall white woman called Scomalt... She could create whatever she wished."

"For many years the white giants lived at peace, but at last they quarrelled amongst themselves. Quarrelling grew into war. The noise of battle was heard, and many people were killed. Schomalt was made very, very angry... She drove the wicked giants to one end of the White Man's Island. When they were gathered together in one place, she broke off the piece of land and pushed it into the sea. For many days the floating island drifted on the water, tossed by waves and wind. All the people on it died except one man and one woman...Seeing that their island was about to sink they built a canoe... after paddling for many days and nights, they came to some islands. They steered their way through them and at last reached the mainland."

Alan Alford suggests that if you replace 'island' with 'planet' and 'sea' with 'space', then Schomalt's annihilation of White Man's Island is actually an account of the destruction of a planet. The Okanagan Legend is the account of an actual war causing the destruction of a planet containing life – the white giants. However, the Legend says that the surviving giants made their way through some islands, enduring waves and wind after building a canoe. Afterwards, they reach the mainland.

From the above, when considering the 'mainland', it is quite clear that 'islands' cannot be planets, and the mainland should be 'planet'. Therefore, the islands could actually be the Asteroid Belt – the remains of a previously exploded planet. This would also be in-line with Van Flandern's revised Multiple-Exploded Planet Hypothesis; the waves and wind could be plasma energy.

In summary, the Okanagan Legend is an account of a war which exploded a planet. This planet contained life, in the form of intelligent giants, ruled by a woman named Schomalt, and they built a spacecraft (acting as an Ark) to journey (dangerously) through space, to a new planet, on which they could live.

Zecharia Sitchin's interpretation of Enuma Elish is very similar to the Okanagan Legend. In Sitchin's view, Marduk originates from the abyss of space as an intruder planet, and proceeds to undergo various encounters with the outer planets of our Solar System. What follows is a catastrophic encounter with the planet Tiamat. Sitchin states that one of Marduk's moons struck Tiamat and split it into two. Then on Marduk's return (after 3,600 years), Marduk itself struck the broken fragments. One half of Tiamat became Earth and the remaining half became the asteroid belt.

Earth acquired a Moon (named Kingu) which was previously the satellite of Tiamat. Marduk then proceeded to move off into space to begin a very large elliptical orbit. In this orbit, Marduk will return to the location of the celestial battle/destruction of Tiamat every 3,600 years.

This supports Dr. Flandern's revised Exploded Planet Hypothesis, by considering that there may have been at least two planets in orbit between Mars and Jupiter, which exploded during different periods.

Note: According to Sitchin, Marduk's original name was Nibiru. Nibiru got replaced with Marduk in the original legends by the Babylonian ruler of the same name.

In sports today, such as the Olympic Games, medals (competence symbols) are given to the three winners: gold, silver and bronze. These three actually have astrological significance. The gold medal represents the Sun, silver represents the Moon, and bronze symbolises the Earth. Bronze and brown are colours of the earth.

This is the point I am making: Is anyone aware of the bronze sculpture by Italian sculptor Arnaldo Pomodoro? This sculpture can be seen in different locations worldwide, including the Vatican and the United Nations Headquarters in New York. Hence, this specific sculpture is possessed by extremely powerful entities. The name of this sculpture is Sphere Within Sphere. And this sculpture looks very much like a sphere crashed into another sphere. The sculpture is made of bronze. Could this be Sphere (Nibiru) Within Sphere (Tiamat) = Bronze (Earth)?

NIBIRU AND THE ANUNNAKI

So, Earth was formed by the destruction of a planet, Tiamat, which was struck by Nibiru. I must say something here. If Nibiru struck Tiamat then why didn't Nibiru break away into pieces like Tiamat? My view is that either Nibiru was somehow protected by a technically sophisticated shield, or, it blasted Tiamat with one of its moons – which was actually similar to the Death Star from *Star Wars*. And it makes you wonder, did the Anunnaki purposely destroy Tiamat or was it an accident?

As stated earlier, according to Sitchin, clay tablets describe the Anunnaki, who came to earth to mine for gold and take it back to their home planet, Nibiru, because they needed gold for their atmosphere, as the gold content in their atmosphere was depleting. Several Sumerian clay tablets depict the

Anunnaki (nephilim/giants) and flying vehicles used by them to descend to the Earth.

How do we know the Anunnaki created us to be their slaves? From the Atrahasis clay tablets, which include the Creation and Flood accounts. The 18th Century BC Akkadian epic is written on three tablets (now held in the British Museum, London, England). In the text:

- Atrahasis means 'extra-wise'
- Mankind is referred to as 'Igigi' in the tablets
- Sky is ruled by Anu
- Earth is ruled by Enlil
- Sea is ruled by Enki
- War is ruled by Ninurta
- Irrigation is ruled by Ennugi
- Belet-Ili (or Mami) is the goddess of the womb
- Nintu is the mother goddess
- Adad is the god of storms
- Nissaba is the goddess of grasses, reeds and cereals
- Nergal is one of the sons of Enlil and Ninlil, and presides over the underworld
- Anunna is the collective sky and Earth gods, the assembly of the high gods
- Shullat is a minor god, an attendant of the sun god Shamash
- Hanish is a servant to the weather god
- Ninurta is the god of war
- Anzu is the fire- and water-breathing son of the bird goddess Siris

Atrahasis epic:

When the gods instead of man
Did the work, bore the loads,
The gods' load was too great,
The work too hard, the trouble too much.
The great Anunnaki made the Igigi
Carry the workload sevenfold.
Anu their father was king,
Their counsellor warrior Enlil,

Their chamberlain was Ninurta,
Their canal-controller Ennugi,
They took the box [of lots]...,
Cast the lots; the gods made the division.
Anu went up to the sky,
[And Enlil(?)] took the earth for his people...
They were counting the years of loads.
For 3600 years they bore the excess,
Hard work night and day.
They groaned and blamed each other,
Grumbled over the masses of excavated soil;
"Let us confront our [ ] the chamberlin,
And get him to relieve us of our hard work!
Come, let us carry [the Lord (?)],
The counsellor of gods, the warrior, from his dwelling..."

The passages so far tell us how tired the 'gods' were of the workload. They are on the verge of revolting, and they demand to see the 'chamberlain'. The rise of the rebellion now threatens to become an open war:

"Every single one of us gods declared war!
We have put [a stop] to the digging.
The load is excessive, it is killing us!
Our work is too hard, the trouble is too much!
So every single one of us gods
Has agreed to complain to Enlil."

As Sitchin said, the gods now see the opportunity to ease their workload by creating mankind to do their work, as slaves:

Ea made his voice heard
And spoke to the gods his brothers...
"There is [ ]
Belet-ili the womb goddess is present –
Let her create primeval man
So that he may bear the yoke [( )],

So that he may bear the yoke, [the work of Enlil],
Let man bear the load of the gods!"
The creation of man is described in detail:

Enki made his voice heard,
And spoke to the great gods,
"On the first, seventh, and fifteenth of the month
I shall make a purification by washing.
Then one god should be slaughtered.
And the gods can be purified by immersion.
Nintu shall mix clay
With his flesh and his blood.
Then a god and a man
Will be mixed together in clay.
Let us hear the drumbeat forever after,
Let a ghost come into existence from the god's flesh,
Let her proclaim it as his living sign,
And let the ghost exist so as not to forget (the slain god)."
They answered "Yes!" in the assembly,
The great Anunnaki who assign the fates.

The Anunnaki agreed with Enki's proposition, and killed one of their own to create man, their slaves. This killing shows the morality of the Anunnaki who don't mind killing one of their own to ease the workload of the rest. Man seems to be in constant personal conflict between actions of good and evil. Is the evil-side from the Anunnaki? And are our Reptilian Brains from the Anunnaki's DNA?

Also it should be noted, when Enlil was a young god, he was banished from Dilmun (home of the gods) to Kur (the underworld) for raping a goddess named Ninlil. So our gods created humanity to be their slaves, and the gods rape each other! Doesn't this now tell us why we do evil things? Because it is in our DNA from the gods, the Anunnaki I wonder what modern-man would be like without the Anunnaki's DNA. I don't believe, for example, there would be anywhere near as many laws and jails around the globe as there are now, because we wouldn't be conducting the kinds of actions to get us locked up in jails!

In the Babylonian Creation myth, *Enuma Elis*, man is created to be slaves of the gods. Marduk destroys Tiamat's husband, Kingu, the evil leader of the enemy gods, and Marduk uses his blood to create man with the help of Ea/Enki. Clay is not mentioned.

In Genesis of the *Bible*, Chapter 2.7: "And the Lord God formed [as a potter] man [Adam] of the dust of the ground, and breathed into his nostrils the breath that is life; and man became a living soul."

The Sumerian and Babylonian creation accounts are linked with the Biblical creation account, in the sense that they use something from a god to create man, in this case, blood, clay, perhaps dirt and breath. However, with the Sumerian account, 'man' was mixed with the god's blood, in order to form us. Man was already in existence!

As Joseph P. Farrell puts it: "For the theologically inclined, these observations suggest a method of reconciliation between the Mesopotamian and the Biblical traditions, for it there was an already existing human or human-like creature from which 'primeval' worker-man was engineered, as the Atrahasis suggests, then the biblical account in Genesis would appear to be referring to this creature, while its subsequent mention of the creation of a hybrid race brought about by the intermarriage of the Nephilim and the daughters of men in Genesis 6 would then be the hybrid race referred to here as the creation of man by the gods in the Atrahasis."

Here is what follows in the Atrahasis epic:

Far-sighted Enki and wise Mami
Went into the room of fate.
The womb-goddesses were assembled
He trod the clay in her presence;
She kept reciting an incantation,
For Enki, staying in her presence, made her recite it.
When she had finished her incantation,
She pinched off fourteen pieces (of clay),
(And set) seven pieces on the right,
Seven on the left.
Between them she put down a mud brick.
She made use of a reed, opened it to cut the umbilical cord,
Called up the wise and knowledgeable

Womb-goddesses, seven and seven.
Seven created males,
Seven created females.

There is an important connection between the Atrahasis account of the creation of this hybrid man (made from a God and a man) and the Genesis account of the Nephilim and their hybrid offspring (made from Anunnaki and daughters of men). The connection is that they are the reason for the deluge.

Genesis 6:1–4 claims that the Anunnaki interbred with the daughters of men and gave birth to a race of giants: "And the Lord saw that the wickedness of man was great in the earth, and that every imagination of the thoughts of his heart was only evil continually." God decided to destroy what he had made and start again with the righteous Noah. God chose the flood as the instrument for destruction.

However, in the Atrahasis account, the reasoning behind the flood was very different. Here, the reason for destroying this new race of hybrid man was because of their long life and resulting over-population of the earth:

And the country became too wide, the people too numerous.
The country was as noisy as a bellowing bull.
The God grew restless at their racket,
Enlil had to listen to their noise.
He addressed the great gods,
"The noise of mankind has become too much,
I am losing sleep over their racket."

Enlil then introduced a deadly disease among the hybrid population in order to reduce their numbers:

"Give the order that suruppu-disease shall break out..."

This is familiar with the Greek epic, Cypria, in which Zeus planned to reduce overpopulation by war.

Have you heard of the Georgia Guidestones? They form a structure over 19 feet tall and just under 109,000 kg, located in Elbert County, Georgia, USA. The stones consist of messages in four ancient languages: Babylonian,

Sanskrit, Egyptian and Greek. Other languages are also included, such as English, Hindu, Arabic, Chinese, Russian, Spanish and Swahili.
What does this structure say? One statement says that humanity should be maintained at a population of 500 million. However, the population currently stands at roughly 6.5 billion. How was the population reduced in the creation accounts? By flood ('natural' disaster) or disease. I'm sure there are other ways too, such as war. I wonder who planned and built the Georgia Guidestones, and how they plan to reduce/kill much of the world's population. I also wonder why questions aren't being asked about this structure.

I do not believe the world is over-populated, but I do believe that humanity is becoming more conscious of its true ability, and thus rebelling against 'the norm'. I wonder if this is what happened in our past with the different creations of man – our ancestors.

Continuing with the Atrahasis epic. It seems that one man created from the hybrid race, called Atrahasis (after whom this epic is named), begs Enki to do something about humanity's unfortunate situation:

Now there was one Atrahasis
Whose ear was open to his god Enki.
He would speak with his god
And his god would speak with him.
Atrahasis made his voice heard
And spoke to his lord,
How long will the gods make us suffer?
Will they make us suffer illness forever?
*   Enki made his voice heard*
And spoke to his servant:
"Call the elders, the senior men!
Start an uprising in your own house,
Let the heralds proclaim...
Let them make a loud noise in the land:
Do not revere your gods,
Do not pray to your goddesses..."

From the above, it is obvious that Enki told Atrahasis to form a rebellion against all the gods, strike and refuse to work. This would leave the

Anunnaki council in the same situation which led to the creation of hybrid man in the first place. However, this now leads to disease because Enlil orders (by his authority) that hybrid man should be starved to death, thus reducing the population:

600 years, less than 600, passed
And the country became too wide,
The people too numerous.
The God grew restless at their clamour,
Enlil had to listen to their noise.
He addressed the great gods,
"The noise of mankind has become too much.
I am losing sleep over their racket.
Cut off food supplies to the people!
Let the vegetation be too scant for their hunger!
Let Adad wipe away his rain.
Below (?) let no flood-water flow from the springs.
Let wind go, let it strip the ground bare,
Let clouds gather (but) not drop rain,
Let the field yield a minished harvest,
Let Nissaba stop up her bosom.
No happiness shall come to them.
* Enlil organised his assembly again,*
Addressed the gods his sons:
"The noise of mankind has become too much,
Sleep cannot overtake me because of their racket.
Command that Anu and Adad keep the (air)
Above (earth) locked,
Sin and Nergal keep the middle earth locked."

Therefore, Anu and Adad guarded the heaven, Enlil the Earth, and Enki the waters, so there was no way hybrid man could be nourished with nature. In addition to this staggering assault against mankind, Enlil decrees infertility!:

"Let the womb be too tight to let the baby out".

This lasted six years, and the hybrid man was reduced to cannibalism:

When the second year arrived
They had depleted the storehouse.
When the third year arrived
The people's looks were changed by starvation.
When the fourth year arrived
Their upstanding bearing bowed,
Their well-set shoulders slouched
The people went out in public hunched over.
When the fifth year arrived,
A daughter would eye her mother coming in;
A mother would not even open the door to her daughter...
When the sixth year arrived
They served up a daughter for a meal,
Served up a son for food.

Has any of the text from this epic occurred during our present day?
A council is held again by the Anunnaki, and Enlil complains that the plan to create an obedient slave race, hybrid man, did not work, and he blames Enki for offering support to mankind:

He (Enlil) was furious [with the Igigi]
"We, the great Anunna, all of us,
Agreed together on [a plan].
Anu and [Adad] were to guard [above],
I was to guard the earth [below].
Where Enki [went],
He was to undo the [chain and set (us) free],
He was to release [produce for the people].
He was to exercise [control (?) by holding the balance (?)]."
Now an argument begins between Enlil and Enki:
"[You] imposed your loads on man,
You bestowed noise on mankind,
You slaughtered a god together with his intelligence.
(Enlil to Enki): You must... and [created a flood].

It is indeed your power that shall be used against [your people!]
You agreed to [the wrong (?)] plan!
Have it reversed! (?)
Let us make far-sighted Enki swear...an oath."
  Enki made his voice heard
And spoke to his brother gods,
"Why should you make me swear an oath?
Why should I use my power against my people?
The flood that you mention to me –
What is it? I don't even know!
Could I give birth to a flood?
That is Enlil's kind of work!
Let him choose
Let Shullat and [Hanish] march [ahead]
[Let Erakal pull out] the mooring poles
Let Ninurta march, let him make [the weirs] overflow."

Here you can see Enki refusing to take part in the annihilation of the hybrid race. And Enki warns Atrahasis of their coming deliberate and systematic destruction, also known as genocide!:

Enki made his voice heard
And spoke to his servant,
  "Dismantle the house, build a boat,
Reject possessions, and save living things..."

This is when the deluge begins:

Anzu was tearing at the sky with his talons,
He broke [ ] the Flood [came out (?)].
The kasusu-weapon went against the people like an army.
No one could see anyone else,
They could not be recognised in the catastrophe.
The Flood roared like a bull,
Like a wild ass screaming the winds [howled]
The darkness was total, there was no sun.

Note that it is Anzu who seems to bring the flood, and who also wages a war with the rest of the gods. There are many similarities between the scriptures of the Sumerians, and those in the Vedas. For example, Enki is referred to as Indra, and Anu is referred to as Rama. I will go into the Veda texts in more detail later.

To conclude here, is this the reason we haven't been told the truth for generations? We haven't been told the truth about how Earth and the Moon came into existence? We haven't been told the truth about comets and asteroids? And there hasn't been a thorough and accurate 'official' investigation into our origins? Because it all originates from the fact that the Earth and moon were formed due to the actions of an extra-terrestrial race, called the Anunnaki, who created us to be their slaves. And it is possible that our evil actions stem from the DNA of the Annunaki. I wonder if those of us conducting evil actions such as initiating wars, rape and murder, have more of the Anunnaki's DNA in their bloodline than that of a human.

POSSIBLE REASON BEHIND THE DELUGE

If Earth was formed from Tiamat, then perhaps some of Tiamat's creatures such as giants, elves and fairies survived, and were forced to continue their lives on Earth, whilst the Anunnaki were genetically engineering man. Tiamat was an ocean planet, but from the debris in the collision, some of it must have solidified itself on Tiamat which eventually became Pangaea. Over time, Pangaea then separated, to give us the continents we have today.

So why did catastrophic events, such as the deluge, occur in the first place? Because man protested against being a slave, because he wanted to live a life of freedom and be at one with nature. As already stated in the Atrahasis epic, man already existed. And it seems that modern-man's evil actions of today could stem from the DNA of the anunnaki. How many times has man been created and destroyed by these slave-masters? And why did man even rise up against them? I believe it could be because man is not meant to be a slave and man knows this. Otherwise, there would be no rebellion. Man's soul, the intuition, the subconscious, knows that man has the ability to be much more than just a slave.

For the next few pages, I want to turn your attention to movies and television again for parallels. There is one very interesting scene in the movie *Matrix Reloaded* (2003). This scene is with the Architect. Please note, as with all movies, messages are hidden, and they need to be deciphered. Different interpretations may arise. However, the following has been included to encourage you to think independently and critically and establish possible links. The Oxford English Dictionary definition of an architect is a person who designs buildings and in many cases also supervises their construction; a person who is responsible for inventing or realizing a particular idea or project.

- **Scene**: Neo meets the Architect face-to-face in a large oval room, with the walls covered with many monitors.
  Something to think about: Monitors are used to watch people. Is he watching everyone's actions like some kind of god?
- **Scene**: The very first image on every monitor is the universe.
  Something to think about: Is the Architect the architect of the universe? Or does the image refer to our reality of the universe? And therefore he is a god of the universe in a false reality? The matrix our false-universe? Below, you will see why I say 'a god' and not God.
- **Scene**: The Architect continually says "We".
  Something to think about: Who are 'We'? Being a designer, he was ordered by someone to design the universe, and worked with the builders of it. Is the Architect like one of the sons of God – the Anunnaki?
- **Scene**: The Architect says that the first Matrix failed because it was too perfect.
- **Something to think about**: If something is too perfect, why should it fail? Unless it was perfect for those for whom it was not intended? Was it that the first humans were made perfectly upon creation, used their free will, and immediately refused to be slaves?
- **Scene**: The Architect says that this will be the sixth time that Zion has been destroyed.
  Something to think about: Is Zion the Earth? Was humanity already created and destroyed five times? Was it destroyed because humans began to wake up and rebel against the control imposed on them? Similar to the Sumerian account of creation?
- **Scene**: At one point, the monitors show the reactions of Neo's five predecessors.

Something to think about: Have our individual appearances been created before in the previous five creations? And do our past life experiences stem from the fives times we were initially created?

- **Scene**: The Architect tells Neo that 16 females and 7 males would be required to re-create Zion.
  Something to think about: Doesn't this sound like the Anunnaki creating man to replenish the Earth? In Genesis of the Bible, Adam and Eve were created to replenish the Earth.
- **Scene**: Throughout all the Matrix movies
  Something to think about: The machines harvest humans for their energy, their lives. Their lives power the machines. What/who do the machines represent on Earth? It is important you think about this.

THIRD/MIDDLE EARTH

Considering the concept of cycles of creation and destruction, aside from the *Matrix* being in the sixth cycle, have you noticed terms such as 'Third Earth' and 'Middle Earth'? Is there something to this? In *Lord of the Rings* the story is set in Middle Earth:

During an interview in January 1971, when asked whether the stories take place in a different era, [Tolkein] stated, "No...at a different stage of imagination, yes." However, he did nod to the stories' setting on Earth... "Most people have made this mistake of thinking Middle-earth is a particular kind of earth or in another planet of the science fiction sort but it's just an old fashioned word for this world we live in..." Wikipedia and Valarguild.org

The Pendragon Adventure: A series of science fiction/fantasy novels, in which three friends discover they must prevent the destruction of their world as well as others. Second Earth is the present day. Third Earth is set in the 51st Century, a utopian society with one central government. Years prior to Pendragon and his friend Vandyke arriving on Third Earth, the territory was having overpopulation problems, so people moved underground and colonised other planets in the Solar System.

Thundercats: This was a 1980s animated television series, involving cat-like humanoid aliens from a planet called Thundera in a distant galaxy. In

Episode 1: Exodus, the Thundercats are referred to as the 'nobles', and they seem to form the nobility of their planet. They are forced to leave their home planet. These extra-terrestrials are chased and attacked by their enemies including the reptilian Slithe, and the Thundercats journey to Third Earth. This Third Earth is also home to the demonic priest/sorcerer Mumm-ra, who is on Third Earth from the time when it was First Earth. *Note:* This demon priest exists in the form of a mummy. Upon reciting a spell, he transforms into a more vigorous and muscular form – Mumm-Ra. He rests in a stone sarcophagus (same as the Egyptians) to replenish his energy (same as in the 1994 movie *Stargate* – based on the Egyptians), inside a giant pyramid (same as the Egyptians), and the pyramid seems to absorb/discharge energy (in Stargate, the pyramid was electrical as it was a spacecraft). Also, on Mumm-Ra's chest is the symbol of a two-headed serpent in a red sun disc. In ancient Egypt, the two-headed serpent represented a deity named Nehebkau ('he who harnesses the souls'). This deity guarded the entrance to the underworld.

Lion-O possesses the Sword of Omens, which contains a ruby with the Eye of Thundera. Rubies actually have a magical use – to protect against wicked spirits, foes and negativity. *Note:* the Eye of Thundera looks identical to the Eye of Sauron in the *Lord of the Rings*. When Lion-O uses the sword, looking through the crossbars, he asks for 'Sight Beyond Sight'. The Eye of Thundera is positioned in the middle of, and slightly above, eye-level. At this exact position is the human's pineal gland. The pineal gland is also referred to as the Third Eye. This is a small endocrine gland in the vertebrate brain. Its shape resembles a tiny pine cone.

It is said that the Ancient Egyptians wore crowns which featured a serpent protruding from the third eye region on the crown. To the Egyptians, serpents/snakes denoted wisdom. Even in the *Bible*, the Gospel of Matthew 10.16 says: "be as wise as serpents".

The third-eye (Ajna in Sanskrit) is the site of our seventh energy centre known as the chakras. This chakra deals with visualisation, intuition, imagination and telepathy.

THE PINEAL GLAND

Now I will introduce to you to Dr. Rick Strassman. He is a medical doctor specialising in psychiatry with a fellowship in clinical psychopharmacology research. Strassman embarked on human research with psychedelic and hallucinogenic substances. For twenty years prior to this, research was restricted by law to animal studies only. Dr Strassman's research was conducted at the University of New Mexico's School of Medicine, where he was the Associate Professor of Psychiatry.

DMT, a psychedelic compound of the tryptamine family, is found in plants, and these are commonly used in South American Shamanic practices, such as in the preparation of ayahuasca. DMT can produce powerful psychedelic experiences. Dr. Strassman hypothesised that DMT is produced by the human brain in the pineal gland. DMT is related to human neurotransmitters such as serotonin and melatonin.

It has been said that upon entering the REM stage of sleep, tiny doses of DMT are likely to be released into the bloodstream. REM (Rapid Eye Movement) sleep is a normal stage of sleep, during which rapid and random eye movements occur. REM sleep in adults occupies 20–25% of complete sleep – roughly 90-120 minutes in total per night – usually broken down into four or five periods of REM sleep.

Dr. Strassman has referred to DMT as the "god molecule" or "spirit molecule" because many users have claimed to have contacted non-human or god-like beings. During Strassman's research spanning five years, he administered 400 doses of DMT to 60 human volunteers. Over half of the volunteers reported similar experiences ranging from observing highly detailed, self-transforming geometric patterns, to interacting with non-human beings.

Dr. Strassman has proposed that when someone is near his/her death, the pineal gland releases a large amount of DMT. This explains the imagery reported by survivors of near-death experiences. He has also noted that the pineal gland first becomes visible on the 49th day of foetal development. This is roughly the same time that the gender of the foetus can be determined. This is also the same period of time that the Tibetan Book of the Dead teaches that it takes a soul of the recently deceased to reincarnate.

More information concerning the pineal gland is given later in this book, when discussing the Fourth Root-Race – the third-eye of Cyclopes.

ANUNNAKI AND EARTH'S RESOURCES

I have wondered when exactly the Anunnaki are supposed to have arrived on Earth. I will not speculate on dates, but I will say that as already stated in the Sumerian clay tablets, Man was already here when the Anunnaki began genetically engineering mankind to become their slaves. Why would any human allow an extra-terrestrial to use them in an experiment to create a race of human slaves? It is my belief that they would not! The only way I can see this happening is if the human(s) were held against their will, perhaps tortured and killed. The Anunnaki are invaders. If you think these statements cannot be true, consider the following:

- Anunnaki destroyed an entire planet. I don't think it was accidental, unless their planet, Nibiru, was also smashed in the collision with Tiamat. But how can this be true if the Anunnaki came to Earth (formed from Tiamat) to mine for gold for their atmosphere? Their planet must have remained intact, meaning they used some kind of a plasma weapon to destroy Tiamat.
- If I went to your home and removed items, this constitutes stealing. Isn't this what the Anunnaki did by mining for gold from a planet which was not their own?
- One of the Anunnaki, Enlil, raped another of their kind, Ninlil.
- Anunnaki killed one of their own to create hybrid man, thereby displaying a lack of emotion and murderous intentions.
- Anunnaki created hybrid man to be their slaves.

Before moving on, ask yourself whether the above actions (raping, killing and stealing) still occur today? Slavery existed for many many years in the so-called modern world. I wonder if it has really been abolished from today's world...perhaps you should ask those working in Third-World countries.

However, I do believe there have been other extra-terrestrials who have tried to assist in the development of man. This will be covered later.

Earth can be seen as a microcosm, as opposed to a macrocosm. Consider the following. Just as we have different cultures in different parts of this tiny planet Earth speaking different languages, why can't there be different alien races in the massive galaxy and infinite universe? There is already evidence of aliens, such as those forming Saturn's rings (see section 3 of this book).

How we humans, upon discovering a mass of resources in one location, for example, oil or gold, rush there to take it over and kill others who try to take it for themselves (or even try to defend it) - Why can't Earth be that resource in the galaxy/universe, with different races of extra-terrestrials wanting to have the Earth in their possession?

What resources does the Earth possess? Aside from matter such as humans, water, oil, gold, silver, copper, platinum, titanium and other metals, the Earth contains unique matter which may not be located on the other planets in our Solar System, such as (you may find these can be used for interesting purposes): Aegerine: Agate: Alexandrite: Amazonite: Amber: Amethyst: Ametrine: Anandalite: Angel Aura Quartz: Angelite: Apache Tears: Apatite: Apophyllite: Aqua Aura Quartz: Aquamarine: Aragonite: Atlantisite: Aventurine: Azeztulite: Azurite: Beryl: Bismuth: Bloodstone: Boji Stones: Brandberg Crystals: Brazilanite: Bronzite: Budd Stone: Calcite: Carnelian: Cavansite: Celestite: Chakra Crystals: Chalcedony: Chalcopyrite: Charolite: Chiastolite Cross: Chrysanthemum Stone: Chrysocolla: Chrysoprase: Cinnabar Crystals: Citrine: Coral: Covellite: Danburite: Desert Rose: Diamond: Diopside: Dioptase: Dolomite: Dumortierite: Emerald: Epidot: Euclase: Feldspar: Fluorite: Fulgurite; Galena; Garnet: Goldstone: Heliodor: Hematite: Hemimorphite: Herkimer Diamond; Hiddenite: Howlite: Iolite: Iron Pyrite: Jade: Jasper: Jet: Kunzite: Kyanite: Labradorite: Lapis Lazuli: Larimar Stone: Lepidolite: Lodestone: Magnetite: Malachite: Marcasite: Merlinite: Moldavite: Mookaite: Moonstone: Morganite: Muscovite: Obsidian: Okenite: Onyx: Opal Crystal: Orpiment: Pearl: Peridot: Petalite: Petrified Wood: Phenacite: Pietersite: Prehnite: Preseli Blue Stone: Quantum Quattro: Quartz – Clear Quartz: Quartz – Crackle: Quartz – Lemurian Seed Crystals: Quartz – Rose Quartz: Quartz – Smoky Quartz: Quartz – Snow Quartz: Quartz – Specialist Points: Quartz – Spirit Quartz: Realgar: Rhodochrosite: Rhodonite: Rhyolite: Rock Salt: Rose Crystalline: Ruby: Rudraksha Seed Beads: Rutile – Golden: Sapphire: Scapolite: Scheelite: Selenite: Seraphinite: Serpentine: Shaman Stones: Shattuckite: Shiva Lingham Stones: Shungite: Smithsonite: Soladite: Spectrolite (Rainbow Moonstone): Sphalerite: Sphene Crystals: Spinel: Spodumene: Staurolite-fairy Cross: Stibnite: Stichtite: Stilbite: Stromatolites: Sugilite: Sulfur: Sunstone: Tanzanite: Tekite Meteorites: Tiger Eye: Titanium Rainbow Aura Quartz: Topaz: Tourmaline: Turquoise: Unakite: Variscite: Vesuvianite: Wavellite: Wulfenite: Zincite: Zircon: Zoisite & Ruby

What we will focus on now is what man was like before the invasion of this alien race, before they manipulated our DNA from being pure man, to being mixed with alien DNA and the attribute/gene of slavery. What was it in the hybrid humans which made them rise up and rebel against being slaves of the Anunnaki? Was it the soul/spirit within humans which the Anunnaki did not understand and therefore could not suppress? I am now reminded of the 1983 and 2009 V television series. Before I describe it, ask yourself, is this what could have happened when the Annunaki invaded Earth? The television series involves an extra-terrestrial race arriving on Earth with seemingly good intentions. However, they slowly reveal their true intentions as they become more integrated within society.

At the beginning of the television series, a giant spacecraft appears in each of 29 major cities in the world. Anna (the leader of the extra-terrestrial visitors (Anunnaki)), declares they come in peace. They claim they require a small amount of Earth's resources, and in exchange they will share their advanced technological and medical knowledge. While a small number of humans start to doubt the Visitors' intentions, Erica (an FBI agent) discovers that the aliens are actually reptilian humanoids wearing pseudo-human skin and that the Visitors have spent many years infiltrating human governments, businesses and religious institutions, and they are now in the final stages of their plan to fully take over Earth. Erica joins the resistance movement which includes a Visitor sleeper agent named Ryan. Over time, Ryan seems to develop human emotions and now wants to save humankind (doesn't this sound like Enki?) The rebellion is challenged as the Visitors win the trust of humans on Earth (by curing diseases with their advanced knowledge and equipment), and they begin to use the Earth's youth unknowingly as spies.

Initially the true purpose of the Vistors' arrival was to conquer and control the planet, steal Earth's water (or gold as with the Anunnaki), and harvest the human race as food, leaving only slaves and cannon fodder for the Visitors' wars with other alien races from outer space. However, in later episodes, the Visitors attempt to destroy the human soul because they see it as a threat to man's subservience to the queen and her race. Is the plot of V, similar to what could have happened in the distant past with the Anunnaki? Considering the Sumerian epic, doesn't it sound plausible?

AN ANCIENT WAY OF LIFE

As mentioned earlier, ancient texts of Sumer, Egypt and India predate the *Bible* by thousands of years. I will now delve into the Veda texts, and show you its similarities with other texts.

In volume 1 of the translated Mahabharata, regarding the Veda's history, it states "Even as all the senses rest on the manifold workings of the mind, so all works and virtues rest upon this narrative. No story is found on earth that doesn't rest on this epic – nobody endures without living off its food. Even as servants that strive for preferment live off a high-born master, so all the best poets live off this epic."I believe some of these "best poets" exist today, such as Steven Spielberg, George Lucas and James Cameron.

Astaka said, "Whose are these five golden chariots we see before us, which stand there shining high, ablaze like flame crests?"
Yayati said, "They shall carry yourselves, these golden chariots, which stand there shining high, ablaze like flame crests!"
Astaka said, "King, you ascend your chariots and stride wide in the sky! We shall come after you whenever our time comes.
Yayati said, "We must now go altogether; we have conquered heaven together. See how our path goes beyond the sky to the seat of the Gods!"

Astaki is possibly one of the kings of the Puru Dynasty and Yayati a Puranic king. The chariot's horses are very strange: "The thunderbolt of the baronage is their steeds – the steeds are known to be indestructible. Vadava gave birth to the chariot steed – hence the name suta for those who drive the horses. Gandharva bred horses take on any colour or speed, they can be approached for any whim, and they fulfil any desire."

Haven't we seen flying horses in history elsewhere? How about Pegasus of Ancient Greece? I believe animals were used as a type of military symbolism, such as those used for today's aircrafts:

- F-14D Super Tomcat
- F-111 Aardvark
- F-14D E-2 Hawkeye
- NASA: "The Eagle has landed" – on the Moon, referring to a spacecraft, not an eagle!

In Egyptian texts, Amen-Ra (known as the Egyptian Sun God) was referred to as the Travelor, who ... "dost pass over and dost travel through untold spaces requiring millions and hundreds of thousands of years to pass over;

though passest through them in peace, and thou steerest thy way across the watery abyss to the place which thou lovest; sink down and dost make an end of the hours".

In the Rigveda, an ancient Indian sacred collection of Vedic Sanskrit hymns, ships that can pass from water to air are described: "You brought him back, Asvins, in ships that were alive, that swam through the realm of air far from the water."

Have you seen the 1989 movie *The Abyss*, directed by James Cameron? The movie contains an alien ship passing from within the ocean abyss to the open air. In March 2012, James Cameron dived seven miles down in a one-man green submarine in the abyss of the Mariana Trench in the South Pacific Ocean. This location is said to be Earth's deepest, and perhaps most alien, realm. Why do you think he spent millions of dollars of his own money to build the submarine and dive to this mysterious location? For the fun of it? Or to explore what is really down there?

Back to the Egyptians... in their hieroglyphs, why have hawk-headed or dog-headed gods? This is symbolism too, just as with the aircrafts. Hawk-headed gods seem to imply flying vehicles, dog-headed gods imply alert and keen trouble-shooters, perhaps relating to the underworld – like Anubis. The Veda tells us it is not so much symbolism that the monkeys (i.e. Hanuman), lions, bulls, crocodiles and hawks are groups of people (perhaps hybrid), similar to today's military units such as the Wolverines, Blue Angels, or the U.S. army's 1st Cavalry Division whose patch was of a horse, or even the U.S. 34th Infantry Platoon Dog patch. Hawks, vultures and falcons are aerial military units. The apes and monkeys are infantry and artillery units.

In the Mahabharata, Mothers hope that their sons "shall become like Indra to reign alone over the birds. A heroic bird; esteemed by all the world, he will have every power in his grasp." This means that mothers hope their sons will become a part of a star fleet (*Star Trek*). What is the calibre of those who are permitted to be amongst the ranks of those on those spacecrafts? Only the wisest, most intelligent and most courageous of individuals. Even the Hindu God Krishna was referred to as the "Bird-bannered God".

In both the Egyptian and Veda scriptures, the gods always walk around their space crafts to check everything is in order for take-off. Some of the crafts seem to be open vehicles or the type of small flying crafts seen in the *Flash Gordon* movie (1980).

In the *Mahabharata*: "The generous Matali, and expert in the science of horses, started the steeds, which sped like thought and the wind, in the proper fashion. The charioteer looked at my face as I stood on the swinging chariot, king, and he said in surprise, 'This appears to me most marvellous and wonderful today that you have not moved a foot while riding on this celestial chariot! Even he king of the Gods I have always found to stagger at the first upward start of the horse, bull of the Bharatas. But you stand right there on the swinging chariot, scion of Kuru, and me thinks your mettle surpasses Sakra's.'"

- **Matali**: Charioteer of Indra, who took Arjuna to the kingdom of gods.
- **Indra**: Leader of the Devas or gods, and god of war and thunder.
- **Arjuna**: Third of the Pandavas – the five acknowledged sons of Pandu, all married to the same woman (Draupadi).
- **Pandu**: A king and son of Ved Vyasa, who ruled Hastinapur.
- **Ved Vyasa**: Is said to be the one who classified the Vedas into four sections. He is author of the Mahabharata and considered to be the scribe of both the Vedas.
- **Hastinapur**: A town in the Indian state of Uttar Pradesh. Hastinapur was the capital of the Kuru dynasty of kings. Most or even all of the incidents in the epic Mahabharata were believed to have occurred in the city of Hastinapur.
- **Bharata**: A legendary emperor of India, who established the Bharat Empire – covering the entire Indian subcontinent, and parts of Pakistan, Afghanistan, China, Iran, Tajikistan, Uzbekistan, Kyrgyzstan, Russia, Turkmenistan, North-west Tibet, Nepal and Bangladesh.
- **Kuru**: The name of the Indo-Aryan clan.
- **Sakra**: An epithet/characterisation of Indra.

There seem to be many battles over the fuel of the aircrafts, which is referred to as 'blood' or 'Elixir'.

There are multiple parallels between the Sumerian and Egyptian texts, the Bible and the Veda, such as those concerning Enoch (said to be the great-grandfather of Noah) of the Bible and his Vedic counterpart, who was taken up in a "... large celestial crystalline chariot in the sky, which it is the Gods' privilege to enjoy, this airborne chariot will come to you as my gift. Among all mortals you alone shall stand upon a grand and skygoing chariot, and indeed, you will ride there above, like a God come to Flesh!"

Some were ecstatic at the privilege of being aboard an aircraft: "for before, when I rode around heaven in a celestial chariot, I was so drunk with self-grandeur that I did not think of anyone else."

An Egyptian scripture states: "Ferry me over speedily to the landing place of that field which the gods made, on which the gods carouse on those their days of annual festivals." The Veda describes temples which move in the sky, "mansions made in the image of celestial chariots, colourful, gem-studded, opulent with superb wealth."

In Sumerian scriptures, 'Edins' (Edens) were created but they were not gardens at all. They were instead enclosed, protected areas where one could reside, safe from impurities of the environment (couldn't this be the Garden of Eden in the Bible?).

The Vedic text also refers to these Edins, which could fly: "... this lovely airborne city, with the splendour of good works, piled with all precious stones, and impregnable even to the Immortals, the bands of Yaksas and Gandharvas, and Snakes, Asuras, and Raksasas, filled with all desires and virtues, free from sorrow and disease, was created from the Kalaleyas by Brahma, O best of the Bharatas. The Immortals shun this celestial, sky-going city, O hero, which is by the Pauloma and Kalakeyas Asuras. This great city is called Hiranyapura, the City-of-Gold, and it is defended by the grand Pauloma and Kalakeya Asuras."

- *Yaksha*: These appear in Hindu, Buddhist and Jain mythology. The name of a class of nature-spirits, said to be caretakers of the natural treasures/resources hidden in the Earth and tree roots. The Yaksha had a dual personality, where they could be kind nature-fairies associated with the woods and mountains; but on the other hand, they could also be ghosts haunting the wilderness, ambushers and devourers travellers, similar to the Raksasas.
- *Gandharvas:* Male nature-spirits, (husbands of the Apsaras), which sing in the court of Gods. Some of the Gandharvaas are part animal, usually a bird or a horse, and possess very good musical skills. (Most of us have heard of winged cherubs playing harps). With the Devas, they act as singers and dancers, and with the Yaksha, they were formidable warriors.

- *Devas*: Deities, also known as Suras, are in regular conflict with their equally powerful counterparts, the Asuras.
- *Snakes:* Serpent deities are actually worshipped in several cultures. Snakes are seen as knowledgeable, wise and strong. They represent rebirth, death and mortality due to a snake's continuous casting of its skin.

Among some in India, if a cobra is accidentally killed it is burned like a human being. Lord Shiva wears a snake around his neck.

- Shiva is a major deity, 'the Destroyer' among the Trimurti, the Hindu Trinity.
- The Trimurti is made up of the three deities Brahma (the creator), Vishnu (the preserver) and Shiva (the destroyer)... of the cosmos.
- Asuras: These are power-seeking deities opposed to the Devas. Both the Asuras and Devas are children of Kasyapa.
- Kasyapa: An ancient sage, also known as a Rishi. He was also father of the Nagas – the snake deities.

Rakshasa: A race of wicked humanoid beings or unrighteous spirits (also in the Buddhist religion). They are referred to as man-eaters, and Rakshasa and Asura are often used interchangeably. They are notorious for possessing human beings, amongst other things, and they are seen to be shape-shifters and black magicians.

One of the official marks of the Gods was their strong liking for flags. In fact, the Egyptian hieroglyphic symbol for the Gods is a flag. In the Veda, the Gods are described as waving masts on the aircrafts. It's interesting to know that a flag is representative of a god, and in the present day, each country has their own flag. Have you noticed that nearly every flag of the world uses only two or three colours? I wonder why independent countries all have something in common. The symbols on flags can be of great interest too.

Regarding weaponry, both the Veda and Egyptians mention the "dreadful club" that "flashed like lightning in the sky with many arrows that had been wetted on stone...The fearfully whistling missile..." In Egyptian hieroglyphics, the "dreadful club" looks very similar to a modern-day missile.

Staffs or sceptres were known to be held by a ruling monarch as an item of royal or imperial insignia:

- The Code of Hammurabi Stele, a 1772 BC Babylonian code of law existing on a human-sized stone, depicts a seated ruler holding a staff
- Statue of Jupiter in the Hermitage, holding the sceptre and an orb
- In an 1873 portrait, Emperor Pedro II of Brazil, is seen holding an imperial sceptre.

The staff is also well-represented in Sumer, Egypt and Vedic literature, long before Moses' use of it in the *Bible*. In the Vedas, the gods battle with staffs. To "wield the staff" was "to be dreaded, and to protect the people." In the Veda, it seems like when anyone is mad, they "burn like Brahma's staff". The staffs were made of gold, copper or iron – the first two being very good electrical conductors. One passage in the *Veda* refers to it as a "staff of Death". The famous symbol of the devil in modern-days, the trident staff, is also possessed by the Greek God Poseidon, and also by Indra. Egyptian and Sumerian pictographs often show the staffs (or rods) with a 'disc' in the sky. The staffs had immense power and those who used them were greatly feared: "When I heard that the divine spear, which had to be granted by the king of the Gods, had been spirited away by Madhava to the abominable demon Ghatotkaca – then, Samjaya, I lost hope of victory..."

- Ghatotkaca: Son of Bhima and the giantess Hidimbi. His parentage made him half-rakshasa, giving him magical powers such as the ability to fly.
- Bhima is the second of the Pandava brothers, and symbolic of great strength.

According to the Sumerian Epic of *Aquat*, the staff can act as a magician's wand, and the user can disappear and reappear at a different location. Haven't we seen magicians with staffs in movies? Think, for example, of the wizards in *Lord of The Rings*, or Loki in *Thor and The Avengers*? Do you still think these kinds of movies are simply pure fantasy and entertainment?

Considering the above, can't it be said that the sceptres were used as electromagnetic weapons? If the ancients had spacecrafts, flying temples, and missiles, then I don't see why not.

Just as animals have represented military units, one can infer that the snakes in *Veda* texts are actually entities/people trained in some sort of electro-magnetic technology. Snakes represent the waves and erratic movement of electrical emanations. There is a relationship between a staff and a snake. The Egyptian god Ra is shown holding snakes, just as Moses did.

Figurines of a Snake Goddess, holding a snake in each hand, have been found during an excavation of Minoan archaeological sites in Crete, dating from 1600 BC. The snake goddess is linked with the Egyptian snake goddess Wadjet.

The snake was used for transmitting and receiving electricity. The Egyptian god Unas was said to have worn a 'serpent-guide' upon his brow, and with it he was endowed with power and sailed the heavens. The Egyptian texts tell us that 'snake' meant 'word', 'thing' and 'matter'. The sound of snake was 'tchet'. It was said that when Ra spoke to his assistants, his voice sounded like the "humming of bees". This seems to refer to a transmitted voice. The assistants answer in a voice resembling "weeping women" or "bulls", like garbled transmissions.

According to the *Veda*, our present history accounts from around 12,000 years after the flood.

The *Mahabharata* states: "In the Beginning, after the destruction of the entire universe, O, tiger among men there is the Krta age, which, they say, lasts four thousand years, preceded by a dawn and followed by a dusk of four hundred. The Treta age is said, to last for three thousand years, preceded by a dawn and followed by a dusk of three hundred each. The Dvapara lasts two thousand years, with a dawn and a dusk of two hundred years each, the Kali age is taught to be one thousand years long, with a hundred years each of dawn and dusk; When the Kali age has been spent the Krta comes around again. This total period of twelve thousand years is called, the Eon. The unit of a thousand such eons is cited as a Day of Brahma. When the entire universe reverts to its home in Brahma, O tiger among men, the wise know this as the reabsorption of the world."

"At the end of the Eon the population increases, tiger among men, and odor becomes stench, and flavours putrid. When the Eon perishes women will have too many children, O king, be short of stature, cast off all morals, and have intercourse through the mouth. At the end of the Eon the countryside will bristle with towers, the crossroads with jackals, the women with hair."

How much of the latter paragraph is true today?

The *Veda* tells us that at the time of man's fall, thousands of years ago, the basic primal instinctive laws of man changed progressively, altering man's genetics: "Some people know four Vedas, others three or two or one, while some have no hymns at all. While the scriptures are thus broken up, the ritual becomes multitudinous; and bent upon austerities and gifts, the creatures fall under the sway of the Constituent of Passion. Because the single Veda is no longer known, the Vedas multiply; and because there is now a collapse of truthfulness, few abide by truth. Many diseases strike those who have lapsed from the truth, and lusts and disasters caused by fate arise, afflicted by which some men perform very severe austerities, while others, motivated by desires or the wish for heaven, hold sacrifices. Thus, having come to the Dvaparayuga, the creatures perish from lawlessness."

Regarding how the universe came into being, the method, or 'big bang', is not known, but according to the *Veda*, the gods were created from It and not by a Him, and the gods supposedly are none the wiser: "There was neither non-existence nor existence then, there was neither the realm of space nor the sky which is beyond. What stirred? Where? In whose protection? Was there water, bottomlessly deep? There was neither death nor immortality then. There was no distinguishing sign of night nor of day. That one breathes, windless, by its own impulse. Other than that there was nothing beyond. Darkness was hidden by darkness in the beginning; with no distinguishing sign, all this was water. The life force that was covered with emptiness, that one arose through the power of heat. Desire came upon that one in the beginning; that was the first seed of mind. Poets seeking in their heart with wisdom found the bond of existence in non-existence. Their cord was extended across. Was there below? Was there above? There were seed-placers; there were powers. There was impulse beneath, there was giving forth above. Who really knows? Who will here proclaim it? Whence was it produced? Whence is this creation. The gods came afterwards, with the creation of this universe? Who then knows whence it has arisen? Whence this creation has arisen – perhaps it formed itself, or perhaps it did not – the one who looks down on it in the highest heaven, only he knows – or perhaps he does not know."

There are many similarities between the scriptures of the Sumerians and those in the *Vedas*. For example, Enki is referred to as Indra, and Anu is referred to as Rama. I will go into the *Veda* texts in more detail later.

As I have said, Indra is referred to as Enki, and Rama is referred to as Anu. These different versions must come from a source. The source is unknown, or perhaps one of these ancient texts is the 'original'.

A war erupted amongst the anunnaki. It is not so clear what the reason was behind it, but the war seems to have been nuclear. Yet, as Joseph P. Farrell puts it: It seems that the Atrahasis is more than a mere epic, for it hints at dark designs and agendas at work in the pantheon, and moreover clearly suggests that mankind, whether in his hybrid form or not, is perhaps both battlefield and prize in a much larger cosmic conflict. In the aftermath of this nuclear war, as Dr. Lana Cantrell has said, the radiation had badly damaged the DNA of the gods, and they were not as powerful as they had previously been.

People living in and around the area of nuclear disasters, such as those in Fukushima and Chernobyl, were obviously affected by the radiation. Even three generations of butterflies which live near the Fukushima nuclear plant have recently been reported to have undergone genetic mutations. Without a doubt, other species would also have been affected. I have previously referred to the Anunnaki as the Nephilim. Nephilim is derived from 'to fall'. This is exactly what happened to the Anunnaki, because of the radiation.

Again, what were humans like before being genetically invaded by these extra-terrestrials, which seem to be the Elohim of the Bible?

HUMAN ANCESTORS

Continuing with the concept of creation and destruction, and observing how the terms First Earth, Second Earth, Third Earth and Middle-Earth have been used for many years on television, have these concepts and terms been explored in the 'real world'? Yes.

One individual to explore them was Madame Helena Petrovna Blavatsky (1831–1891). Blavatsky was a scholar of ancient wisdom literature, conducting extensive research into various spiritual traditions of the world. Blavatsky's work was read by many, especially *The Secret Doctrine*, which is considered to be her magnum-opus, her most renowned achievement. Manly P. Hall in *Blavatsky and The Secret Doctrine*, by Max Heindel (1933) commented: "The Secret Doctrine is one of the most remarkable books in the world... Behind her stood the real teachers, the guardians of the Secret Wisdom of the ages, who taught her all the occult lore which she transmitted in her writings."

Blavatsky had published two volumes of *The Secret Doctrine*, with the intention of writing two further volumes. Unfortunately, she died before being able to do this. I do wonder what we may have learnt from her two additional volumes.

According to *The Secret Doctrine* and Blavatsky's study of *The Book of Dzyan* (ancient texts of Tibetan origin), man actually lived in a non-physical state. Human history comprises seven evolutionary stages, of which we humans are the fifth. Each of the evolutionary stages (called the 'Root Races') is associated with a Continent. Blavatsky finds that the *Book of Dzyan* teaches the evolution of seven human groups on seven different portions of the Earth.

The doctrine of seven Races, seven Rounds and Evolution is also found in Revelation 17.10: "And there are seven kings: five are fallen, and one is, and the other is not yet come; and when he cometh, he must continue a short space."

In summary:

- *First Root Race*: Polarians, or, Chhayas. Continent: The Sacred Land in the Polar region (North and/or South Poles).
- *Second Root Race*: Hyperboreans. Continent: Hyperborea or Plaksha, which was located west of the North Pole, now known as Northern Asia.
- *Third Root Race*: Lemurians. Continent: Lemuria, which stretched from the Indian Ocean to Australia.
- *Fourth Root Race*: Atlanteans. Continent: Atlantis, which stretched from Iceland to South America, including the Gulf of Mexico, across the ocean to Scotland and Ireland.
- *Fifth Root Race*: Aryans. Continent: Europe and Asia Minor. *Note*: We are of the Aryan Race.
- *Sixth Root Race*: Unnamed.

From this point in this book, I will provide more information of the Races from studying the *Stanzas of Dzyan* using Blavatsky's great work, *The Secret Doctrine*.

Blavatsky claims that every Root Race has seven Sub-races. Every Sub-race has seven Family-races. Unless otherwise stated, all quotations from this point will be taken from the *Stanzas of Dzyan* and/or *The Secret Doctrine*.

First Root-Race

The very first Root-Race, called the Chhayas, are said to have been astral/etheric in nature, and therefore have no physical body.

Chhaya...is the astral image

But men, during the first and second races, were not physical beings, but merely rudiments [astral entities] of the future men: Bhutas...

Hence we believe in races of beings other than our own in far remote geological periods; in races of ethereal, following incorporeal, 'Arupa', men, with form but no solid substance.

... primeval humanity had at first an ethereal... form, evolved by gods or natural 'forces', which grew, condensed throughout millions of ages, and became gigantic in its physical impulse and tendency, until it settled into the huge, physical form of the Fourth Race Man...

In those early ages, astral evolution was alone in progress, and the two planes, the astral and the physical, though developing on parallel lines, had no direct point of contact with one another.

The astral bodies of the Chhyas were created by the Lunar Pitris. Lunar means belonging to the moon and Pitris is a Sanskrit word meaning father. Lunar Pitris is a term used in Theosophy. Specifically, it signifies the seven or ten grades of evolving entities, which at the end of the lunar manvantara, pass into a nirvanic state, to leave it aeons later as the seven or tenfold hierarchy of beings which inform the planetary chain of Earth. A manvantara is the period of activity between any two manus. A manu is a title granted to the ancestor/progenitor of mankind, and also the very first king to rule this Earth, who saved mankind from the universal flood. A general definition of Lunar Pitri covers all entities which originally came from the moon-chain to the earth-chain. Another term for Lunar Pitris is lunar ancestors, or barhishads. These lunar ancestors are usually of seven classes, three being Arupa (without a body), and four being Rupa (with a body).

... the progenitors created man out of their own astral bodies...

The Progenitors of Man, called in India 'Fathers', Pitara or Pitris, are the creators of our bodies and lower principles...As stated, they were 'lunar Beings'.

¿en qué quedamos? ¿no fueron los Anunakis quien nos crearon?

It is from the material Worlds that descend they, who fashion physical man at the new Manvantaras. They are inferior Lha (Spirits), possessed of a dual body (an astral within an ethereal form). They are the fashioners and creators of our body of illusion.

As to their fashioners or 'Ancestors' – those Angels who, in the exoteric legends, obeyed the law – they must be identical with the Barhishad Pitris, or the Pitar-Devata, i.e. those possessed of the physical creative fire.

The astral bodies of the Fourth-Round Chhyas were created from astral matter carried over from the Third Round.

The astral prototypes of the mineral, vegetable and animal kingdoms up to man have taken that time (300 million years) to evolve, re-forming out of the cast-off materials of the preceding Round, which, though very dense and physical in their own cycle, are relatively ethereal as compared with the materiality of our present middle Round. At the expiration of these 300 million years, Nature, on the way to the physical and material, down the arc of descent, begins with mankind and works downwards, hardening or materialising forms as it proceeds.

The Chhayas are called The Sons of the Self-Born, or, Shadows, because they only existed on the astral plane, lacking physical bodies.

The 'shadows' or Chhayas, are called the sons of the 'self-born', as the latter name is applied to all the gods and Beings born through the Will, whether of Deity or Adept.

The Chhayas are also referred to as The Sons of Yoga.

The Commentaries explain that the first Race – the ethereal or astral Sons of Yoga [are] also called 'Self-born'.
The First [Race] were the Sons of Yoga.

These 'Forms' are called 'Sons of Yoga' because Yoga (union with Brahma exoterically) is the supreme condition of the passive infinite deity, since it contains all the divine energies and is the essence of Brahma, who is said to create everything through the power of Yoga. The Chhayas are also called the Sons of the Sons of Twilight. Chhayas (The First Race) initially appeared as astral off-shoots from the Progenitors (and did not have physical bodies).

The First Race, the 'Self-born', [were] the (astral) shadows of their Progenitors.It is [The Barhishad]... who project the senseless model (the Astral) of the physical Being...they could only give birth to the outer man, or rather to the model of the physical, the astral man.

The process by which the Chhayas were created was called Fission.

Fission... As seen in the division of the nucleated cell, in which the cell-nucleus splits into two sub-nuclei... and multiply outside as independent entities.

The Chhayas have completely disappeared.

The 'moon coloured' (i.e. the First and the Second Races) [are] gone for ever – ay, without leaving any traces whatever...

Second Root-Race:
The Hyperboreans, like the Chhayas before, only existed on the astral plane (without physical bodies).

But men, during the first and the second races, were not physical beings, but merely rudiments [astral entities] of the future men: Bhutas...

The Hyperboreans initially appeared as astral buds from the Chhayas.

The Second Race was the product by budding and expansion...
What will be most contested by scientific authorities is this a-sexual Race, the Second, the fathers of the 'Sweat-born'...'Budding' is the very word used in the Stanza [to describe how they procreated]. How could these Chhayas reproduce themselves otherwise; viz., procreate the Second Race, since they were ethereal, a-sexual, and even devoid, as yet, of the vehicle of desire, or Kama Rupa, which evolved only in the Third Race? They evolved the Second Race unconsciously, as do some plants.
When the season of reproduction arrives, the sub-astral [Chhayas] 'extrudes' a miniature of itself from the egg of surrounding aura. This germ grows and feeds on the aura till it becomes fully developed, when it gradually separates from its parent, carrying with it its own sphere of

aura; just as we see living cells reproducing their like by growth and subsequent division into two.

The Hyperboreans are called the Sweat-Born, because later members of their race were produced by budding.

The Sons of Wisdom... spurned the Sweat-born.

The early Second (Root) Race were the Fathers of the 'Sweat-born'; the later Second (Root) Race were 'Sweat-born' themselves.

When the race became old, the old waters [Chhayas] mixed with the fresher waters [Hyperboreans]; When the drops became turbid, they vanished and disappeared, in the new stream, in the hot stream of life. The outer of the First became the inner of the Second... The old (primitive) Race merged in the second race, and became one with it... This is the mysterious process of transformation and evolution of mankind. The material of the first forms – shadowy, ethereal, and negative – was drawn or absorbed into, and thus become the complement of, the forms of the Second Race. The Commentary explains this by saying that, as the First Race was simply composed of the astral shadows of the creative progenitors, having of course neither astral nor physical bodies of their own – this Race never died. Its 'men' melted gradually away, becoming absorbed in the bodies of their own 'sweat-born' progeny, more solid than their own. The old form vanished and was absorbed by, disappeared in, the new form, more human and physical. There was no death in those days of a period more blissful than the Golden Age; but the first, or parent material was used for the formation of the new being, to form the body and even the inner or lower principles or bodies of the progeny... When the shadow retires, i.e. when the Astral body becomes covered with more solid flesh, man develops a physical body. The 'wing', or the ethereal form that produced its shadow and image, became the shadow of the astral body and its own progeny.

The Chhayas lived their entire lives in a single astral body, and eventually changed into the Hyperboreans. The significant differences between the two races were not discussed in *The Secret Doctrine*. Perhaps Blavatsky planned to include the information in her two further volumes. No physical remains exist of the Chhayas and the Hyperboreans.

The 'moon coloured' (i.e. the First and Second Races) gone for ever – ay, without leaving any traces whatever...

Third Root-Race: — *separation of the sexes*
The Lemurians were the first race to live in physical bodies. ←

... the Lemurian, the first physical man... ←

The Third Race were said to have formed by 'budding' from the previous race, the Hyperboreans.

The Second Race... evolved out of itself... the Third Androgyne Race... the very earliest of that race were – The Sons of Passive Yoga. They issued from the second Manushyas (human race), and became oviparous. The emanations that came out of their bodies during the seasons of procreation were ovulary; the small spheroidal nuclei developing into a large soft, egg-like vehicle, gradually hardened, when, after a period of gestation, it broke and the young human animal issued from it unaided, as the fowls do in our race.
This Third Race is sometimes called collectively 'the Sons of Passive Yoga', i.e. it was produced unconsciously by the second Race, which, as it was intellectually inactive, is supposed to have been constantly plunged in a kind of blank of abstract contemplation, as required by the conditions of the Yoga state. In the first or earlier portion of the existence of this third race, while it was yet in its state of purity, the 'Sons of Wisdom' who, as will be seen, incarnated in this Third Race...

The next generations of the Third Race were named, 'Egg-born', referring to Budding on the physical plane.

¿ de dónde salió el sweat

The early Third Race, then, is formed from drops of 'sweat', which, after many a transformation, grow into human bodies.
The First Race having created the Second by 'budding', the Second Race gives birth to the Third – which itself is separated into three distinct divisions, consisting of men differently procreated. The first two of these are produced by an oviparous method, presumably unknown to modern

Natural History. While the early sub-races of the Third Humanity procreated their species by a kind of exudation of moisture or vital fluid, the drops of which coalescing formed an oviform ball – or shall we say egg? – which served as an extraneous vehicle for the generation therein of a foetus and child, the mode of procreation by the later races changed, in its results at all events.

The separation of the sexes, male and female, occurred in the period of the Lemurian Root-Race.

...the men of the Third Race became physiologically and physically ready... when they had separated into sexes.

If you think the idea of humans being androgynous (possessing both male and female characteristics in terms of reproduction) is unlikely, I ask you, are you sure you haven't read something like this in the *Bible*? I believe the following passage supports the case for androgyny in humans: Genesis 6.1: *"Now it came to pass, when men began to multiply on the face of the earth, and daughters were born to them."* Genesis 6.2: *"...that the sons of God saw the daughters of men"* The men multiplied? Daughters of men? I sense androgyny.

The Third Race can be divided into three periods: (1) Early Period – Sweat-Born, the same reproductive period as the Second Race: (2) Middle Period – Egg-Born: (3) Final Period – Sex-Born, the same reproductive process as today.

The Fall of Man
The fall of man occurred in three generations:

- Primordial Fall
- Fall of the Asura
- Fall of humans into generation

The fall of man occurred due to the separation of the sexes. When humans separated male and female, sexual activity started, and led to Half-Human Abominsations. *abominations*

...the so-called SONS OF WILL AND YOGA... were generated sexually after the separation of sexes, the Fall of Man.
The third race fell – and created [single-person procreated] no longer: it begot [sexually] its progeny. Being still mindless at the period of separation it begot, moreover, anomalous offspring, until its physiological nature had adjusted its instincts in the right direction. Like the 'lords the gods' of the Bible, the 'Sons of Wisdom'', the Dhyan-Chohans, had warned them to leave alone the fruit forbidden by Nature: but the warning proved of no value. Men realised the unfitness – we must not say sin – of what they had done, only when too late: after the angelic monads from higher spheres had incarnated in, and endowed them with understanding.

The early Lemurians are referred to as being androgynous or a-sexual. The middle-period of Lemurians are referred to as the hermaphrodite or bi-sexual.

Intermediate Hermaphroditism – Male and female organs inhering in the same individual; e.g. the majority of plants, worms, and snails, etc. allied to budding.

The final period of Lemurians are referred to as normally-sexual, male and female.

True sexual union: (cf. later Third Root Race)
Once that Androgyne 'humanity' separated into sexes, transformed by Nature into child-bearing engines, it ceased to procreate its like through drops of vital energy oozing out of the body.
The little ones of the earlier races were entirely sexless – shapeless even for all one knows; but those of the later races were born androgynous. It is in the Third Race that the separation of sexes occurred. From being previously a-sexual, Humanity became distinctly hermaphrodite or bi-sexual; and finally the man-bearing eggs began to give birth, gradually and almost imperceptibly in their evolutionary development, first, to Beings in which one sex predominated over the other, and, finally, to distinct men and women.

The History of the Races begins at the separation of the Sexes, when the preceding egg-bearing androgynous race perished rapidly, and the subsequent sub-races of the Third physiologically.
Though we apply the term 'truly human' only to the Fourth Atlantean Root-Race, yet the Third Race is almost human in its latest portion, since it is during its fifth sub-race that mankind separated sexually, and that the first man was born according to the now normal process. This 'first man' answers in the Bible (Genesis) to Enos or Henoch, son of Seth.

Enoch

The physical component of humanity (within the Third Race) is eighteen million years old.

Humanity is eighteen million and odd years old. We say, yes; but only so far as physical, or approximately physical, man is concerned, who dates from the close of the Third Root-Race. Beyond that period MAN, or his filmy image, may have existed for 300 million years, for all we know...

Over what period of time did this process of evolution occur?

...this mode of procreation [sexual intercourse] did not occur suddenly, as one may think, and required long ages before it became the one 'natural' way.

The Third Race is grouped into three classes:

- *First class:* The Sons of Wisdom who incarnated into human bodies, and humans who had "prematurely developed intellects".
- *Second class:* Humans who were "'half-ready', who received 'but a spark' [constituting] the average humanity..."
- *Third class:* "...those which 'were not ready' at all, the latest Monads, which hardly evolved from their last transitional and lower animal forms at the close of the Third Round, remained the 'narrow-brained'..."

Early members of the Third Race were grouped into three classes – advanced, intermediate and poor. The Solar Pitris chose the first group, and incarnated into bodies of that group. The Solar Pitris were the Divine Leaders, the Divine Kings that are referred to in the titles of British monarchy.

Today's Ceylon was part of the Lemurian continent:

> *The sinking and transformation of Lemuria beginning nearly at the Artic Circle (Norway), the Third Race ended its career in Lanka, or rather on that which became Lanka with the Atlanteans. The small remnant now known as Ceylon is the Northern highland of ancient Lanka, while the enormous island of that name was, in the Lemurian period, the gigantic continent described a few pages back.*

Problems began to emerge from a lack of mind-principle and half-human abominations.

Lack of Mind Principle

The Lunar Pitris were able to provide astral forms for the new humans, but they were not able to provide Manas or higher minds.

> *The Barhishad [Lunar Pitris], though possessed of creative fire, were devoid of the higher MAHAT-mic element. Being on a level with the lower principles – those which precede gross objective matter – they could only give birth to the outer man, or rather to the model of the physical, the astral man.*
>
> *... We find primeval man, issued from the bodies of his spiritually fireless progenitors, described as aeriform, devoid of compactness, and MINDLESS. He had no middle principle to serve him as a medium between the highest and the lowest, the spiritual man and the physical brain, for he lacked Manas. The Monads which incarnated in those empty SHELLS, remained as unconscious as when separated from their previous incomplete forms and vehicles.*
>
> *Thus physical nature, when left to herself in the creation of animal and man, is shown to have failed. She can produce the first two and the lower animal kingdoms, but when it comes to the turn of man, spiritual, independent and intelligent powers are required for his creation, besides the 'coats of skin' and the 'Breath of animal Life.' The human Monads of*

preceding Rounds need something higher than purely physical materials to build their personalities with, under the penalty of remaining even below any 'Frankenstein' animal.

More was needed.

... Two connecting principles are needed: Manas and Kama. This requires a living Spiritual Fire of the middle principle form the fifth and third states of Pleroma. But this fire is the possession of the... 'Flames' (the Agnishwatta) who, as shown in [Shloka ii-3-13], 'remain behind' instead of going along with the others to create men on Earth. But the true esoteric meaning is that most of them were destined to incarnate as the Egos of the forthcoming crop of Mankind. The human Ego is neither Atman nor Buddhi, but the higher Manas: the intellectual fruition and the efflorescence of the intellectual self-conscious Egotism – in the higher spiritual sense.

Finally, humans developed Manas or intelligence.

Then all men became endowed with Manas. They saw the sin of the Mindless.

'Nature', the physical evolutionary Power, could never evolve intelligence unaided – she can only create 'senseless forms'... The 'Lunar Monads' cannot progress, for they have not yet had sufficient touch with the forms created by 'Nature' to allow of their accumulating experiences through its means. It is the Manasa-Dhyanis who fill up the gap, and they represent the evolutionary power of Intelligence and Mind, the link between 'Spirit' and 'Matter' – in this Round.

The Dhyanis who incarnate in the human forms of the Third Root-Race and endow them with intellect (Manas) are called the chyuta, for they fall into generation.

'The subtle bodies remain without understanding (Manas) until the advent of the Suras (Gods) now called Asuras (not Gods)', says the Commentary.

... the Third Root-Race shows three distinct divisions or aspects physiologically and psychically; the earliest, sinless; the middle portions

131

Manas or intelligence appeared in the third Race, the intellectual, on the physical plane was reached during the Fourth Root-Race.

awakening to intelligence; and the third and last decidedly animal: i.e. Manas succumbs to the temptations of Kama. (*desire*)

The monad of the animal is as immortal as that of man, yet the brute knows nothing of this; it lives an animal life of sensation just as the first human would have lived, when attaining physical development in the Third Race, had it not been for the Agnishwatta and the Manasa Pitris.

… the Manasaputras, the Sons of Wisdom who informed the mindless man, and endowed him with his mind (manas).

Manas, or intelligence, first appeared in the Third Race and continued to the Fourth Race.

It is only at the mid-point of the 3rd Root Race that man was endowed with Manas.

The intellectual, on the physical plane, was reached during the Fourth Root-Race.

Half-Human Abominations

Strange, half-human creatures such as Minotaurs, Satyrs and Mermaids appeared.

Oannes (or Dagon, the Chaldean 'Man-fish') divides his Cosmogony and Genesis into two portions. First the abyss of waters and darkness, wherein resided most hideous beings – men with wings, four and two-faced men, human beings with two heads, with the legs and horns of a goat (our 'goat-men'), hippocentaurs, bulls with the heads of men, and dogs with tails of fishes. In short, combinations of various animals and men, of fishes, reptiles and other monstrous animals assuming each other's shapes and countenances.

According to the [Chinese] commentator Kwoh P'oh, in the work called Shan-Hai-King, 'Wonders by Sea and Land', a work which was written by the historiographer Chung Ku from engravings on nine urns made by the Emperor Yu, (B.C. 2255), an interview is mentioned with men having two distinct faces on their heads, before and behind, monsters with bodies of goats and human faces, etc.

beget – to procreate
create – to cause to come into existence

In the initial period of man's Fourth evolution, the human kingdom branched off in several and various directions. The outward shape of its first specimens was not uniform, for the vehicles (the egg-like, external shells, in which the future fully physical man gestated) were often tampered with, before they hardened, by huge animals, of species now unknown, and which belonged to the tentative efforts of Nature. The result was that intermediate races of monsters, half animals, half men, were produced. But as they were failures, they were not allowed to breathe long and live, though the intrinsically paramount power of psychic over physical nature being yet very weak, and hardly established, the 'Egg-Born' Sons had taken several of their females unto themselves as mates, and bred other human monsters. Later, animal species and human races becoming gradually equilibrized, they separated and mated no longer. Man created no more – he begot. But he also begot animals, as well as men in days of old.

But who were the Nephilim of Genesis vi. 4? There were Palaeolithic and Neolithic men in Palestine ages before the events recorded in the book of the Beginnings. The theological tradition identifies these Nephilim with hairy men or Satyrs, the latter being mythical in the Fifth Race and the former historical in both the Fourth and Fifth Races. We have stated elsewhere what the prototypes of these Satyrs were, and have spoken of the bestiality of the early and later Atlantean race.

Those races... which 'remained destitute of knowledge', or those again which were left 'mindless', remained as they were, even after the natural separation of the sexes. It is these who committed the first cross-breeding, so to speak, and bred monsters... Adam and Eve were supposed, with Cain and Abel, to be the only human family on Earth. Yet we see Cain going to the land of Nod and taking there a wife.

These monsters, the first result of ensouling physical bodies, are called the Second Humanity.

... The First Root-Race, the 'Shadows' of the Progenitors, could not be injured, or destroyed by death. Being so ethereal and so little human in constitution, they could not be affected by any element – flood or fire. But their 'Sons', the Second Root-Race, could be and were so destroyed.

As the 'progenitors' merged wholly in their own astral bodies, which were their progeny; so that progeny was absorbed in its descendants, the 'Sweat-born'. These were the second Humanity – composed of the most heterogeneous gigantic semi-human monsters – the first attempts of material nature at building human bodies.

The Lords of the Flame hesitated at the thought of incarnating into those bodies.

"She evolved water-men, terrible and bad."
The water-men terrible and bad She [Earth] herself created. From the remains of others (from the mineral, vegetable and animal remains) from the first, second, and third (Rounds) She formed them... The Dhyani came and looked... Displeased they were... This is no fit rupa for our Brothers of the Fifth.

At that point, earthly evolution could be referred to as a failure. *"failure" ha quedado*

The Chaldean fragments of Cosmogony on the Cuneiform inscriptions, and elsewhere, show two distinct creations of animals and men, the first being destroyed, as it was a failure.

The physical abominations were destroyed.

The explanations given in our Stanzas are far more clear than that which the legend of creation from the Cutha tablet would give, even were it complete. What is preserved on it, however, corroborates them. For, in the tablet. 'the Lord of Angels' destroys the men in the abyss... who 'were destroyed because they were not 'perfect'...

Fall of the Asura
The Fall of the Asura, involved three falls; The Primordial Fall: The Fall of the Asura: The Fall of humans into generation

The history begins by the descent on Earth of the 'Gods' who incarnate in mankind, and this is the FALL.

Satan and his rebellious host would thus prove, when the meaning of the allegory is explained, to have refused to create physical man, only to become the direct Saviours and the Creators of 'divine Man'. The symbolic teaching is more than mystical and religious, it is purely scientific, as will be seen later on. For, instead of remaining a mere blind, functioning medium, impelled and guided by fathomless LAW, the 'rebellious' Angel claimed and enforced his right of independent judgement and will, his right of free-agency and responsibility, since man and angel are alike under Karmic Law. [Footnote: Explaining Kabalistic views, the author of the 'New Aspects of Life' says of the Fallen Angels that, 'According to the symbolical teaching, Spirit, from being simply a functionary agent of God, became volitional in its developed and developing action; and, substituting its own will for the Divine desire in its regard, so fell. Hence the Kingdom and reign of Spirits and spiritual action, which flow from and are the product of Spirit-volition, are outside, and contrasted with, and in contradiction to, the Kingdom of Souls and Divine action.' So far, so good; but what does the Author mean by saying, 'When man was created, he was human in constitution, with human affections, human hopes and aspirations. From this state he fell – into the brute and savage'? This is diametrically opposite to our Eastern teaching, and even to the Kabalistic notion so far as we understand it, and to the Bible itself. This looks llike Corporealism and Substantialism colouring positive philosophy, though it is rather hard to feel quite sure of the Author's meaning. A FALL, however, 'from the natural into the supernatural and the animal' – supernatural meaning the purely spiritual in this case – means what we suggest.]

... The 'Self-created' and the 'Self-existent' projected their pale shadows; but group the Third, the Fire-Angels, rebelled and refused to join their Fellow Devas.

... Tradition shows the celestial Yogis offering themselves as voluntary victims in order to redeem Humanity – created god-like and perfect at first – and to endow him with human affections and aspirations. To do this they had to give up their natural status and, descending on our globe, take up their abode on it for the whole cycle of the Mahayuga, thus exchanging their impersonal individualities for individual personalities – the bliss of sidereal existence for the curse of terrestrial

life. This voluntary sacrifice of the Fiery Angels, whose nature was Knowledge and Love, was construed by the exoteric theologies into a statement that shows 'the rebel angels hurled down from heaven into the darkness of Hell' – our Earth.

yo siempre lo he dicho, que la Tierra es el infierno.

Arrival of the Lords of the Flame

The Lords of the Flame (Solar Pitris) came down to assist human evolution. These Lords succeeded in helping humans to develop to mental abilities.

The Endowers of man with his conscious, immortal EGO, are the 'Solar Angels' – whether so regarded metaphorically or literally... It has already been explained why the trans-Himilayan Occultists regard them as evidently identical with those who in India are termed Kumaras, Agnishwattas...

... The Kumaras, Asuras, and other rulers and Pitris, who incarnated in the Third Race, and in this and various other ways endowed mankind with Mind.

Fourth Root-Race:

... The Atlanteans were a very ancient northern nation, long prior to the Hindus, the Phoenicians, and the Egyptians.

Atlanteans were developed from a nucleus of Northern Lemurian Third Race Men, centred, roughly speaking, toward a point of land in what is now the mid-Atlantic Ocean. Their continent was formed by the coalescence of many islands and peninsulas which were upheaved in the ordinary course of time and became ultimately the true home of the great Race known as the Atlanteans.

The term 'Atlantean' must not mislead the reader to regard these as one race only, or even a nation. It is as though one said 'Asiatics'. Many, multityped, and various were the Atlanteans, who represented several humanities, and almost a countless number of races and nations, more varied indeed than would be the 'Europeans' were this name to be given indiscriminately to the five existing parts of the world; which, at the rate colonization is proceeding, will be the case, perhaps, in less than two or three hundred years. There were brown, red, yellow, white and black

Atlanteans; giants and dwarfs (as some African tribes comparatively are, even now).

... The Mediterranean barbarians... marvelled at the prowess of the Atlanteans. 'Their physical strength was extraordinary (witness indeed their cyclopean buildings), the earth shaking sometimes under their tread.'

The Atlanteans were the first physical, intellect-using race.

... It is only from the time of the Atlantean, brown and yellow giant Races, that one ought to speak of MAN, since it was the Fourth race only which was the first completely human species, however much larger in size than we are now.

... The Atlanteans were really the first purely human and terrestrial race – those that preceded it being more divine and ethereal than human and solid.

Some of the Races overlapped.

Since the beginning of the Atlantean Race many million years have passed, yet we find the last of the Atlanteans, still mixed up with the Aryan element, 11,000 years ago. This shows the enormous overlapping of one race over the race which succeeds it, though in character and external type the elder loses its characteristics, and assumes the new features of the younger race. This is proved in all the formations of mixed human races.

As mentioned earlier, some Atlanteans were giants.

The giants of Genesis are the historical Atlanteans of Lanka, and the Greek Titans... if Noah was an Atlantean, then he was a Titan, a giant

Atlantis ended when its continent sank in the ocean:

... the Atlanteans were post diluvian to the Lemurians, and Lemuria was not submerged as Atlantis was...

Atlantis was the last part of history where the newly-individualised humans experienced their first incarnation.

> *No fresh Monads have incarnated since the middle-point of the Atlanteans.*

The Greeks originated from the Atlanteans:

> *... The Greeks were but the dwarfed and weak remnant of that once glorious nation... What was this nation? The secret doctrine teaches that it was the latest, seventh sub-race of the Atlanteans, already swallowed up in one of the early sub-races of the Aryan stock...*

The end of Atlantis seems to have been a time of negativity.

> *...many of us are now working off the effects of the evil Karmic causes produced by us in Atlantean bodies.*
>
> *The Atlantean races were many, and lasted in their evolution for millions of years; all were not bad. They became so toward their end, as we (the fifth) are fast becoming now.*
>
> *It was the Atlanteans, the first progeny of semi-divine man after his separation into sexes – hence the first-begotten and humanly-born mortals – who became the first 'Sacrificers' to the god of matter. They stand in the far-away dim past, in ages more than prehistoric, as the prototype on which the great symbol of Cain was built, as the first anthromorphists who worshipped form and matter. That worship generated very soon into self-worship, thence led to phallicism, or that which reigns supreme to this day in the symbolisms of every exoteric religion of ritual, dogma, and form.*
>
> *Thus the first Altantean races, born on the Lemurian Continent, separated from their earliest tribes into the righteous and the unrighteous; into those who worshipped the one unseen Spirit of Nature, the ray of which man feels within himself – or the Pantheists, and those who offered fanatical worship to the Spirits of the Earth, the dark Cosmic, anthropomorphic Powers, with whom they made alliance.*

... The 'Lemurians' and the Atlanteans, 'those children of Heaven and Earth', were indeed marked with a character of SORCERY...

...The ungodly Atlanteans perished, and 'were seen no more...'

The mysteries of Heaven and Earth, revealed to the Third Race by their celestial teachers in the days of their purity, became a great focus of light, the rays from which became necessarily weakened as they were diffused and shed upon an uncongenial, because too material, soil. With the masses they degenerated into Sorcery, taking later on the shape of exoteric religions, of idolatry full of superstitions, and man- or hero-worship.

... The Atlanteans became the terrible sorcerers, now celebrated in so many of the oldest [manuscripts] of India, only toward their fall, the submersion of their continent having been brought on by it.

The negativity of Lemuria and Atlantis led to the creation of today's mystery religions. An impenetrable veil of secrecy was thrown over the occult and religious mysteries taught, after the submersion of the last remnant of the Atlantean race, some 12,000 years ago, lest they should be shared by the unworthy, and so desecrated... It is this secrecy which led the Fifth Race to the establishment, or rather the re-establishment of the religious mysteries, in which ancient truths might be taught to the coming generations under the veil of allegory and symbolism.

The Third and Fourth Root-races were marked by certain physical characteristics. They were Giants and Cyclops Humans.

Giants

... All ancient writings – prose and poetry – are full of the reminiscences of the Lemuro-Atlanteans, the first physical races, though the Third and the Fourth in number. Hesiod records the tradition about the men of the age of Bronze, whom Jupiter had made out of ash-wood and who had hearts harder than diamond. Clad in bronze from head to foot they passed their lives in fighting. Monstrous in size, endowed with a terrible strength, invincible arms and hands descended from their shoulders, says the poet. Such were the giants of the first physical races.

Hesiod was a Greek poet from the era between 750 and 650 BC, approximately the same as that of Homer.

... The Mediterranean barbarians... marvelled at the prowess of the Atlanteans. 'Their physical strength was extraordinary (witness indeed their cyclopean buildings), the earth shaking sometimes under their tread. Whatever they did, was done speedily... They were wise and communicated their wisdom to men'

That Third and holy Race consisted of men who, at their zenith, were described as, 'towering giants of godly strength and beauty...'

... The Atlanteans [were] giants whose physical beauty and strength reached their climax, in accordance with evolutionary law, toward the middle period of their fourth sub-race.

While it is very probable that the Gibborim (the giants) of the Bible are the Rakshasas of the Hindus, it is still more certain that both are Atlanteans, and belong to the submerged races.

To speak of a race nine yatis, or 27 feet high, in a work claiming a more scientific character than 'Jack the Giant-Killer' is a somewhat unusual proceeding. 'Where are your proofs?' the writer will be asked. In History and tradition, is the answer. Traditions about a race of giants in days of old are universal; they exist in oral and written lore. India had her Danavas and Daityas; Ceylon had her Rakshasas; Greece, her Titans; Egypt, her colossal Heroes; Chaldea, her Izdubars (Nimrod); and the Jews their Emims of the land of Moab, with the famous giants, Anakim. Moses speaks of Og, a king who was nine cubits high (15 feet and 4 inches) and four wide, and Goliath was 'six cubits and a span in height' (or 10 feet and 7 inches).

Quotations from the *Bible* have already been mentioned, however, for their relevance here, they will be included:

Genesis 6.4: "There were giants in the earth in those days..."
Numbers 13.33: "And there we saw the giants..."
Deuteronomy 2.11: "Which also were accounted giants..."
Deuteronomy 3.11: "For only Og king of Bashan remained the remnant of giants..."

However, over time, the giants began to be phased out, getting shorter and shorter, until mankind reached his current average height of five to six feet.

Gradually, mankind went down in stature, for, even before the real advent of the Fourth or Atlantean race, the majority of mankind had fallen into iniquity and sin, save the hierarchy of the 'Elect', the followers and disciples of the 'Sons of Will and Yoga' – referred to later as the 'Sons of the Fire Mist.'

... It is after the destruction of 'Lemuria' by subterranean fires that man went on steadily decreasing in stature – a process already commenced after their physical FALL – and that finally, some millions of years after, they reached between six and seven feet, and are now dwindling down (as the older Asiatic races) to nearer five than six feet.

Evidence of giants has already been mentioned in this book. However, here is further evidence.

...we may turn to the scientific journals of 1858, which spoke of a sarcophagus of giants found that year on the site of that same city. As to the ancient pagan writers – we have the evidence of Philostratus, who speaks of a giant skeleton twenty-two cubits long, as well as another of twelve cubits...nevertheless, it was that of a giant, as well as that other one discovered by Messecrates of Stire, at Lemnos – 'horrible to behold,' according to Philostratus...

...the Abbe Pegues (citied in de Mirville's Pneumatologie) affirms in his curious work on 'The Volcanoes of Greece' that 'in the neighbourhood of the volcanoes of the isle of Thera, giants with enormous skulls were found laid out under colossal stones...'

Certain excavations in America in mounds and in caves, have already yielded in isolated cases groups of skeletons of nine and twelve feet high. These belong to tribes of the early Fifth Race, now degenerated to an average size of between five and six feet. But we can easily believe that the Titans and Cyclopes of old really belonged to the Fourth (Atlantean) Race, and that all the subsequent legends and allegories found in the Hindu Puranas and the Greek Hesiod and Homer, were based on the hazy reminiscences of real Titans – men of a superhuman tremendous physical power...

It is at the entrance of some of these [viharas in Bamian] that five enormous statues, of what is regarded as Buddha, have been discovered or rather rediscovered in our century, as the famous Chinese traveller, Hiouen-Thsang, speaks of, and saw them, when he visited Bamian in the VIIth century... The Buddhist Arhats and Ascetics found the five statues, and many more, now crumbled down to dust... The largest is made to represent the First Race of mankind, its ethereal body being commemorated in hard, everlasting stone, for the instruction of future generations, as its remembrance would otherwise never have survived the Atlantean Deluge. The second – 120 feet high – represents the sweat-born; and the third – measuring 60 feet – immortalises the race that fell, and thereby inaugurated the first physical race, born of father and mother, the last descendants of which are represented in the Statues found on Easter Isle: but they were only from 20 to 25 feet in stature at the epoch when Lemuria was submerged, after it had been nearly destroyed by volcanic fires. The Fourth Race was still smaller, though gigantic in comparison with our present Fifth Race, and the series culminated finally in the latter... These are, then, the 'Giants' of antiquity, the ante- and post-diluvian Gibborim of the Bible. They lived and flourished one million rather than between three and four thousand years ago.

What are the Bamian statues? The Bamian valley in Afghanistan contains ancient caves of the Kushan Dynasty. It lies northwest of Kabul, the capital of Afghanistan. Bamian is first mentioned in 5th Century AD by Chinese sources. It was first visited by Chinese travellers to Fa-hsien in 400 AD, and Hsuan-tsang in 630 AD. There are giant statues located in the Bamian valley, carved from the living rock, finished with fine plaster. When Hsuan-tsang saw them, he said they were decorated with gold and fine jewels. It is believed that these statues are not Buddhist in origin, but they were built by initiates of the Fourth Race Atlanteans. One statue is a stunning 53 metres high, and another is 120 feet high. There are five statues in total, and they are said to show the occult history of the decrease in Man's stature as his form consolidated into gross physical matter. These five statues represent this decrease in size of the average human frame beginning over a million years ago.

Here is what Blavatsky has to say specifically about the Bamian statues, in *The Secret Doctrine*:

Who cut the Bamian statues, the tallest and the most gigantic in the whole world? Burne, and several learned Jesuits who have visited the place, speak of a mountain "all honeycombed with gigantic cells" with two immense giants cut in the same rock. They are referred to as the modern Miaotse [in Chinese legend, an antediluvian race of giants], the last surviving witnesses of the Miaotse who had "troubled the earth"; the Jesuits are right, and the Archaeologists, who see Buddhas in the largest of these statues, are mistaken. For all those numberless gigantic ruins one after the other in our day, are the work of the Cyclopes, the true and actual Giants of old.

Central Asian traditions say the same of the Bamian statues. What are they, and what is the place where they have stood for countless ages, defying the cataclysms around them, and even the hand of man, as in the instance of the hordes of Timoor and the Vandal-warriors of Nadir-Shah? Bamian is a small, miserable, half-ruined town in Central Asia, half-way between Kabul and Balkh, at the foot of Kobhibaba, a huge mountain of the Paropamisian (or Hindu-Kush) chain, some 8,500 feet above the level of the sea. In days of old, Bamian was a portion of the ancient city of Gholgola, ruined and destroyed to the last stone by Genghis Khan in the 13th Century. The whole valley is hemmed in by colossal rocks, which are full of partially natural and partially artificial caves and grottoes, once the dwellings of Buddhist monks who had established in them their viharas. Such viharas are to be met with in abundance, to this day, in the rock-cut temples of India and the valleys of Jalalabad. It is at the entrance to some of these that five enormous statues, that what is regarded as Buddha, have been discovered or rather re-discovered in our century. The famous Chinese traveller, Hsuan-tsang, saw and spoke of them when he visited Bamian in the 17th Century.

When it is maintained that no larger statues exist on the whole globe, the fact is easily proven on the evidence of all the travellers who have examined them and taken their measurements. Thus, the largest is 173 feet high, or seventy feet higher than the Statue of Liberty. The famous Colossus of Rhodes itself, between whose limbs passed easily the largest vessels of those days, measured only 120 to 130 feet in height. The second statue, cut out in rock like the first, is only 120 feet (15 feet taller than the Statue of Liberty). The third statue is only 60 feet high, the two others still smaller and the last only a little larger than the average tall man of our present race. The first and largest of the Colossi represents a man draped in a kind of toga; M. de Nadeylac thinks that the general appearance of the figure, the lines of the head, the drapery, and especially the large hanging ears, point out undeniably that Buddha was meant to be represented. But this proves nothing. Notwithstanding the fact that most of the now existing figures of Buddha, represented in the posture of Samadhi, have large drooping ears, this is a later innovation and an afterthought. The primitive idea was the result of esoteric allegory.

The Buddhist monks, who turned the grottos of the Miaotse into Viharas and cells, came into Central Asia about or in the first century AD. Therefore Hsuan-tsang, speaking of the colossal statue, says that "the shining of the gold ornamentation that overlaid the statue" in his day "dazzled one's eyes", but of such gliding there remains not a vestige in modern times. The very drapery, in contrast to the figure itself, cut out in the standing rock, is made of plaster and modelled over the stone image. Talbot, who has made the most careful examination, found that this drapery belonged to a far later epoch. The statue itself therefore has to be assigned to a far earlier period than Buddhism. Whom does it represent in such a case?

Once more, tradition, corroborated by written records, answers the query, and explains the mystery. The Buddhist Arhats and Ascetics found the five statues, and many more, now crumbled down to dust. As the three were found by them in colossal niches at the entrance to their future abode, they covered the figures with plaster, and, over the old, modelled new statues made to represent Lord Tathagata. The interior walls of the niches are covered to this day with bright paintings of human figures, and the sacred image of Buddha is repeated in every group. These frescoes and ornaments – which remind one of the Byzantine style of painting – are all due to the piety of the ascetic monks, as are some other minor figures and rock-cut ornamentations. But the five statues belong to the handiwork of the Initiates of the Fourth Race, who sought refuge after the submersion of their continent, in the fastnesses and on the summits of the Central Asian mountain chains.

Moreover, the five statues are an imperishable record of the esoteric teaching of the gradual evolution of races.

The largest is made to represent the First Race of mankind, its ethereal body being commemorated in hard, everlasting stone, for the instruction of future generations. Its remembrance would never otherwise have survived the Atlantean Deluge. The second – 120 feet high – represents the sweat-born [second root-race]; and the third – measuring 60 feet – immortalises the race that fell, and thereby inaugurated the first physical race, born of father and mother, the last descendants of which are represented in the statues found on Easter Isle; but they were only from 20 to 25 feet in stature at the epoch when Lemuria was submerged, after it had been nearly destroyed by volcanic fires. The Fourth Race was still smaller, though gigantic in comparison with our present Fifth Race, and the series culminated finally in the latter.

These are, then, the 'Giants' of antiquity, the ante- and post- diluvian Gibborim of the Bible. They lived and flourished one million rather than between three and four thousand years ago. The Anakim of Joshua, whose hosts were as 'grasshoppers' in comparison with them, are thus a piece of Israelite fancy, unless indeed the people of Israel change the millenniums of their chronology into millions of years.

In the next section we'll focus back on the *Book of Dzyan* and *The Secret Doctrine*.

Cyclops and the Third Eye

Cyclops, well-known in Greek and later Roman mythologies, actually existed.

The evidence for the Cyclopes – a race of giants – will be pointed out in the forthcoming Sections, in the Cyclopean remnants, so called to this day.

... We can easily believe that the Titans and Cyclopes of old really belonged to the Fourth (Atlantean) Race, and that all the subsequent legends and allegories found in the Hindu Puranas and the Greek Hesoid and Homer, were based on the hazy reminiscences of real Titans – men of a superhuman tremendous physical power, which enabled them to defend themselves, and hold at bay the gigantic monsters of the

hermaphrodites — male-females

Mesozoic and early Cenozoic times – and of actual Cyclopes – three-eyed mortals.

The oldest remains of Cyclopean buildings [of Lemurian sixth sub-race buildings] were all the handiwork of the Lemurians of the last sub-races; and an occultist shows, therefore, no wonder on learning that the stone relics found on the small piece of land called Easter Island by Captain Cook, are 'very much like the walls of the Temple of Pachacamac or the Ruins of Tia-Huanuco in Peru', and that they are in the CYCLOPEAN STYLE.

Then, 'the third eye acted no longer', says the Stanza, because MAN had sunk too deep into the mire of matter.

There were...armed human creatures in those early days of the male-females (hermaphrodites); with one head, yet three eyes. They could see before them and behind them. A KALPA later (after the separation of these sexes) men having fallen into matter, their spiritual vision became dim; and co-ordinately the third eye commenced to lose its power... The third eye, likewise, getting gradually PETRIFIED, soon disappeared... The Inner sight could henceforth be acquired only through training and initiation, save in the cases of 'natural and born magicians', sensitives and mediums, as they are called now... The 'deva-eye' exists no more for the majority of mankind. The third eye is dead, and acts no longer; but it has left behind a witness to its existence. This witness is now the PINEAL GLAND.

...As the cycle ran down toward that point when the physiological senses were developed by, and went pari passu with, the growth and consolidation of the physical man, the interminable and complex vicissitudes and tribulations of zoological development, that median 'eye' ended by atrophying along with the early spiritual and purely psychic characteristics in man.

The [third eye] did not become entirely atrophied before the close of the Fourth Race. When spirituality and all the divine powers and attributes of the deva-man of the Third had been made the hand-maidens of the newly-awakened physiological and psychic passions of the physical man, instead of the reverse, the eye lost its powers. But such was the law of Evolution, and it was, in strict accuracy, no FALL. The sin was not in using those newly-developed powers, but in misusing them; in making of the tabernacle, designed to contain a god, the fane of every spiritual iniquity.

The pineal gland/third-eye does exist. However, its power of giving psychic abilities withered away as man became mired in the physical world.

The possession of a physical third eye, we are told, was enjoyed by the men of the Third Root-Race down to nearly the middle period of Third SUB-race of the Fourth root-Race, when the consolidation and perfection of the human frame made it disappear from the outward anatomy of man. Psychically and spiritually, however, its mental and visual perceptions lasted till nearly the end of the Fourth Race, when its functions, owing to the materiality and depraved condition of mankind, died out altogether before the submersion of the bulk of the Atlantean continent.

... After the separation of the sexes [Men fell into matter, and] their spiritual vision became dim; and co-ordinately the third eye commenced to lose its power... The third eye, likewise, getting gradually PETRIFIED, soon disappeared.

On the Acropolis of Argos, there was a [Zoanon], a rudely carved wooden statue (attributed to Daedalus), representing a three-eyed colossus, which was consecrated to Zeus Triopas (three-eyed). The head of the 'god' has two eyes in its face and one above on the top of the forehead.

Even at the date of Cook's visit [to Easter Island], some of the statues, measuring 27 feet in height and eight across the shoulders were lying overthrown, while others still standing appeared much larger. One of the latter was so lofty that the shade was sufficient to shelter a party of thirty persons from the heat of the sun. The platforms on which these colossal images stood averaged from thirty to forty feet in length, twelve to sixteen broad...all built of hewn stone in the Cyclopean style, very much like the walls of the Temple of Pachacamac, or the ruins of Tia-Huanuco in Peru.

Noah and the Flood

Atlantis... sunk and its chief portions...disappeared before the end of the Miocene period.

[It has been] "... 850,000 [years] since the submersion of the last large peninsula of the great Atlantis..."

... Most of the later islander Atlanteans perished in the interval

between 850,000 and 700,000 years ago, and that the Aryans were 200,000 years old when the first great 'island' or continent was submerged...

It is the submersion of the great Atlantis which is the most interesting. It is of this cataclysm that the old records (See the 'Book of Enoch') say that 'the ends of the Earth got loose:' and upon which the legends and allegories of Vaivasvata, Xisuthrus, Noah, Deukalion and all the tutti quanti of the Elect saved, have been built... The cataclysm which destroyed the huge continent of which Australia is the largest relic, was due to a series of subterranean convulsions and the breaking asunder of the ocean floors. That which put an end to its successor – the fourth continent – was brought on by successive disturbances in the axial rotation. It began during the earliest tertiary periods, and, continuing for long ages, carried away successively the last vestige of Atlantis, with the exception, perhaps, of Ceylon and a small portion of what is now Africa. It changed the face of the globe, and no memory of its flourishing continents and isles, of its civilisations and sciences, remained in the annals of history, save in the Sacred records of the East.

Lemuria [was] destroyed by fire, Atlantis by water. The Flood.

The remnants of the first two races disappear[ed] for ever [except for groups] of the various Atlantean races saved from the Deluge along with the Forefathers of the Fifth.

... Is...the story of Moses himself and many others, simply another version of the legends told of the Atlanteans... [with] finally the Egyptians and their Pharaoh drowned in the Red Sea...[?]

Noah's Deluge is astronomical and allegorical, but it is not mythical, for the story is based upon the same archaic tradition of men – or rather of nations – which were saved during the cataclysms, in canoes, arks, and ships. No one would presume to say that the Chaldean Xisuthrus, the Hindu Vaivasvata, the Chinese Periun – the 'beloved of the gods', who rescued him from the flood in a canoe – or the Swedish Belgamer, for whom the gods did the same in the north, are all identical as a personage. But their legends have all sprung from the catastrophe which involved both the continent and the island of Atlantis.

Noah [symbolises] both the Root-Manu and the Seed-Manu, or the Power which developed the planetary chain, and our earth, and the Seed

Race (the Fifth) which was saved while the last sub-races of the Fourth perished – Vaivasvata Manu – the number Seven will be seen to recur at every step. It is he (Noah), who represents, as Jehovah's permutation, the septenary (the Preserver) of all animal life. Hence versus 2 and 3 of chapter 7 of Genesis, 'Of every clean beast thou shalt take to thee by sevens, the male (3), and the female (4); of fowls also of the air by sevens', etc., etc., followed by all the sevening of days and the rest.

Vaivasvata Manu... saves the Fifth Race during the destruction of the last Atlanteans, the remnants that perished 850,000 years ago, after which there was no great submersion until the day of Plato's Atlantis, or Poseidonis, known to the Egyptians only because it happened in such relatively recent times.

There have been several Floods throughout history – not a single Flood, as written in the *Bible*.

The 'Deluge' is undeniably an universal tradition. 'Glacial periods' were numerous, and so were the 'Deluges', for various reasons. Stockwell and Croll enumerate some half dozen Glacial Periods and subsequent Deluges – the earliest of all being dated by them 850,000, and the last about 100,000 years ago. But which was our Deluge? Assuredly the former, the one which to this date remains recorded in the traditions of all the peoples, from the remotest antiquity; the one that finally swept away the last peninsulas of Atlantis, beginning with Ruta and Daitya and ending with the (comparatively) small island mentioned by Plato. This is shown by the agreement of certain details in all the legends. It was the last of its gigantic character. The little deluge, the traces of which Baron Bunsen found in Central Asia, and which he places at about 10,000 BC, had nothing to do with either the semi-universal Deluge, or Noah's flood – the latter being a purely mythical rendering of old traditions – nor even with the submersion of the last Atlantean island; at least, only a moral connection.

Our Fifth Race (the non-initiated portions), hearing of many deluges, confused them, and now know of but one. This one altered the whole aspect of the globe in its interchange and shifting of land and sea.

... Neither the Chaldean nor the Biblical deluge (the stories of Xisuthrus

and Noah) is based on the universal or even on the Atlantean deluges...
... That there were many such deluges as that mentioned in Genesis, and three far more important ones, which will be mentioned and described in the Section devoted to the subject of pre-historic continents.

The Biblical flood was by no means the first flood to occur.

The Second Flood – the so-called 'universal' – which affected the Fourth Root Race (now conveniently regarded by theology as "the accursed race of giants", the CAINITES, and "the sons of Ham") is that flood which was first perceived by geology.

In Theosophy, 'Flood' refers to several different events.

The First Cosmic Flood refers to primordial creation, or the formation of Heaven and the Earths; in which case Chaos and the great Deep stand for the 'Flood', and the Moon for the 'Mother', from whom proceed all the life-germs. But the terrestrial Deluge and its story has also its dual application. In one case it has reference to that mystery when mankind was saved form utter destruction, but the mortal woman being made the receptacle of the human seed at the end of the Third Race, and in the other to the real and historical Atlantean submersion. In both cases the 'Host' – or the Manu which saved the seed – is called Vaivasvata Manu. Hence the diversity between the Puranic and other versions; while in the Sathapatha Brahmana, Vaivasvata produces a daughter and begets from her the race of Manu; which is a reference to the first human Manushyas, who had to create women by will (Kriyasakti), before they were naturally born from the hermaphrodites as an independent sex, and who were, therefore, regarded as their creator's daughters. The Puranic accounts make of her (Ida or Ila) the wife of Buddha (Wisdom), the latter version referring to the events of the Atlantean flood, when Vaivasvata, the great Sage on Earth, saved the Fifth Root-race from being destroyed along with the remnants of the Fourth.

Ulysses, Homer and the Odyssey

Ulysses derives from Ulixes, the Latin name for Odysseus, a character in ancient Greece literature. Mentioned earlier, Homer is a great Greek poet and author of the *Iliad* and *Odyssey* poems. Finally, Homer's *Odyssey* is a sequel to the Iliad. The Odyssey focuses on the Greek hero Odysseus (Ulysses in Roman mythology) and his journey home after the fall of Troy. It took Odysseus ten years to reach Ithaca after the ten-year Trojan War. In his absence, everyone assumed he had died, and his wife Penelope and son Telemachus dealt with a group of unruly suitors who competed for the hand of Penelope. It also seems the Odyssey refers to actual interactions between today's average-sized humans and Atlantean giants.

Troy was an actual city in northwest Anatolia – now Turkey. It is famously known as the setting of the Trojan War, the war waged against Troy by the Achaeans (Greeks). Homer described the Trojan War in his Greek epic, the *Iliad*.

All the 'fables' of Greece were built on historical facts, if that history had only passed unadulterated by myths to posterity. The 'one-eyed' Cyclopes, the giants fabled as the sons of Coelus and Terra – three in number, according to Hesiod – were the last three sub-races of the Lemurians, the 'one-eye' referring to the Wisdom eye; for the two front eyes were fully developed as physical organs only in beginning of the Fourth Race. The allegory of Ulysses, whose companions were devoured while the king of Ithaca was saved by putting out a fire-brand the eye of Polyphemus, is based upon the psycho-physiological atrophy of the 'third' eye. Ulysses belongs to the cycle of the heroes of the Forth Race, and, though a 'sage' in the sight of the latter, must have been a profligate in the opinion of the pastoral Cyclopes. His adventure with the latter – a savage gigantic race, the antithesis of cultured civilisation in the Odyssey – is an allegorical record of the gradual passage from the Cyclopean civilisation of stone and colossal buildings to the more sensual and physical culture of the Atlanteans, which finally caused the last of the Third Race to lose their all-penetrating spiritual eye. That other allegory, which makes Apollo kill the Cyclops to avenge the death of his son Asclepios, does not refer to the three races represented by the three sons of Heaven and Earth, but to the Hyperborean Arimaspian Cyclopses, the last of the race endowed with the 'Wisdom-eye'.

Ulysses was wrecked on the isle of Aeaea, where Circe changed all his companions into pigs for their voluptuousness; and after that he was thrown into Ogygia, the island of Calypso, where for some seven years he lived with the nymph in illicit connection (Odyssey and elsewhere). Now Calypso was a daughter of Atlas, and all the traditional ancient versions, when speaking of the Isle of Ogygia, say that it was very distant from Greece, and right in the middle of the ocean: thus identifying it with Atlantis.

There are, in addition to this, other stories of a small race fighting with a race of giants:

... From the first appearance of the Aryan race, when the Pliocene portions of the once great Atlantis began gradually sinking and other continents to appear on the surface, down to the final disappearance of Plato's small island of Atlantis, the Aryan races had never ceased to fight with the descendants of the first giant races. This war lasted till nearly the close of the age which preceded the Kali Yug, and was the Mahabharatean war so famous in Indian History.

Easter Island

Easter Island is a Polynesian island in the south-eastern region of the Pacific Ocean.

The Easter Island relics are, for instance, the most astounding and eloquent memorials of the primeval giants. They are as grand as they are mysterious; and one has but to examine the heads of the colossal statues, that have remained unbroken on that island, to recognise in them at a glance the features of the type and character attributed to the Fourth Race giants.

Easter Island was... taken possession of... by some Atlanteans; who, having escaped form the cataclysm which befell their own land, settled on that remnant of Lemuria only to perish thereon, when destroyed in one day by its volcanic fires and lava.

... Most of the gigantic statues discovered on Easter Island, a portion of an undeniably submerged continent – as also those found on the

giants { 27' height / 8' across the shoulders (handwritten note)

outskirts of Gobi, a region which had been submerged for untold ages – are all between 20 and 30 feet high. The statues found by Cook on Easter Island measured almost all twenty-seven feet in height, and eight feet across the shoulders.

The Easter Isles in 'mid Pacific' present the feature of the remaining peaks of the mountains of a submerged continent, for the reason that these peaks are thickly studded with Cyclopean statues, remnants of the civilisation of a dense and cultivated people, who must have of necessity occupied a widely extended area.

Even at the date of Cook's visit, some of the [Easter Island] statues, measuring 27 feet in height and eight across the shoulders were lying overthrown, while others still standing appeared much larger. One of the latter was so lofty that the shade was sufficient to shelter a party of thirty persons from the heat of the sun. The platforms on which these colossal images stood averaged from thirty to forty feet in length, twelve to sixteen broad...all built of hewn stone in the Cyclopean style, very much like the walls of the Temple of Pachacamac, or the ruins of Tia-Huanuco in Peru... 'THERE IS NO REASON TO BELIEVE THAT ANY OF THE STATUES HAVE BEEN BUILT UP, BIT BY BIT, BY SCAFFOLDING ERECTED AROUND THEM' – adds the journal very suggestively – without explaining how they could be built otherwise, unless made by the giants of the same size as the statues themselves.

Egypt and the Pyramids

Pyramids are associated with the Egyptians. However, if they have been found worldwide (for example, the Bosnian, Aztec, Mayan pyramids, and those found off the coast of Japan), then why assume the source of pyramids to be Egyptian? The Egyptians were descendants of the Atlanteans.

The civilisation of the Atlanteans was greater even than that of the Egyptians. It is their degenerate descendants, the nation of Plato's Atlantis, which built the first Pyramids in the country...

The Pyramids are closely connected with the ideas of both the Great Dragon (the constellation), the 'Dragons of Wisdom', or the great Initiates of the Third and Fourth Races, and the Floods of the Nile, regarded as a divine reminder of the great Atlantic Flood.

The human Dynasty of the older Egyptians, beginning with Menes, had all the knowledge of the Atlanteans, though there was no more Atlantean blood in their veins.

The Egyptian culture was a remnant of older cultures.

... The civilisations of such archaic nations as the Egyptians, Aryans of India, Chaldeans, Chinese, and Assyrians are the result of preceding civilisations during "myriads of centuries"; and the latter points to the fact that, "Egypt at the beginning appears mature, old, and entirely without mythical and heroic ages, as if the country had never known youth. Its civilisation has no infancy, and its art no archaic period. The civilisation of the Old Monarchy did not begin with infancy. It was already mature." To this Professor R. Owen adds that, "Egypt is recorded to have been a civilised and governed community before the time of Menes"; and Winchell, that "at the epoch of Menes the Egyptians were already a civilised and numerous people."

Egypt is far older than Europe as now traced on the map. Atlanto-Aryan tribes began to settle on it, when the British Islands and France were not even in existence.

Here is what Robert Temple, a famous American author, says of the pyramids in his great book, *The Sirius Mystery*:

I certainly believe that there is much undiscovered – possibly under the silt and mud of the Nile Delta – concerning the high civilisation of Predynastic Egypt. But the 'Atlantis' which is postulated today is too far back, and it leaves several thousand years of 'nothingness' in between it and Egypt and Sumer. John Anthony West's suggestion leaves a 'blank' of between 22,000 and 27,000 years! I cannot accept such suggestions. Nor can I accept that the Sphinx is 12,500 years old, even though I believe it and the pyramids were probably built long before the lifetimes of the Pharaohs Cheops and Khephren. But these things are all a matter of degree. In my view, there was ancient extraterrestrial contact with Earth. And I believe that the period of interaction with extraterrestrials and the founding of Egyptian and Sumerian civilisation with their help probably fell between 5000 and 3000 BC. We can call the time of this interaction, whenever it was, the Contact Period. I believe that the pyramids and the Sphinx were probably built by the extraterrestrials themselves during the Contact Period, and that the Step Pyramid of Saqqara was a later and magnificent attempt by men working unaided under the human architect Imhotep – since the extraterrestrials had long since vanished – to match those mysterious earlier achievements and show that humans could do such things too. Many of the other Egyptian pyramids then imitated the Step Pyramid...a lot of them have crumbled into dust and were not very well constructed.

Stonehenge

Stonehenge is a prehistoric monument located in the English county of Wiltshire, two miles west of Amesbury and eight miles north of Salisbury. Stonehenge is a circular setting of very large standing-stones. According to the *Book of Dzyan*, Stonehenge was built by the Cyclopean giants.

...The rocking stones of Ireland, or those of Brinham, in Yorkshire...them are evidently the relics of the Atlanteans...

... Had there been no giants to move about such colossal rocks [as in Stonehenge], there could never have been a Stonehenge... Who then, if not giants, could ever raise such masses (especially those at Carac and West Hoadley), range them in such symmetrical order that they should represent the planisphere, and place them in such wonderful equipoise that they seem to hardly touch the ground, are set in motion at the slightest touch of the finger, and would yet resist the efforts of twenty men who should attempt to displace them. We say, that most of these stones are the relics of the last Atlanteans.

Fifth Root-Race

It is believed the Aryan Race migrated to the area now known as the Gobi Desert, a large desert region in Asia covering parts of northern and north-western China and southern Mongolia. During the beginning of the Aryan Race, the Gobi Desert was a fertile basin with a large body of water. Five sub-races were produced, which migrated throughout the world. For Blavatsky, the term 'Aryan' referred to a stage of spiritual evolution for humanity as a whole. It does not have racial connotations. All the major races of man today are of the Aryan Root Race.

The Aryan race was born and developed in the far north, though after the sinking of the continent of Atlantis its tribes emigrated further south into Asia.

The rapid progress of anthropomorphism and idolatry led the early Fifth, as it had already led the Fourth Race, into sorcery...

The Aryan races, for instance, now varying from dark brown, almost black, red-brown-yellow, down to the whitest creamy colour, are yet all of one and the same stock – the Fifth Root-Race – and spring from one single progenitor, called in Hindu exotericism by the generic name of Vaivasvata Manu...

Nor is Bailly wrong again in assuring us that the Hindus, Egyptians, and Phoenicians came after the Atlanteans, for the latter belonged to the Fourth, while the Aryans and their Semitic Branch are of the Fifth Race.

The Aryan nations... trace their descent through the Atlanteans from the more spiritual races of the Lemurians, in whom the 'Sons of Wisdom' had personally incarnated.

From verse 24 to 34, ch. xxv. of Genesis contains the allegorical history of the birth of the Fifth Race.

Sixth Root-Race

... The Sixth will [rapidly grow] out of its bonds of matter, and even of flesh.

The Fifth will overlap the Sixth Race for many hundreds of millenniums, changing with it slower than its new successor, still changing in stature, general physique, and mentality, just as the Fourth overlapped our Aryan race, and the Third had overlapped the Atlanteans.

In the Sixth Root-Race... new forms – though fewer and ever wider apart as ages pass on and the close of the Manvantara approaches – will develop from their 'cast off' types of the human races as they revert once again to astral, out of the mire of physical, life.

[Some day, in the distant future,] ... the Sixth Root-Race will have appeared on the stage of our Round. When shall this be? Who knows

save the great Masters of Wisdom, perchance, and they are as silent upon the subject as the snow-capped peaks that tower above them. All we know is, that it will silently come into existence; so silently, indeed, that for long millenniums shall its pioneers – the peculiar children who will grow into peculiar men and women – be regarded as anomalous lusus naturae, abnormal oddities physically and mentally. Then, as they increase, and their numbers become with every age greater, one day they will awake to find themselves in a majority.

Since the beginning of the Atlantean Race many million years have passed, yet we find the last of the Atlanteans, still mixed up with the Aryan element, 11,000 years ago. This shows the enormous overlapping of one race over the race which succeeds it, though in character and external type the elder loses its characteristics, and assumes the new features of the younger race. This is proved in all the formations of mixed human races. Now, Occult philosophy teaches that even now, under our very eyes, the new Race and Races are preparing to be formed, and that it is in America that the transformation will take place, and has already silently commenced... Thus the Americans have become in only three centuries a 'primary race', pro tem., before becoming a race apart, and strongly separated from all other now existing races. They are, in short, the germs of the Sixth sub-race, and in some few hundred years more, will become most decidedly the pioneers of that race which must succeed to the present European or fifth sub-race, in all its new characteristics. After this, in about 25,000 years, they will launch into preparations for the seventh sub-race; until in consequence of cataclysms – the first series of those which must one day destroy Europe, and still later the whole Aryan race (and thus affect both Americas), as also most of the lands directly connected with the confines of our continent and isles – the Sixth Root-Race will have appeared on the stage of our Round.

[The] process of preparation for the Sixth great Race must last throughout the whole sixth and seventh sub-races. But the last remnants of the Fifth Continent will not disappear until some time after the birth of the new Race; when another and new dwelling, the sixth continent, will have appeared above the new waters on the face of the globe, so as to receive the new stranger. To it also will emigrate and settle all those

who shall be fortunate enough to escape the general disaster.

Mankind will not grow again into giant bodies as in the case of the Lemurians and the Atlanteans; because while the evolution of the Fourth race led the latter down to the very bottom of materiality in its physical development, the present Race is on its ascending arc; and the Sixth will be rapidly growing out of its bonds of matter, and even of flesh.

Seventh Root-Race (Unnamed) –

... The great Adepts and Initiated ascetics will 'multiply', i.e. once more produce Mind-born immaculate Sons – in the Seventh Root-Race.

This is the end of the analysis of the races of mankind.

SIRIUS STAR SYSTEM

From Madam Blavatsky and the *Book of Dzyan*, we have discovered some phenomenal information about out past and our ancestors. We have also examined information about an extra-terrestrial race called the Anunnaki, the Elohim, the gods, who seem to be our creators. I would like to ask you, have we ever been visited and influenced by another species?

For a long time, I have been interested in the Genesis account involving the Tree of Knowledge, in the Garden of Eden. In this story, it is said that Eve was tempted by the serpent to eat the fruit (an apple) from the tree. Adam also ate from the tree. The serpent was said to be the devil, a fallen angel, created by God prior to the creation of Man. The devil is also known as Satan, or Lucifer. Let me clarify.Satan simply means 'Opponent' and Lucifer means 'the morning star' or 'light-bringer' Why is the devil referred to as the Prince of Darkness if his name actually refers to light?

Our creator, the Anunnaki, who created us to be slaves (righteous gods?), have an opponent, referred to as the light-bringer. Does a light-bringer sound like someone with evil intentions? As I mentioned earlier, the ancient Egyptians wore crowns which featured a serpent, and serpents denoted wisdom.

In the Genesis story, the serpent tempts Eve to eat an apple from the Tree of Knowledge. Surely you can see that it wasn't a physical apple, but it was knowledge (from the Tree of Knowledge) which the light-bringer tried to bring to the attention of Eve. The Anunnaki became angry and banished Adam and Eve from the Garden of Eden.

- Who sounds Good and Evil according to the above account?
- If Lucifer was created by God, must he not have been an earlier creation of the Anunnaki?
- Was Lucifer, the light-bringer actually trying to help Adam and Eve by giving them knowledge, in order to free them from the shackles of slavery? *Yo creo que sí.*
- Why would Lucifer help mankind? He was a prior creation of the Anunnaki (and, as they used the DNA of man), Lucifer was like a cousin to us.

Note: As stated earlier, Indra and Enki were one and the same being. According to Blavatsky, Lucifer is also the same being as Indra and Enki.

This story of the Tree of Knowledge now brings me to the final topic of this chapter. I have already asked you whether we have ever been visited and influenced by another species. Now, I will make an addition to this question: have we ever been visited and influenced by another species of extra-terrestrials? In R. Boulay's book, *Flying Serpents and Dragons*: "The Book of Dzyan... (states that) the Sarpa or Great Dragons were the Fifth Race to inhabit the world. The Fourth Race was a race of giants who had lived before the Deluge but were wiped out by that catastrophe. The book relates how the serpent gods or dragons redescended after the Deluge and instructed man in the arts of civilisation. These serpent-gods had a human face and the tail of a dragon: they founded divine dynasties on Earth and are believed to be the ancestors of our current civilisation, the Fifth Race of the Book of Dzyan."

I do often wonder whether the serpent in the story of the Tree of Knowledge was not representative of Lucifer, but actually these serpent gods. In any case, the point remains, the serpent tried to help and free mankind, whereas the Anunnaki wanted to keep mankind in slavery.

Why has this section of the book been termed Sirius? It has been said that Earth has been visited by intelligent beings from the system of the star Sirius. Who first said this? A supposedly primitive African tribe called the Dogon, who live in the present state of Mali. It should have been impossible for any primitive tribe to have known about the Sirius star system.

Concerning the background of the Dogon Tribe, research leads us to believe the Dogon to be descendants of Lemnian Greeks (who claimed to be descended from Argonauts), travelled to Libya, then forced to the south-west, reaching the River Niger in Mali. They intermarried with the local Negroes in Mali.

In the book entitled *African Worlds*, translated into English from the eminent French anthropologists Marcel Griaule and Germaine Dieterlen, a chapter describing the cosmological theories of the Dogon Tribe states: "The starting-point of creation is the star which revolves round Sirius and is actually named the 'Digitaria star'; it is regarded by the Dogon as the smallest and heaviest of all the stars; it contains the germs of all things. Its movement on its own axis and around Sirius upholds all creation in space. We shall see that its orbit determines the calendar."

The star, Sirius B, which revolves around Sirius (Sirius A), is actually invisible to us. It was only discovered in 1970 by using a telescope. So how did the Dogon tribe know of it? Even more astonishing was their knowledge of another orbiting star, Sirius C, only recently discovered.

Carl Sagan (American astronomer, astrophysicist, cosmologist, author, science populariser and science communicator in astronomy and natural sciences), in his book, *Intelligent life in the Universe*, discussed some fascinating amphibious creatures which he says founded the Sumerian civilisation. Sagan says the amphibians were happier to return to the sea at night, and back to dry land in the daytime. The creatures were described as semi-demons, and never gods. They were even described as being superhuman in terms of knowledge and lifespan, eventually returning to a ship and carrying representatives of Earth's fauna.

The founder of the Sumerian civilisation is referred to as the collective name – Nommo (or Nommos), the amphibious creatures who came from the Sirius system to help society on Earth. The Sirius system is actually known as 'Land of the Fish'. The landing of the Nommos onto Earth is known as the 'Day of the Fish'.

The Nommos are said to be more fish-like than human. There are references in the oral traditions, drawings and cuneiform tablets of the Dogons, describing them as human-looking but with a large fish skin running down their bodies. The Nommos could live on land but dwelled most of the time in the water. They were part-fish, similar to merfolk (mermaids and mermen). The Nommos bear some physical resemblance to beings from other ancient civilisations:

- Babylon = Oannes
- Sumeria = Enki
- Egypt = Isis
- Akkadian = Ea
- China = Fuxi
- Philistine = Dagon
- Greece = Nereus

According to the Dogon legend, the Nommos live on a planet which orbits another star in the Sirius system. They landed on Earth in an ark that made a spinning descent to the ground with great noise and wind. It was the Nommos who gave the Dogon the knowledge about Sirius B.

Did the Egyptians know of Sirius? Indeed they did, and Sirius was very important to them. The ancient Egyptians believed that once someone died, their spirit would travel to the Sirius system. The Dogon believe this too. The Egyptians and Dogon were/are very smart people. Is the Sirius system, our Heaven?

Like our Sun is the most important star in the sky to us, for the Egyptians, Sirius was the most important star in the sky to them. Perhaps we all should investigate Sirius in serious detail and ask why the Egyptians neglected our Sun? What did the Egyptians know that we do not? Perhaps the sun we think we see in the sky, is actually Sirius? Again, the ancient Egyptians were very smart people.

The Egyptian calendar was based on Sirius, and Sirius was identified with their chief goddess Isis. Osiris, the chief god, was the companion of Isis. The companion of the constellation of the Great Dog (including Sirius) is the constellation Orion. Osiris occasionally represents Orion, but infact, the companion of Sirius os Sirius B. Osiris represents Sirius B, the companion of Isis. It has been investigated that the original hieroglyph for Osiris, was a throne and an eye. Related to the Dogon tribe, the Bozo tribe of Mali, refer to Sirius B, Osiris, as the 'Eye star'

It seems that today's human civilisation on Earth was taught by visiting extra-terrestrials. In this book we have encountered the Anunnaki, those who created us as slaves, and now the Nommos, those who taught us how to be civilised, and to survive. Are these just two extra-terrestrials out of many in our infinite universe, some good and some bad? Could extra-terrestrials be monitoring us? As discussed in the next chapter, there are various moons in our Solar System. Moons are regarded as satellites. What are satellites on and around the Earth used for?

You will discover some weird and wonderful information in the following, final section of this book.

The Anunnaki - those who created us as slaves.
the Nommos - those who taught us how
to be civilised + to survive.

PART 3
ABOVE AND BEYOND

What are we generally taught about the planets in our Solar System? We are taught about their appearance, size, mass, temperature, whether they are gaseous, whether they have rings, their distance from the sun and their orbit trajectory. But is this really all that there is to know? Absolutely not! There is something deep and mysterious we are not being told about these planets – more than what is uncovered in any book of this world.

THE MOON

When defining the Moon, I have found multiple statements such as this from Wikipedia: "The Moon is the only natural satellite of the Earth". In this section, I argue that the moon is not 'natural' and it is not 'of the Earth'. There are also other anomalies relating to the Moon, which I will go into. Before delving into the above arguments, I will recap some general information about the Moon:

- The Moon is said to be 4.5 billion years old
- Its diameter is around 2,000 miles
- The moon's surface contains craters, mountains, valleys and lava plains
- There is no atmosphere on the moon
- The Moon travels counter-clockwise around the Earth (looking from above the north pole), in a circle called an orbit
- The orbit is a slightly flattened circle called an ellipse
- The Moon always keeps one face towards the Earth. Is something on the other side? yes!
- It takes roughly 27 days for the Moon to orbit the Earth (around 1,423,000 miles), returning to its starting position
- The Moon orbits the Earth at an average speed of 2,288 miles per hour. The speed changes during different phases of orbit. Its speed slows farthest from the Earth, and speeds up when closer to the Earth

The Moon has its own cycle of phases, in order:

a. *New Moon*: The Moon is positioned and approximately aligned between the Earth and Sun. Only the Moon's back side is illuminated, which cannot be seen from Earth
b. *Waxing crescent*: The sunlit portion accounts for around one-third

c. *First quarter/Half Moon*: The sunlit portion accounts for one-half. The moon is at a 90 degree angle corresponding to the Earth and Sun

d. *Waxing Gibbous*: The sunlit portion accounts for around two-thirds

e. *Full Moon:* The Moon again, is in approximate alignment with the Earth and Sun, however, the moon is on the opposite side of Earth. The Moon's front-side is illuminated, which can be seen from Earth

f. *Waning Gibbous*: The sunlit portion accounts for around two-thirds, but from the opposite end of Waxing Gibbous

g. *Third Quarter/Half Moon*: The sunlit portion accounts for one-half again, but on the opposite side of First Quarter. The moon again is at a 90 degree angle corresponding to the Earth and Sun

h. *Waning Crescent:* The sunlit portion accounts for around one-third, but from the opposite side of Waxing crescent

New Moon once again, and so on. In Latin, the name for the Moon is Luna and a Lunar Month is the time it takes for the Moon to pass through its complete cycle of phases. This period lasts around 29.5 days. A Lunar month is around 2.5 days longer than the Moon takes to orbit the Earth because while the Moon is orbiting the Earth, the Earth is in its orbit of the Sun. So, the Moon travels a little more than 360 degrees to complete its cycle of phases. Therefore, a Lunar month is longer. The Moon rises in the east and sets in the west. That's the basics over with.

It is strange that the moon, although much smaller than the sun, looks to be the same size as the Sun, to us on Earth. This is obviously because the Moon is a lot closer to us than the Sun. However, the Moon is 400 times smaller than the Sun, and yet it is 1/400th the distance between the Sun and Earth. This is some coincidence. Another strange phenomenon is the relationship that the Moon and Sun share. In the middle of winter, the Sun is at its lowest point and dimmest and the moon is at its highest point and brightest. In the middle of summer, the exact opposite occurs – the Sun is at its highest point, and the Moon at its lowest point and most dim.

Our yearly calendar is based on the Sun. Well, do you know that the calendar used to be based on the Moon, not the Sun? From ancient records, the world used the Lunar Calendar, which changed to the Egyptian (Solar) Calendar, which changed to the Roman (Julian) Calendar and finally to what we have now (adopted from the 16th Century), the Gregorian Calendar.

The purpose of the calendar was to calculate time of the past and future, to convey the number of days for a certain event to occur, i.e. a traditional festival. Farmers would not harvest or plant anything without referring to the Moon. The Lunar calendar became the basis of the calendars used by the Sumerians, Babylonians, Chinese, Greeks, Jews and Arabs. Lunar calendars were and still are important to our understanding of our development and environment. The Moon's movement was observed to be (and still remains) relational to Earth.

Another strange phenomenon is the fact that in the phases of New Moon and Full Moon, the Earth's sea level rises. We are told this is due to the gravitational force between the Moon and Earth. But why is it that the Earth is able to hold onto everything except water? Why don't solids rise in the air towards the Earth like water does?

Another phenomenon: Why do women's menstrual cycles follow the Lunar cycle? Gravitational force again? I don't think so. From puberty, women lose blood once every complete Moon cycle. Also, in many studies, one being Dr. Winnifred Cutler's 1980 study of the lunar cycle's influence on menstrual cycles, it was proved that the lunar cycle and a fertile menstrual cycle are the same!

Considering the Moon's different phases, as the Moon waxes, oestrogen levels increase, peaking at Full Moon. During the waning Moon, higher progesterone prepares the womb for new life. Birth rates are lower in the three-day period during the New Moon. The most fertile days are when the mid-cycle ovulation matches with the natal Lunar phase. A woman's average gestation period is around nine lunar cycles. All this cannot simply be due to 'gravitational force'.

The ancients were fully aware of the Moon-Earth connection. How do we know this? A 25,000 year-old Venus figurine, named Venus of Laussel, was discovered in 1911 by a physician named J. G. Lalanne. This 1.5-foot tall figurine was carved into the wall of limestone rock in southwestern France (currently displayed at the Museum of Aquitaine, in Bordeux, France). This figure can be seen holding a wisent horn which has 13 notches. According to some researchers, the 13 notches symbolise the number of Full Moons or menstrual cycles in one year.

There are four seasons per year, and generally three Full Moons occur in every season, giving us twelve Full Moons in a year. This is why the word 'month' actually comes from the word 'Moon' or 'Moonth'. Note, the word 'menstrual' comes from the Latin word mensis, which means 'month'.

Remember the 13 notches supposedly being the number of Full Moons in one year? Well, in the previous paragraph I did say there are 'generally' three Full Moons per season. In some years, a month will have two Full Moons, at the start and end (also referred to as a 'Blue Moon'). Therefore, these years would have thirteen Full Moons – symbolising the thirteen notches on the Venus figurine.

Figurines showing fertility were quite common during the Palaeolithic and Neolithic Eras. Such figurines could have been symbols of a fertility-based deity. There are a vast array of these fertility/Moon-based deities from the Aztec, Celtic, Inca, Hindu, Maya and many other mythologies. Most of these deities were female, not male.

As I have made clear in The Futuristic Past, I do not believe the past was so primitive. Evidence of detailed knowledge of the Moon was found by Dr. Philip J. Stooke at a megalithic site named Knowth, of the Boyne Valley in Ireland. He found a carving more than 5,000 years old consisting of lines and dots, which to his astonishment lined up with a map of the Moon!

It is obvious that the Moon has played an extremely important role in humanity, in the ancient past, to the present day. Have you heard of the 'Lunar Effect'? It is a theory that there is a relationship between the Lunar cycle and a human's deviant behaviour. Examples of this have been found in ancient Babylonian texts.

More recently than Babylonian times, Europe in the Middle Ages believed the Full Moon caused mental disorders and strange behaviour, including aggression, suicides and accidents.

And now to the present day. The *Daily Mail*, in 2007, reported "A full moon doesn't just encourage werewolves. It also brings out the worse in the Great British Hooligan, police have discovered." Relating to this quotation, Inspector Parr, who led the study, said its findings are too striking to dismiss as mere coincidence. He compared the number of violent crimes recorded in Brighton in 2006 with the date of each Full Moon and he discovered a distinct correlation. Inspector Parr said: "I'm aware that this is just one of many things that can influence public disorder but if you speak to ambulance staff they will tell you exactly the same."

Something interesting to note here: The word 'lunatic' is derived from the Latin word luna, meaning 'Moon'.

In the 2006 movie *Apocalypto*, set during the Mayan civilisation, one scene shows a very frightened population when the moon 'devoured' the sun – the scene of the solar eclipse. Human sacrifices were made by the priests in order to please the god Kulkulkan, to allow light to return to the world.

The Moon's origin has been one of the most complicated problems for cosmologists. It has been subject to multiple theories, including:

- *Fission Theory*: The Moon was once part of the Earth, and separated from Earth (in its molten state) by Earth's spin. In the 1920s, the British Astronomer, Harold Jeffries, proved this theory to be incorrect.
- *Capture Theory*: The Moon formed elsewhere in the Solar System and it was captured by Earth's gravitational force. This is not possible, one reason being that something the size of the Moon would not have 'docked' safely into an Earth orbit; it would have smashed into the Earth or slightly bounced off the atmosphere, taking it elsewhere.
- *Coaccretion Theory:* The formed Earth accumulated a disc of particles similar to Saturn's rings, and these joined together to form the Moon. This theory has problems because if the Moon and Earth were formed from the same matter, and the same distance from the sun, their density should be the same, which is not the case.
- *Giant Impact Theory*: A giant object, similar to the size of Mars, struck the Earth, ejecting large volumes of Earth's matter, which formed to create the Moon. This impact set the Earth spinning faster than its normal rate. However, this theory fails to satisfy many requirements as the logical explanation of the Moon's origin. One reason for this is due to the supposed fast-spinning of the Earth, which could not be possible. Unless, there was a second collision from another planet, in the opposite direction, which would cancel the fast spin of the Earth. This was actually seriously suggested and named 'Big Whack 2'. But the chance of this happening is so unlikely that the theory is counted implausible.

All the theories have too many flaws to be true. However, there has still been no 'official' theory of the Moon's origin. Lets now take a look at a specific event which raises an interesting question and a very interesting theory. I have been searching for information relating to the Moon's interior structure. I am shown the same concept that the Moon has a crust and a mantle, with a fluid outer core and a solid inner core (similar to Earth).

However, I will now turn your attention to an Apollo 13 space mission in April 1970. Just under 56 hours into the Fra Mauro mission to the moon, the crew found themselves in danger when three fuel cells in the service module suddenly became inactive. Fortunately they discovered they could use the engine of the lunar module to return back to Earth, sacrificing their intended moon landing in Fra Mauro Hills. Attached to the Apollo spacecraft was Saturn V. Saturn V (Saturn Five) was a rocket NASA built in the 1960s and 1970s, in order to send a space-crew to the Moon. It was 111 metres tall, weighed 2.8 million kilograms and generated an immensely powerful 7.6 million pounds of thrust at launch. For Apollo missions, Saturn V worked in three stages. Each stage burnt its engines until no more fuel remained, then separated from the rocket. Whilst this occurred, the rocket would continue travelling into space.

- *Stage 1*: Contained the most powerful engines because their job was to lift the fully-fuelled rocket off the ground – no easy task! The rocket would be lifted to an altitude of around 42 miles.
- *Stage 2:* Carried the rocket until it was virtually in orbit.
- *Stage 3*: Placed the Apollo spacecraft into Earth orbit and pushed the spacecraft towards the Moon.

Stages 1 and 2 fell into the ocean after separating from the rocket. Stage 3, remained in space or it collided into the Moon.

Now back to Apollo 13's mission. On 14th April, Apollo 13 began its journey back to Earth, and initiated stage three of the Saturn V. The huge fifteen-tonne vehicle crashed into the Moon with a force equal to 11.5 tonnes of the explosive, TNT. The point of impact was at a site where Apollo 12 astronauts had previously installed a seismometer – an instrument which measures motions of the ground.

As soon as Saturn V plunged into the Moon, reports from NASA indicated the following reaction of scientists on Earth: "The Moon rang like a bell!" Shock waves built up to a peak after seven minutes, and echoes (reflected sound waves) lasted for over three hours, travelling down the Moon to a depth of twenty-five miles! This has led to the conclusion that the Moon has a very light inner core, or no core at all.

The second strange comment was made by CAPCOM at the NASA headquarters in Houston to the crew of Apollo 13: "We see the results now from 12's seismometer. Looks like your booster just hit the Moon, and it's rocking a little bit."

So not only did the Moon ring like a bell, but it also wobbled! The act of rocking is very strange. If something was to collide with a large stationary object in space, and as a result this object moved, surely it would cause a shift (however slight) in the object's position? But to describe the movement as "rocking", meaning a side-to-side motion, as the moon is not held in place by an external object, it must have something holding it in place – an internal object – like shock absorbers inside the Moon! People obviously began to speculate that the Moon may be hollow. Given the information above, I would say it absolutely is hollow! Solid objects do not and cannot ring like a bell. What did scientists say about the possibility of the Moon being hollow?

In 1962, the NASA scientist Dr. Gordon McDonald, stated in *Astronauts* magazine: "According to an analysis of the moon's motion, it appears that the moon is hollow. Indeed, it would seem that the moon is more like a hollow than a homogenous sphere."

In 1969, a space mission, led by Apollo 12, plunged their 2.5-tonne lunar module into the Moon. In 1970, former SS Nazi and director at NASA, Dr. Wernher Von Braun wrote in an article entitled 'How APOLLO 13 Will Probe the Moon's Interior': "The moon rang like a bell for nearly an hour, indicating some strange and unearthly underground structure."

Apollo 14 (of 1971) astronaut, Dr. Edgar Mitchell, admitted it is quite possible that giant caverns exist within the Moon.

MIT's Dr. Sean C. Solomon wrote: "The lunar orbiter experiments vastly improved our knowledge of the Moon's gravitational field... indicating the frightening possibility that the Moon might be hollow." Why is this frightening? In his book Intelligent Life in the Universe, 1966. Carl Sagan said "A natural satellite cannot be a hollow object." Therefore, if the Moon is hollow (which it is), someone or something artificially created it!

Another strange phenomenon: The Moon maintains the Earth's angle around the Sun. The Earth does not rotate around the Sun in a completely vertical/upright position. It rotates around the sun at an angle of around

22.5 degrees – which is also the reason as to why we have the four seasons. If the Earth was upright, the equators of both the Sun and Earth would directly face each other, creating a temperature around Earth's equator which is too hot to survive. Life would be virtually impossible across most of the Earth. How did (and does) the Moon 'know' to maintain this angle? Maintaining this angle means we all survive on Earth (in relation to temperature), hence, the moon is keeping us alive! Why is the Moon protecting us? Is the Moon's presence a coincidence?

What if the Moon did not exist? What effect would this have on the Earth? Earlier in this section I mentioned that the Earth's sea level tends to rise when the Moon is at a Full Moon and New Moon. We will now take a look into this at a deeper level. Neil F. Comins, a professor in Astronomy, wrote a series of articles for *Astronomy Magazine* between 1991 and 1993. Regarding the effect on the Earth if the Moon ceased to exist, it was concluded:

- *Day length*: The length of a day would shorten from 24 hours to 8 hours. As well as the Moon, the Sun's gravitational pull also produces tides on the Earth, accounting for around one-third of the tides we see today. Tides slow the Earth's rotation, as they cause friction. So, with only the Sun's gravitational pull, there would be fewer tides, hence less friction, thus resulting in a faster-rotating Earth.
- *Winds*: This faster rotation on Earth would obviously cause faster winds. Jupiter rotates every 10 hours and its wind speed ranges between 100–200 mph! Therefore, as the Earth would rotate every 8 hours, the wind speed would be much higher than this on a daily basis, causing disasters such as hurricanes.
- *Day-to-day life*: Shorter days would drastically change the internal biological clocks of humans and animals. They would sleep when they should be awake, hunt when they should mate, etc. Life would be vulnerable to attack by better-adjusted predators. In an 8-hour day, with only 3 or 4 hours of sunlight, there would not be enough time for humans to work in order to make a living for their families. The entire present way of life would be dismantled.

Faster or stronger winds would knock down and drag anything and anything not stabilised by its weight. People would be flung around, trees would come apart from their roots, homes and buildings would collapse, etc. We would all have to become more responsive to this new environment. Those who have mental or physical disabilities would be more at risk than those who don't, but no one would be safe on the planet from the winds.

Now I hope you can understand the vital importance of the Moon. Without it, there is no hope for us on Earth.

In the information presented thus far, I have shown that the moon has a profound impact on human emotions and the Earth's system. The Moon is an artificial satellite and it is not natural. It has been made by something or someone. Remember, what is a satellite used for? Observation. Therefore, can it not be said that; (1) We are intentionally being kept alive by someone or something? But why?: (2) This something knows and understands the Earth, our human bodies and behaviour?: (3) We are being observed from their satellite, called the Moon?

I now refer to something I said in Part 1 of this book:

- In a park, I once saw a parent ask his son where God is. The son pointed to the sky. I thought to myself, "Isn't that where extra-terrestrials are supposed to come from?"
- In contrast to the above, I have heard that God is 'everywhere'. Consciousness/energy is also everywhere, isn't it? I have seen this concept somewhere before... in the movie Star Wars – the power of The Force.
- If there is a God – in terms of an all-powerful being, and God is righteous, then why do innocent people get killed? And why does God allow wars to commence?

To the last statement above: now we know that during Full Moons and New Moons, humans are increasingly violent, can God (whatever God is for those who believe in God) truly be righteous? Let us look at this another way. If God is righteous (again, if you believe in God – It/Him/Her), then wouldn't this mean that by creating a Full Moon and New Moon to cause us to be violent to each other, God actually wants us to destroy ourselves? Perhaps this could be because we have not developed according to how God intended (for better or worse).

Note: It is not only Full and New Moons that cause us to be violent. Again, consider war – how many wars have actually occurred? The number could be higher than you think. And how many innocent people have been killed in these wars? And why do such evil people who are behind the wars exist? Is there more than one God? Some 'good' and some 'bad'? This is what ancient civilisations believed. Wouldn't a righteous God have created righteous people, so we can all live a righteous life?

WE ARE MICRO-ORGANISMS

In 1675, a Dutch scientist, Anton van Leeuwenhoek, was the first to discover micro-organisms, and thus he is known as The Father of Microbiology and the first microbiologist. How can we, without a doubt, say that we are not micro-organisms?

Now I'm reminded of the very last scene of the movie *Men In Black 2* (2002). In the movie, Tommy Lee Jones (Agent K) opens a standard-sized locker at Grand Central Terminal. The locker reveals hundreds of miniature aliens in a miniature city, similar to a miniature civilisation. Now at the very end of the movie, Will Smith (Agent J) says to Agent K: "We need to let them out of there... they need to know that the world is bigger than that."

Now both agents stand beside a door labelled 'Danger! Do NOT Open!' In direct response to Agent J's comment, Agent K opens the door to reveal arguably the most stunning scene of the entire movie. We ourselves are a miniature civilisation, living alongside other miniature civilisations, and with aliens who are exponentially larger than us. We are a world, amongst worlds, living inside a bigger world. Perhaps you should be asking questions of the producer of this movie, because it sends a stunning message.

NASA website, Planets Around Other Stars, 2012: "If you think the idea that humans being are micro-organisms absurd, and you are convinced that there cannot be any macro-organisms in relation to us, consider this...As we came to understand the stars in the sky are other suns, and that the galaxies consist of billions of stars, it appeared a near certainty that other planets must orbit other stars. And yet, it could not be proven, until the early 1990s. Then, radio and optical astronomers detected small changes in stellar emission which revealed the presence of first a few, and now many, planetary systems around other stars. We call these planets 'exoplanets' to distinguish them from our own Solar System neighbours."

As mentioned earlier, planets orbit stars. Our Sun, as you know is a star. The Sun is the largest planet in our Solar System.

Now, take a look at the following three illustrations. *Figure 6: Our Gigantic Sun – Largest Planet in the Solar System.* Now look at *figure 7: Our Sun cannot even be seen in comparison to the other suns.* Shocked? What if I told you that Betelgeuse is not the largest Sun that we know of? Refer to *Figure 8: Our Sun – A Speechless Sight of Comparison.* The following quote springs to mind: "A picture paints a thousand words." – Frederick R. Barnard. Now I ask you once more, are you still convinced we cannot be micro-organisms?

Figure 6: Our Gigantic Sun – Largest Planet in Solar System

Figure 7: Our Sun – Too Small to be Seen

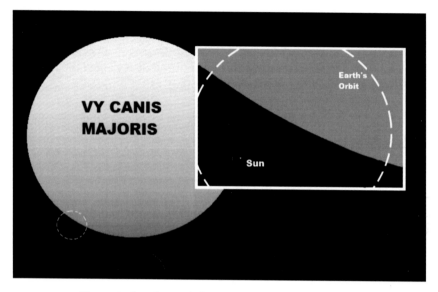

Figure 8: Our Sun – A Speechless Sight of Comparison

SATURN

Saturn blows me away. Its nickname should be 'Mysteriously Astounding!' Aside from what we can deduce ourselves from the above statements, this is what we are generally told about the planet Saturn:

- A very light gas giant, made up of more hydrogen than helium
- The planet contains a small rocky core covered with liquid gas
- Its system of rings spread into space for thousands for miles
- Saturn's rings were named in the order of their discovery. These names are extremely basic. Working outwards from the planet, the rings are named: D, C, B, A, F, G, E
- The rings are made from millions of ice crystals
- Saturn encounters many storms, at an alarmingly high speed of around 500 miles per hour!
- There is a very strong magnetic field which traps energy particles, resulting in Saturn's high levels of radiation
- Saturn orbits the Sun once every 29.5 Earth years
- A day on Saturn lasts 10 hours and 25 minutes

Two spacecrafts, Voyager 1 and Voyager 2 were launched by NASA in 1977 from Cape Canaveral, Florida, US. These spacecrafts served as space probes – robotic spacecrafts on an exploration mission. The Voyagers were to conduct detailed observations of Jupiter and Saturn, including Saturn's rings, and the larger moons of these two planets. Another space probe, Cassini-Huygens, was sent to Saturn in 1997.

So... why have I chosen to research and include Saturn in this book? Because of its rings. The information is shocking. Before I go into this, I will inform you of two very strange things about Saturn. Images taken by Voyager 1 and Voyager 2, show Saturn's North Pole as a giant six-sided hexagon revolving around the entire North Pole. The hexagon is so large that it is in fact 15,000 miles across and 60 miles deep. Saturn is transmitting radio signals! The Cassini space probe has recorded audio transmissions, reported by Wired.com as "eerie whistling, epic whooshing and warbling echoes". It sounds very spooky.

The rings of Saturn have puzzled and fascinated astronomers and scientists ever since Galileo Galilei (an Italian physicist, mathematician, astronomer and philosopher) discovered them in 1610 using a telescope. In the 17th Century, upon observing Saturn's ring, Galileo saw them as planets – solid circles. Other observers viewed a solid elliptical plane, but containing circular and diamond-shaped openings. The rings were also disappearing and reappearing.

In addition to this, the ring plane would somehow change in thickness between 10 miles and 280 miles. Throughout the 17th and 18th Centuries, the reason given for this dramatic change was, believe it or not, put down to the poor quality of the telescope. Due to the disappearance and reappearance of Saturn's rings, the matter of whether Saturn had any rings at all came into question in the 19th Century.

In the present day, Saturn's rings are said to be very thin. This was initially concluded by the English astronomer William Rutter Dawes in 1862, when in an experiment a shadow was expected to be cast on the ring plane from Saturn's largest moon, Titan. No shadow occurred, leading to the conclusion that it had thin rings.

Note: Saturn has a staggering 62 moons (at least) with confirmed orbits!

In the 18th and 19th Centuries, light sources would be seen glowing temporarily on the edge of the ring plane. As they were temporary (less than 20 hours glow) and one of these points changed position, they were not viewed as satellites.

A dramatic event occurred in February 1917. Two British astronomers, John Knight and Maurice Anderson Ainslie, both independently reported the observation of a light source shining so bright that they thought it was a star. But the star moved! It travelled in a straight line, and subtended a cord across the rings. Observing this for 1 hour 40 minutes, the length of the cord stretched to around 77,000 miles, with an average speed of 46,800 miles per hour! This is an astounding speed. (Voyager 1's average speed through space was 38,000 miles per hour, with Voyager 2 at 35,000 miles per hour). In case you are thinking this moving 'star' was a comet or asteroid or some other kind of rock with the Sun's light reflecting from it, this is not the case. Why not? Because as the star crossed the rings (supposedly ice and rocks), it did not collide with the ice/rocks, and none of these were seen to move out of the star's path upon close contact. Instead, the star seemed to consume the ice and rocks in its path. Plus, during the observation, the rings never blocked out the light from the 'star'.

In addition to this, the results from Voyager 1 showed 'spokes' of light, perhaps electrical discharges, extending across the F ring of Saturn (the third most outer ring). Another strange aspect is that Saturn's third largest moon, Iapetus, is around ten times brighter on the face away from the Sun than the face exposed to the Sun. Aren't we taught that the Sun is the source of light in our Solar System?!

In August 1981, Voyager 2 produced another mystery. As mentioned earlier, in the 17th Century, Saturn's ring plane was reportedly changing from 10 miles to 280 miles. Voyager 2 indicated the thickness to be around 600 miles! Were 18th Century telescopes of such poor quality that they gave incorrect results? I don't think so! And remember, the observers were astronomers, not children. Astronomers don't use toy telescopes. You would be amazed at how immensely small our Solar System is compared to the vastness of the universe. Have you heard of a quasar (lengthier name: quasi-stellar radio source)? Wikipedia defines a Quasar as "A very energetic and distant active galactic nucleus" It is an extremely large star-like radio source. How large is extremely large? A light-year across! If anyone is unaware of the measurement (distance) of a light-year:

- *One Light second* = 186,000 miles per second
- *One Light year* = 186,000 x 60 (seconds) x 60 (minutes) x 24 (hours) x 365 days, which gives: 5, 865, 696, 000 miles (five trillion, eight hundred and sixty-five million, six hundred and ninety-six thousand miles)

Quasars were discovered in 1960s, and only around 13,000 have been discovered overall. In terms of being energetic, a quasar can produce energy equivalent to 10 trillion Suns. An active galactic nucleus (AGN) is a class of galaxies, which give out huge amounts of this powerful energy from their centres. This is far more than ordinary galaxies. Astronomers believe that super black holes (regions of space-time where gravity prevents everything from escaping, including light) at the centre of these galaxies may be behind the explosive energy being delivered into space.

These quasars are located in isolated regions of space, far away from our galaxy, the Milky Way. The signals from quasars could take many millions of years to reach Earth, at the speed of light. The placing of the planets in our Solar System with respect to the Sun can be measured with sunlight. For example, the Sun's light takes around 14 minutes to reach the Earth. Pluto is the furthest planet in our Solar System and yet light from the Sun only takes around 5.5 hours to reach it. This shows you how small our Solar System is in comparison to the rest of the known universe.

The distance between the Earth and Saturn is nearly 800 million miles. This is a lot in terms of Earth concepts, but remember, we live in Space. The Earth is in Space. 800 million miles in space is nothing. Voyager 1 spent 3 years and 2 months to reach Saturn.

Saturn's rings span twenty-two diameters of Earth. When looking at Saturn's rings from Earth, they are seen to be separated by thin black gaps. There are multiple gaps, and these 'thin' black gaps are actually enormous. One is called the Cassini Division – the gap separating ring A and ring B – which is 3,000 miles! A gap exists in the outermost segment of ring A, spanning 200 miles. This gap is called the Enke division. The astronomer James Edward Keeler discovered the Encke division. Another division is seen in the A ring, named the Keeler Gap, discovered by Voyager. This gap is 26 miles thick.

Of the minimum of 62 moons which Saturn has orbiting around it, only 8 of these are spheres: Dione, Mimas, Enceladus, Tethys, Titan, Rhea, Iapetus and Phoebe. The first four of these are positioned within the E-Ring. Rhea orbits just outside of the E-ring, the outer-most ring. Titan, Iapetus and Phoebe are situated farther away from Saturn itself, much further than Rhea. Phoebe has defined the boundary of Saturn's system (16 millions miles) because it is the furthest moon orbiting Saturn.

Another mystery surrounding Saturn is its ring geometry. When the gap was discovered in ring A, the Enke Division, some other observers could not find it. Those who did reported the gap to be at different distances from A ring's outer edge.

The thickness of the ring-plane has altered in reports. The width of the Cassini gap has also varied in reports by as much as 33 percent!

Let us now move onto the 1997 space probe, Cassini. Cassini has indicated that each ring of Saturn may have formed at different times and in different ways. Some rings also apparently renew themselves.

If you were to read in the newspaper of a cigar-shaped object, following a path in an orbit along the edge of Saturn's ring, would you believe it? I am betting you would. Well, it was reported in the French newspaper, *L'actualite insolite*. More than one of these colossal cigar-shaped vehicles was seen in the vicinity of Saturn, with sizes ranging from that of Earth to four times its size! And in case you are wondering, these objects were not rocks. If you have doubts over authenticity, I suggest you contact the French newspaper. You can even find images of the article on the Internet.

Dr. Norman R. Bergrun in his book *Ringmakers of Saturn* reveals Saturn's rings to appear to be created and changed by material flowing from cigar-shaped vehicles around Saturn: "The A and B rings are formed by slender mobile vehicles trailing massive efflux. The Cassini division and the Enke gap within the A ring are created simply by definite radial spacing of the respective formative bodies. The C-ring and the F-ring formations apparently depend upon the presence of a nearby vehicle. At birth, the A and B rings appear to have electromagnetic properties. In view of the generating mechanism, heretofore confusing variations in observational results now become explicable."

Who is in those vehicles? Who is ordering those vehicles to create and change the rings? What exactly is in that material? What is the purpose of these rings? And do these vehicles exist elsewhere in our Solar System?

We are told that the rings are made of matter (ice and rocks) which have existed from the beginning of the Solar System. However there is evidence, in the French newspaper, and images from the book *Ringmakers of Saturn*, that several electromagnetic cigar-shaped vehicles are continuously spewing the material to form the A and B rings. This book provides photos showing enormous machines on the moon Dione. In addition to this, the moon Iapetus is described as being invisible for over a month at a time, since its discovery in 1671. The moon/satellite only appeared in some regions of its orbit. Aside from this masterpiece by Bergrun, I am sure ample detail can be viewed from genuine and unedited images taken by our space probes. Dr. Norman R. Bergrun: "Evidence is 100 percent positive that propulsive vehicles generate the inner-and-outer-Enke A rings of Saturn."

From my own extensive research into Saturn, it appears there is too much evidence proving not only their existence but also the existence highly advanced extra-terrestrial life. Electromagnetic vehicles prove advanced knowledge of nuclear physics, aeronautics, engineering and more. Although there is no evidence of beings, can such vehicles be built and controlled by themselves? Saturn, its rings and moons, are without a doubt full of activity.

I wonder, do they believe in God (as a being) as we do? If so, do they believe in the same God? As they are much more technologically advanced than us, surely they know a lot more than us about the universe? If so, what is the probability that their views about life are incorrect and our views are correct? Do you really think they follow the same religions as we do?

To the ancient Greeks and Romans, Saturn (also known as Cronos) was the God of time, and one of the Titans. He killed his father to become ruler of the universe. To prevent a prophecy becoming true (Cronos being killed by one of his sons), he committed a monstrous act by devouring his own children as soon as they were born. Later Zeus was born and hidden by his mother, Rhea, wife of Cronos. Zeus overthrew his father and sent him to Tartaros – a prison for the worst of villains.

Saturn – Cronos (the god of time) + one of the Titans

Rhea – wife of Cronos – mother of Zeus.

CONCLUSION

A variety of interesting topics have been covered in this book, revealing some of humanity's biggest secrets. We must continuously ask ourselves the main question: why? We shouldn't simply conform to ways of living, but we should uncover the foundation of all things. By doing this, only then will you start to unravel the hidden mysteries of the world. Open your eyes, open your ears and deploy constructive critical thinking at all times. One door will open another, and another, and lead you on to a path quite unimaginable.

Sumer and Egypt, two of the oldest civilisations have seemed to have co-existed during the same periods. However, it has been discovered that some Egyptoligists are convinced that both the Sumerian and Egyptian cultures had risen from a common and extremely ancient origin. The remains of this very ancient origin have been forgotten by the many, but what about the few? I wonder what ancient societies, which U.S President John F. Kennedy had spoken of in a famous speech, constitute 'the few'. This famous speech was given to the American Newspaper Publishers Association on 27th April 1961, two and a half years before his assassination (November 22, 1963).

Is the one creator God worshipped not just by us, but also by the Annunaki, Nommos, and others?

However, as wars are ongoing on Earth and the manipulation of resources continues and kills, and as people pray to an almighty God (creator of the universe), bad prevails. Surely common sense tells us that one of the following could very well be true:

- We are unknowingly praying to an evil god *yes!*
- We are praying to a righteous god who for some reason cannot listen or chooses not to listen *porque se le importa un cara. (es sadis)*
- We are praying to a god based on free will, who doesn't follow the concepts of 'good' and 'bad'
- There is no god of the universe – the One God
- The One God (possibly not limited to the Earth, our solar system or our universe) is infact Consciousness. In addition to this One God, the entity which has been taught to be our God by the mainstream, is actually the Elohim – who are said to have genetically engineered us to be their slaves. They changed our DNA from beings of high intellect and spiritual

ability (the initial Root-Races) to beings which have been dumbed-down, subservient, and lacking spiritual capability. Therefore, this Elohim may be considered to be our God, the creators of modern man, but they are not the One God - the true God of all things.

Who is said to have created the current form of humans, mankind? The Annunaki. The Annunaki created us to be slaves to mine for gold for their planet. Therefore, as they created us, are they not our God? The same gods who wanted us, their creation, to be their slaves.

We pray to God now for good and peace, but do we get them? Have wars and innocent killings ended? No. Are manipulations and controls ongoing? Yes.

I believe the final bullet-point above, is the accurate description of our god and the One true God. They are two very different entities. I believe our god (not the universe creator god) is the Anunnaki, and as they created us to be slaves, they do not have good intentions for us. And I ask you, aren't we slaves still? Isn't the education system built on the system that we learn skills to work every day 9 until 5.30, until we're old and frail? Isn't this slavery? What do you think would happen if everyone around the world united in agreement to completely stop working for just one month? We humans are powerful. Do not give your power away by submitting to slavery.

Is a slave master good or bad? How much does a master care about his slave? How much does a master want to be praised by his slave? Why would a slave master (which in essence is what the Annunaki are) want to free slaves? They want us to remain as slaves, which is why suffering continues on this planet. They want it to remain this way. I believe our god is the Annunaki, slave masters, and these are who we to this day are unknowingly praying to.

Ladies and gentlemen, have our prayers stopped murder, rape and war? NO! So please start to use your common sense. I believe the Anunnaki are still here and they're very much still in charge. If you think nothing can live forever except God, so the Anunnaki must have died long ago from something like old age, then consider the following examples of life-spans of living entities:

- The oldest dog, Bluey, has lived for under 30 years
- The oldest known human, Besse Cooper, has lived for approximately 116 years
- The arguably oldest tree, Methuselah, has lived for over 4800 years

183

According to Zecharia Sitchin, human civilisation was set up under the guidance of these gods, and human kingship was introduced to create intermediaries between mankind and the Anunnaki. This created the 'divine right of kings', the monarchy. I also believe this to be true.

Read the above paragraph again, and try to understand its implications. There is evidence of extra-terrestrials, i.e. the Nommos, in and around our Solar System. Their actions, possibly portrayed in the concept of Adam and Eve with the serpent, potentially indicate their attempt to free us from our slavery.

There are many mysteries on Earth itself, as well as in outer space. Remember, although the Earth contains many wonderful secrets, our planet is a micro-organism compared to other planets. Considering this, how significant is our daily working life which we conduct until we're old and frail? What should we be doing instead with our lives in the universe? We need to remove fear from our minds, and like James Cameron who plunged into the deepest part of the ocean, we need to take risks, and adventure the unknown and learn about our true, powerful potential. We are attracted to movies of fantasy and science because our subconscious knows that they are full of information from our true past.

We are born into the world as individuals, and we die as individuals. But why do we live as a collective, through the system of education and uniforms? An individual mind is an independent, critical, free-thinking mind. And it should remain so. You know and you feel there is more to life than just studying, working and paying taxes. Why would a life full of wonders be given to you for only these reasons? If you are content with your life, let it be. But I believe you really want to live life, and to do this, you first need to open your mind. Investigate what I have discussed in this book, and you will find many wonders around you.

The truth is gained by looking into the ancient past, when the world was more spiritual. Now, the world is materialist. We must journey back to the past in order to understand our true nature and our true potential. Use all the tools of research available to you, while you can. Things change, and usually for the worse. Use your time wisely. Ask why.

BIBLIOGRAPHY

–Lyricsmode, John Lennon *Imagine* Lyrics, (2012),
http://www.lyricsmode.com/lyrics/j/john_lennon/imagine.html
–Wikipedia, *Pangaea,* (2012), http://en.wikipedia.org/wiki/Pangaea
–Wikipedia, *Continental Drift,* (2012),
http://en.wikipedia.org/wiki/Continental_drift
– Wikipedia, *Abraham Ortelius,* (2012),
http://en.wikipedia.org/wiki/Abraham_Ortelius
– Wikipedia, *Alfred Wegener,* (2012),
http://en.wikipedia.org/wiki/Alfred_Wegener
– Wikipedia, *Francisco Pizarro,* (2012),
http://en.wikipedia.org/wiki/Francisco_Pizarro
– AllAboutScience, *Darwin's Theory of Evolution – A Theory in Crisis,* (2012),
http://www.darwins-theory-of-evolution.com/
– Wikipedia, *Evolution,* (2012), http://en.wikipedia.org/wiki/Evolution
– The Open University, *Darwin's Theory of Evolution,* (2012),
http://www.open.ac.uk/darwin/darwin-theory.php
– The Natural History Museum, *How did Evolutionary Theory Develop?,*
(2012), http://www.nhm.ac.uk/nature-online/evolution/how-did-evol-theory-
develop/index.html
– YouTube, *Scientists: The Theory of Evolution is Wrong (part 1),* (2012),
http://www.youtube.com/watch?v=SWDRz5cSziQ&feature=related
– YouTube, Scientists: *The Theory of Evolution is Wrong (part 2),* (2012),
http://www.youtube.com/watch?v=Z4ylfLqiyRo&feature=relmfu
– YouTube, *Evidence Against Evolution (Part 1 of 6) Evidence for Intelligent
Design,* (2012), http://www.youtube.com/watch?v=fjThfkdAOoQ&feature=related
– Science Museum, *Dolly the Sheep,* (2012),
http://www.sciencemuseum.org.uk/antenna/dolly/
– National Museums Scotland, *Dolly the Sheep,* (2012),
http://www.nms.ac.uk/highlights/star_objects/dolly_the_sheep.aspx
– YouTube, History.com – *Anunnaki and Nibiru,* (2012),
http://www.youtube.com/watch?v=29HCv_8kNM4
– Ancient History Encyclopedia, *Nineveh,* (2012),
http://www.ancient.eu.com/nineveh/
– Wikipedia, *Enuma Elis,* (2012),
http://en.wikipedia.org/wiki/En%C3%BBma_Eli%C5%A1
– Sitchin.com, *The Official Website of Zecharia Sitchin,* (2012),

http://www.sitchin.com/
- Sagan, C., *The Dragons of Eden, Ballantine Books Inc*, Reprint Edition, (1992)
- Sitchin, Z., *The Twelfth Planet*, Harper Collins, Reprint Edition, (2007)
- Sitchin, Z., *Genesis Revisited: Is Modern Science Catching Up with Ancient Knowledge?*, Avon Books, New Ed edition, (1998)
- Sitchin, Z., *The Wars of Gods and Men*, HarperTorch, Reprint edition, (2007)
- Daniken E., *Chariots of the Gods: Was God an Astronaut?*, Souvenir Press Ltd, New Ed edition, (1990)
- Temple, R., *The Sirius Mystery: New Scientific Evidence for Alien Contact 5000 Years Ago*, Arrow Books Ltd, New edition, (1999)
- Boylan, R., *The Star Nations Revision To the Standard Darwinian Explanation of Human Development*, (2012), http://www.drboylan.com/revhxhomosap.html
- Desaulniers, M., *Extraterrestrial Contact in Shamanic Traditions*, (2009), http://suite101.com/article/extraterrestrial-contact-in-shamanic-traditions-a93537
- Wikipedia, *Ancient Astronauts*, (2012), http://en.wikipedia.org/wiki/Ancient_astronauts
- YouTube, *Michael Jackson*, (2012), http://www.youtube.com/watch?v=3lJmQFlosUw
- Project Avalon Chronicles of the Human Awakening, (2012), http://projectavalon.net/forum4/showthread.php?51673-Those-Who-From-Heaven-to-Earth-Came
- Wikipedia, *Bible Translations*, (2012), http://en.wikipedia.org/wiki/Bible_translations
- Wikipedia, *Biblical Languages*, (2012), http://en.wikipedia.org/wiki/Biblical_languages
- Truthnet, *Origin of the Bible*, (2012), http://www.truthnet.org/Bible-Origins/4_How_was_Bible_written/index.htm
- *Biblica, Bible FAQs*, (2012), http://www.biblica.com/bibles/faq/19/
- Wikipedia, *Henotheism*, (2012), http://en.wikipedia.org/wiki/Henotheism
- Palmer, M., *The God of Israel: An Ancient People's Growing Understanding*, (2005), http://www.greek-language.com/bible/palmer/03godofisrael.pdf
- Wikipedia, *Monotheism*, (2012), http://en.wikipedia.org/wiki/Monotheism
- About.com, *What is Monotheism*, (2012), http://atheism.about.com/library/FAQs/religion/blrel_theism_mono.htm
- Heiser, M., *Monotheism, Polytheism, Monolatry, or Henotheism? Toward an Honest (and Orthodox) Assessment of Divine Plurality in the Hebrew Bible*, (2012), http://www.reclaimingthemind.org/papers/ets/2005/Heisermonotheism/Heisermonotheism.pdf

– Gier, N., *Hebrew Henotheism*, (2012),
http://www.class.uidaho.edu/ngier/henotheism.htm
– BibleGateway.com, (2012), http://www.biblegateway.com
– CompanionBibleCondensed.com, *The Psalms*, (2012),
http://www.companionbiblecondensed.com/OT/Psalms..pdf
– CompanionBibleCondensed.com, *Genesis*, (2012),
http://www.companionbiblecondensed.com/OT/Genesis...pdf
– CompanionBibleCondensed.com, *Isaiah*, (2012),
http://www.companionbiblecondensed.com/OT/Isaiah.pdf
– Kais, D., *Verse (49:13)* – English Translation, (2011),
http://corpus.quran.com/translation.jsp?chapter=49&verse=13
– Zahoor, A., Haq, Z., *O Mankind: Verses From The Glorious Qur'an*, (1998),
http://www.cyberistan.org/islamic/mankindq.htm
– CompanionBibleCondensed.com, *Jeremiah*, (2012),
http://www.companionbiblecondensed.com/OT/Jeremiah.pdf
– Wikipedia, *The Spaceships of Ezekiel*, (2012),
http://en.wikipedia.org/wiki/The_Spaceships_of_Ezekiel
– Blumrich, J., *The Spaceships of Ezekiel*, (2012),
http://www.spaceshipsofezekiel.com/html/josef-blumrich-bio.html
– Chatelain, M., *Our Ancestors Came From Outer Space: A NASA Expert Confirms Mankind's Extraterrestrial Origins*, Doubleday, 1st edition, (1978)
– Blumrich, J., *The Spaceships of Ezekiel, Corgi*, Reprinted edition, (1976)
– Salla, M., *Neil Armstrong dies along with secrets of what he saw on moon*, (2012), http://www.examiner.com/article/neil-armstrong-dies-along-with-secrets-of-what-he-saw-on-moon
– Cantrell, L., *The Greatest Story Never Told: A Scientific Inquiry into the Evidence of the Fall of Man from a Higher Civilisation in Antiquity*, First Edition, (1988)
– World-Mysteries.com, *Zecharia Sitchin*, (2009), http://www.world-mysteries.com/pex_2.htm
– Farrell, J., *Genes, Giants, Monsters, and Men: The Surviving Elites of the Cosmic War and Their Hidden Agenda*, Feral House, (2011)
– Colavito, J., *The Secret History of Ancient Astronauts*, (2012),
http://www.jasoncolavito.com/secret-history-of-ancient-astronauts.html
– Acharya, S., *Who are the Anunnaki?*, (2012),
http://www.truthbeknown.com/anunnaki.htm#.UI6gR1Hty4s
– YouTube, *Zecharia Sitchin – Sumerian and the Origins Of Humans*, (2012),
http://www.youtube.com/watch?feature=player_embedded&v=GlccvSikr0w
– Hamilton, L., *Scientology*, (2006), http://en.allexperts.com/q/Scientology-1751/L-Ron-Hubbard-space.htm?zlr=1

- BBC, Panorama: *Road to Total Freedom*, 27 April 1987.
- Farley, R., *Scientology Nearly Ready to Unveil Super Power*, (2006), http://www.sptimes.com/2006/05/06/Tampabay/Scientology_nearly_re.shtml/
- Wikipedia, *Xenu*, (2012), http://en.wikiquote.org/wiki/Xenu
- Minton, B., *Scientology's Core Beliefs*, (2001), http://www.skeptictank.org/gen3/gen01985.htm
- YouTube, *South Park Proved Right About Scientology XENU Story*, (2012), http://www.youtube.com/watch?v=T7EEOMbBIO8
- *Nine Planets, An Overview of the Solar System*, (2012), http://nineplanets.org/overview.html
- Wikipedia, *Molecular Cloud*, (2012), http://en.wikipedia.org/wiki/Molecular_cloud
- Wikipedia, *Solar System*, (2012), http://en.wikipedia.org/wiki/Solar_System
- Wikipedia, *Astronomical Unit*, (2012), http://en.wikipedia.org/wiki/Astronomical_uni
- Wikipedia, *Voyager 1*, (2012), http://en.wikipedia.org/wiki/Voyager_1
- Coffey, J., *How Big is the Solar System?*, (2008), http://www.universetoday.com/15463/how-big-is-the-solar-system/
- Answers Corporation, *How Big is our Solar System?*, (2012), http://wiki.answers.com/Q/How_big_is_our_solar_system
- Wikipedia, *Milky Way*, (2012), http://en.wikipedia.org/wiki/Milky_Way
- Wethington, N., *The Size of the Milky Way*, (2009), http://www.universetoday.com/24182/the-size-of-the-milky-way/
- Cain, F., *How Many Galaxies in the Universe?*, (2009), http://www.universetoday.com/30305/how-many-galaxies-in-the-universe
- Wikipedia, *Wernher von Braun*, (2012), http://en.wikipedia.org/wiki/Wernher_von_Braun
- Williams, R., *Wernher Von Braun*, (2012), http://earthobservatory.nasa.gov/Features/vonBraun/
- Wikipedia, *Carol Rosin*, (2012), http://en.wikipedia.org/wiki/Carol_Rosin
- YouTube, *U.F.O. Disclosure Project*, (2012), http://www.youtube.com/watch?v=7vyVe-6YdUk
- Greer, S., *Disclosure: Military and Government Witnesses Reveal the Greatest Secrets in Modern History*, Crossing Point Inc (2001)
- Hovni, A., *Ronald Reagan's Obsession with an Alien Invasion*, (1995), http://www.theforbiddenknowledge.com/hardtruth/ronald_reagan_ufo.htm
- Leir, R., *Alien Scalpel*, (2012), http://www.alienscalpel.com/aliens-and-ufos/us-president-reagans-extraterrestrial-speech-to-the-united-nations-1987
- Socio-Economics History Blog, *President Ronald Reagan's (1987) Speech About*

UFO Alien Invasion at United Nations, (2012),
http://socioecohistory.wordpress.com/2010/08/23/president-ronald-reagans-1987-speech-about-ufo-alien-invasion-at-united-nations/
- YouTube, *Reagan Comments on ET Alien Threat*, (2012),
http://www.youtube.com/watch?v=CfejBpD_wm4
- Wikipedia, *Mikhail Gorbachev*, (2012),
http://en.wikipedia.org/wiki/Mikhail_Gorbachev
- Kling, P., *Letters to Earth: You Can Survive Armageddon*, Strategic Book Group, (2011)
- MacAskill. E, *US 'Star Wars' Lasers Bring Down Ballistic Missile*, (2010),
http://www.guardian.co.uk/science/2010/feb/12/star-wars-laser-ballistic-missile
- YouTube, *UFOTV Presents: President Reagan's ET Briefing*, (2012),
http://www.youtube.com/watch?v=bN-h-iX_LtU
- Wikipedia, *Tom Van Flandern*, (2012),
http://en.wikipedia.org/wiki/Tom_Van_Flandern
- Flandern, T., *Dark Matter, Missing Planets and New Comets: Paradoxes Resolved, Origins Illuminated*, North Atlantic Books, Rev Sub edition, (1999)
- Flandern, T., *The Exploded Planet Hypothesis 2000*, (2012),
http://metaresearch.org/solar%20system/eph/eph2000.asp
- *Gregory, D., The Elements of Astronomy, Physical and Geometrical*, J. Nicholson, (1715)
- Wikipedia, *Ceres* (Dwarf Planet), (2012),
http://en.wikipedia.org/wiki/Ceres_(dwarf_planet)#Discovery
- Wikipedia, *Pluto*, (2012), http://en.wikipedia.org/wiki/Pluto
- Wikipedia, *Heinrich Wilhelm Matthias Olbers*, (2012),
http://en.wikipedia.org/wiki/Heinrich_Wilhelm_Matth%C3%A4us_Olbers
- Wikipedia, *2 Pallas*, (2012), http://en.wikipedia.org/wiki/2_Pallas
- Hoagland, R., *A Key to the Mystery of Comet Origins*, (1997),
http://www.enterprisemission.com/comets.html
- Janus, Ovenden, Michael William (1926-1987) *Astronomer*, (2012),
http://janus.lib.cam.ac.uk/db/node.xsp?id=CV%2FPers%2FOvenden%2C%20Mich ael%20William%20(1926-1987)%20astronomer
- Wikipedia, *Meteorite*, (2012), http://en.wikipedia.org/wiki/Meteorite
- Wikipedia, *Willamette Meteorite*, (2012),
http://en.wikipedia.org/wiki/Willamette_Meteorite
- Wikipedia, *Diamond*, (2012), http://en.wikipedia.org/wiki/Diamond
- Sol Company, *Neptune*, (2011), http://www.solstation.com/stars/neptune.htm
- Wikipedia, *Roche Limit*, (2012), http://en.wikipedia.org/wiki/Roche_limit
- Wikipedia, *Kuiper Belt*, (2012), http://en.wikipedia.org/wiki/Kuiper_belt
- Wikipedia, *Ocean Planet*, (2012), http://en.wikipedia.org/wiki/Ocean_planet

– McKee, M., *Gas Giants Credited for Solar System Formation*, (2005), http://www.newscientist.com/article/dn7429-gas-giants-credited-for-solar-system-formation.htm

– Shiga, D., *Neptune May Have Eaten a Planet and Stolen its Moon*, (2010), http://www.newscientist.com/article/mg20527522.900-neptune-may-have-eaten-a-planet-and-stolen-its-moon.html

– KidsAstronomy.com, *Astronomy Packet: 6*, (2012), http://www.kidsastronomy.com/academy/lesson110_assignment1_6.htm

– NASA, *Bizarre Lunar Orbits*, (2012), http://science.nasa.gov/science-news/science-at-nasa/2006/06nov_loworbit/

– Wikipedia, *Mass Concentration (astronomy)*, (2012), http://en.wikipedia.org/wiki/Mass_concentration_(astronomy)

– Wikipedia, *Mare Imbrium*, (2012), http://en.wikipedia.org/wiki/Mare_Imbrium

– Wikipedia, *Mare Serenitatis*, (2012), http://en.wikipedia.org/wiki/Mare_Serenitatis

– Wikipedia, *Kepler (spacecraft)*, (2012), http://en.wikipedia.org/wiki/Kepler_(spacecraft)

– YouTube, *Kepler Discovers a Planet with Two Suns*, (2012), http://www.youtube.com/watch?v=R_XqFq3yNDc

– Wikipedia, *Physics and Star Wars*, (2012), http://en.wikipedia.org/wiki/Physics_and_Star_Wars

– Wikipedia, *The Book of the Damned*, (2012), http://en.wikipedia.org/wiki/The_Book_of_the_Damned#Content

– Wikipedia, *Charles Fort*, (2012), http://en.wikipedia.org/wiki/Charles_Fort

– Burtnyk. K, *Did Comets Bring Water to Earth?*, (2012), http://earthsky.org/space/did-comets-bring-water-to-earth

– Nature.com, *News & Comment*, (2012), http://www.nature.com/nature/index.html

– tlonh.com, *The Hollow Earth Theory*, (2012), http://www.hollowearththeory.com/articles/marsFloodPhotos.asp

– Answering-Christianity.com, *Mars: Cydonia Mensae*, (2012), http://www.answering-christianity.com/fakir60/cydonia.htm

– Wikipedia, *Cydonia (region of Mars)*, (2012), http://en.wikipedia.org/wiki/Cydonia_(region_of_Mars)

– Wikipedia, *Mission to Mars*, (2012), http://en.wikipedia.org/wiki/Mission_to_Mars

– IMDB, *Prometheus*, (2012), http://www.imdb.com/title/tt1446714/

– IMDB, *E.T. the Extra-Terrestrial*, (2012), http://www.imdb.com/title/tt0083866/

– Finney, D., *ET – The Movie*, (2012),

http://www.greatdreams.com/ufos/etmovie.htm
- Wikipedia, *Sistine Chapel Ceiling*, (2012),
http://en.wikipedia.org/wiki/Sistine_Chapel_ceiling
- Wikipedia, *Michelangelo*, (2012), http://en.wikipedia.org/wiki/Michelangelo
- Wikipedia, *Sistine Chapel*, (2012), http://en.wikipedia.org/wiki/Sistine_Chapel
- Siriusly, *The Face on Mars Investigation*, (2012),
http://www.dudeman.net/siriusly/cyd/inv.html
- Steve Qualyle.com, *Genesis 6 Giants and Ancient History*, (2012),
http://www.stevequayle.com/index.php?s=30
- Schwartzbauer. A, *The Truth About Giants*, (2012),
http://tccsa.tc/articles/the_truth_about_giants_short.pdf
- Quayle, S., *Aliens & Fallen Angels Offspring of the Gods the Sexual Corruption of the Human Race*, End Time Thunder Publishers, 2nd Edition, (2003)
- Bates. G, *Alien Intrusion*, Creation Book Publishers, (2010)
- Missler. C, Eastman. M, *Alien Encounters*, Koinonia House Inc, (1997)
- World-Mysteries.com, *Strange Artifacts - Unexplained Skulls*, (1996),
http://www.world-mysteries.com/sar_6.htm
- IMDB, *The Cabin in the Woods*, (2012),
http://uk.imdb.com/title/tt1259521/synopsis
- Wikipedia, *Aryan*, (2012), http://en.wikipedia.org/wiki/Aryan
- Wikipedia, *Master Race*, (2012), http://en.wikipedia.org/wiki/Master_race
- The University Society Inc, *The Young Folks Treasury*, (2012),
http://fairytales4u.com/story/jackand.htm
- Wikipedia, *Og*, (2012), http://en.wikipedia.org/wiki/Og
- MDB, *The Chronicles of Narnia: The Lion, the Witch and the Wardrobe*, (2012),
http://www.imdb.com/title/tt0363771/
- Myths Encyclopedia, *Floods*, (2012), http://www.mythencyclopedia.com/Fi-Go/Floods.html#b
- Quayle, S., *Genesis 6 Giants Master Builders of Prehistoric and Ancient Civilisations*, End Time Thunder Publishers, (2002)
- Bandstra, B., *Enuma Elish*, (2012),
http://www.jcu.edu/Bible/200/Readings/EnumaElish.htm
- Alford, A., *Ancient Astronauts - Enuma Elish*, (2012),
http://www.eridu.co.uk/Author/human_origins/AAS_Intro2/Sitchin_Message/enuma.html
- D'Arc, J., *The Late Great Planet Tiamat - Was the Third Rock from the Sun Once the Fifth Rock from the Sun?*, (2002),
http://www.bibliotecapleyades.net/hercolobus/esp_hercolobus_26.htm
- Knight. C, Butler. A, *Who Built the Moon?*, Watkins Publishing, (2005)

- Vasin, M., Shcherbakov, *Is The Moon The Creation of Intelligence*, (2012), http://www.bibliotecapleyades.net/luna/esp_luna_6.htm
- Wikipedia, *Spaceship Moon Theory*, (2012), http://en.wikipedia.org/wiki/Spaceship_Moon_Theory
- Marrs. J, *Who Parked Our Moon?*, (2010), http://www.disinfo.com/2010/09/who-parked-the-moon/
- Wikipedia, *Moon*, (2012), http://en.wikipedia.org/wiki/Moon
- NASA, *Solar System Exploration*, (2012), http://solarsystem.nasa.gov/planets/profile.cfm?Display=Facts&Object=Moon
- Cain. F, *Interesting Facts about the Moon*, (2008), http://www.universetoday.com/20050/10-interesting-facts-about-the-moon/
- Infoplease, *History of the Lunar Calendar*, (2012), http://www.infoplease.com/calendar/lunar.html
- Infoplease, *History of the Calendar*, (2012), http://www.infoplease.com/ipa/A0002061.html
- Cooley, K., *Moon Tides*, (2002), http://home.hiwaay.net/~krcool/Astro/moon/moontides/
- HowStuffWorks, *What Causes High Tide and Low Tide? Why are There Two Tides Each Day?*, (2012), http://science.howstuffworks.com/environmental/earth/geophysics/tide-cause.ht
- Epigee, *Periods and Moons*, (2012), http://www.epigee.org/menstruation_lunar_fertility.html
- Cutler, W., *Lunar and Menstrual Phase Locking*, (1980), http://www.athenainstitute.com/sciencelinks/lunarandmenst.html
- Hall, M., *Fertility and the Moon*, (2012), http://astrology.about.com/od/themoon/a/MoonFertility.htm
- Castell, C., *Understanding the Blue Moon*, (2012), http://shamanicastrology.com/archives/107
- Wikipedia, *Venus of Laussel*, (2012), http://en.wikipedia.org/wiki/Venus_of_Laussel
- Brunner, B., Imbornoni. A, *Once in a Blue Moon*, (2012), http://www.infoplease.com/spot/bluemoon1.html
- Wikipedia, *List of fertility deities*, (2012), http://en.wikipedia.org/wiki/List_of_fertility_deities
- Stooke, P. J., 'Neolithic Lunar Maps at Knowth and Baltinglass, Ireland', Journal for the History of Astronomy, 25, 39–55, (1994)
- Knowth.com, *Knowth Megalithic Passage Tomb*, (2012), http://www.knowth.com/knowth.htm
- Wikipedia, *Lunar Effect*, (2012), http://en.wikipedia.org/wiki/Lunar_effect

– Sims, P., *There's More Violence During Full Moons, Say Police*, (2007), http://www.dailymail.co.uk/news/article-460050/Theres-violence-moons-say-police.html

– Wikipedia, *Apocalypto*, (2012), http://en.wikipedia.org/wiki/Apocalypto

– Cain, F., *Will Earth Survive When the Sun Becomes a Red Giant?*, (2008), http://www.universetoday.com/12648/will-earth-survive-when-the-sun-becomes-a-red-giant/

– ScienceDaily, *First Evidence Discovered of Planet's Destruction by Its Star*, (2012), http://www.sciencedaily.com/releases/2012/08/120820170715.htm

– King, T., *Stages in the Life Cycle of a Star*, (2012), http://www.ehow.com/how-does_5194338_stages-life-cycle-star.html

– Wikipedia, *Albert Einstein*, (2012), http://en.wikiquote.org/wiki/Albert_Einstein

– HowStuffWorks, *How the Moon Was Born*, (2012), http://science.howstuffworks.com/how-the-moon-was-born-info2.htm

– Wikipedia, *Internal structure of the Moon*, (2012), http://en.wikipedia.org/wiki/Internal_structure_of_the_Moon

– *'How Apollo 13 Will Probe the Moon's Interior'*, Popular Science Magazine,(1970), http://books.google.co.uk/books?id=6QAAAAAAMBAJ&pg=PA56&lpg=PA56&dq=apollo+13+saturn+v+rang+like+a+bell&source=bl&ots=Z3OPn6WJZR&sig=r828FIN57sEDuOIWt-SAsCHFM_M&hl=en&sa=X&ei=B_uSUPvSLvOa1AWO-4HICg&ved=0CBOQ6AEwAA#v=onepage&q=apollo%2013%20saturn%20v%20rang%20like%20a%20bell&f=false

– *'Apollo 13 "Houston, we've got a problem."'*, Space Educators' Handbook, (2012), http://www.spaceacts.com/STARSHIP/seh/pg15.htm

– NASA, *Rocketry*, (2012), http://www.nasa.gov/audience/foreducators/rocketry/home/what-was-the-saturn-v-58.html

– Wikipedia, *Seismometer*, (2012), http://en.wikipedia.org/wiki/Seismometer

– Wikipedia, *Apollo 13*, (2012), http://en.wikipedia.org/wiki/Apollo_13

– thenightsky, *Our Hollow Moon*, (2012), http://thenightsky.org/hollow.html

– Wikipedia, *Apollo 14*, (2012), http://en.wikipedia.org/wiki/Apollo_14

– Stueber, J., *What if the Moon Didn't Exist?*, (2012), http://webpages.charter.net/jeffstueber/what%20if%20the%20moon%20didn't%20exist.htm

– Marrs, J., *Who Parked The Moon?*, (2010), http://www.newrealities.com/index.php/articles-on-new-sciences/item/1018-who-parked-the-moon?-by-jim-marrs

– Wikipedia, *Carl Sagan*, (2012), http://en.wikipedia.org/wiki/Carl_Sagan

– Comins, F., *What If the Moon Didn't Exist*, (1996),

http://www.astrosociety.org/edu/publications/tnl/33/33.html
- NASA, *Ocean Tides and the Earth's Rotation*, (2012),
http://bowie.gsfc.nasa.gov/ggfc/tides/intro.html
- Wikipedia, *Tidal Acceleration*, (2012),
http://en.wikipedia.org/wiki/Tidal_acceleration
- Strobel, N., *Tides*, (2001), http://www.astronomynotes.com/gravappl/s10.htm
- Rosenberg, G. D. and Runcorn, S.K., *Growth Rhythms and the History of the Earth's Rotation*, Wiley, (1975)
- Answers Corporation, *What is the Purpose of a Satellite?*, (2012),
http://wiki.answers.com/Q/What_is_the_purpose_of_a_satellite
- Answers Corporation, *Who Discovered the Microbes?*, (2012),
http://wiki.answers.com/Q/Who_discovered_the_microbes
- Wikipedia, *Antonie van Leeuwenhoek*, (2012),
http://en.wikipedia.org/wiki/Antonie_van_Leeuwenhoek
- IMDB, *Men in Black II*, (2012), http://www.imdb.com/title/tt0120912/synopsis
- NASA, *Planets Around Other Stars*, (2012),
http://science.nasa.gov/astrophysics/focus-areas/exoplanet-exploration
- RayFowler.org, *The Size of the Earth Compared to Other Objects in Space*,
(2008), http://www.rayfowler.org/2008/01/14/the-size-of-the-earth-compared-to-other-objects-in-space/
- DidYouKnow.org, *The Size of the Sun in Comparison*, (2012),
http://didyouknow.org/the-size-of-the-sun-in-comparison/
- Wikipedia, *VY Canis Majoris*, (2012),
http://en.wikipedia.org/wiki/VY_Canis_Majoris
- Dictionary.com, *Righteous*, (2012),
http://dictionary.reference.com/browse/righteous
- Alford, A., *Ancient Astronauts: A Civilisation on Mars?*, (2012),
http://www.eridu.co.uk/Author/human_origins/mars.html
- Brandon, J., *Was There a Natural Nuclear Blast on Mars?*, (2011),
http://www.foxnews.com/scitech/2011/04/01/natural-nuclear-blast-mars/
- Wikipedia, *Fukushima Daiichi Nuclear Disaster*, (2012),
http://en.wikipedia.org/wiki/Fukushima_Daiichi_nuclear_disaster
- Wikipedia, *Plasma Physics*, (2012), http://en.wikipedia.org/wiki/Plasma_physics
- Alfven, H., *Electricity in Space*, (1948),
http://www.catastrophism.com/texts/electricity-in-space/
- Wikipedia, *Hannes Alfven*, (2012),
http://en.wikipedia.org/wiki/Hannes_Alfv%C3%A9n
- Wikipedia, *Magnetohydronamics*, (2012),
http://en.wikipedia.org/wiki/Magnetohydrodynamics

Bibliography

– Proceedings Of The American Philosophical Society, *Hannes Alfven*, (2006), http://www.amphilsoc.org/sites/default/files/150412.pdf
– Peratt, A., *Hannes Alfven*, (1988), http://public.lanl.gov/alp/plasma/people/alfven.html
– Wikipedia, *Parsec*, (2012), http://en.wikipedia.org/wiki/Parsec
– Coalition for Plasma Science, *What is Plasma?*, (2010), http://www.plasmacoalition.org/what.htm
– Masursky, H., Colton, G. and El-Baz, F., *Apollo Over The Moon: A View From Orbit*, (1978), http://history.nasa.gov/SP-362/ch6.2.htm
– Wikipedia, *Rille*, (2012), http://en.wikipedia.org/wiki/Rille
– Wikipedia, *Mamers Vallis*, (2012), http://en.wikipedia.org/wiki/Mamers_Vallis
– Encyclopaedia Britannica, *Hadley Rille*, (2012), http://www.britannica.com/EBchecked/topic/251182/Hadley-Rille
– Lerner. E, *The Big Bang Never Happened: A Startling Refutation of the Dominant Theory of the Origin of the Universe*, Vintage Books, (1992)
– Wikipedia, *Magnetism*, (2012), http://en.wikipedia.org/wiki/Magnetism
– Wikipedia, *Plasma Cosmology*, (2012), http://en.wikipedia.org/wiki/Plasma_cosmology
– Wikipedia, *Solar Wind*, (2012), http://en.wikipedia.org/wiki/Solar_wind
– Wikipedia, *Kristian Birkeland*, (2012), http://en.wikipedia.org/wiki/Kristian_Birkeland
– Wikipedia, *Aurora Borealis*, (2012), http://en.wikipedia.org/wiki/Aurora_borealis
– Wikipedia, *Corona*, (2012), http://en.wikipedia.org/wiki/Corona
– Wikipedia, *Winston H. Bostick*, (2012), http://en.wikipedia.org/wiki/Winston_H._Bostick
– IAEA.org, *Nuclear Fusion Basics*, (2010), http://www.iaea.org/newscenter/news/2010/nucfusionbasics.html
– ITER Organisation, *What is Fusion?*, (2012), http://www.iter.org/sci/whatisfusion
– Wikipedia, *Dense Plasma Focus*, (2012), http://en.wikipedia.org/wiki/Dense_plasma_focus
– Wikipedia, *Plasma Weapon* (fiction), (2012), http://en.wikipedia.org/wiki/Plasma_weapon_(fiction)
– Wikipedia, *J. Robert Oppenheimer*, (2012), http://en.wikipedia.org/wiki/J._Robert_Oppenheimer
– Wikipedia, *Manhattan Project*, (2012), http://en.wikipedia.org/wiki/Manhattan_Project
– Wikipedia, *Atomic bomb*, (2012), http://en.wikipedia.org/wiki/Atomic_bomb
– YouTube, *New Mexico July 16 1945*, (2012), http://www.youtube.com/watch?v=l8w3Y-dskeg

- Wikiquote.org, *Robert Oppenheimer,* (2012),
http://en.wikiquote.org/wiki/Robert_Oppenheimer
- Wikipedia, *Anthony Peratt* (physicist), (2012),
http://en.wikipedia.org/wiki/Anthony_Peratt_(physicist)
- Wikipedia, *Petroglyph,* (2012), http://en.wikipedia.org/wiki/Petroglyph
- Scott, D. and Peratt, A., *The Origin of Petroglyphs – Recordings of a Catastrophic
Aurora in Human Prehistory?,* (2012),
http://public.lanl.gov/alp/plasma/downloads/scott.icops2003
- Wikipedia, *David Talbott,* (2012), http://en.wikipedia.org/wiki/David_Talbott
- Marvel Movies, *Tesseract,* (2012), http://marvel-
movies.wikia.com/wiki/Tesseract
- Wikipedia, *Cosmic Cube,* (2012), http://en.wikipedia.org/wiki/Cosmic_Cube
- Wikipedia, *Spark (Transformers),* (2012),
http://en.wikipedia.org/wiki/Spark_(Transformers)
- Wikipedia, *Norse Mythology,* (2012),
http://en.wikipedia.org/wiki/Norse_mythology
- Albert. A, *What is the Cosmic Cube?* (2012),
http://comicbooks.about.com/od/captainamericamovies/a/What-Is-The-Cosmic-
Cube.htm
- Wikia, *Cosmic Cube,* (2012), http://marvel.wikia.com/Cosmic_Cube
- YouTube, *The Cube in Saturn and Subliminal Symbology,* (2012),
http://www.youtube.com/watch?v=fgdWRCbJSYQ
- Wikipedia, *Ouiji,* (2012), http://en.wikipedia.org/wiki/Ouija
- Wikipedia, *Transformers* (film), (2012),
http://en.wikipedia.org/wiki/Transformers_(film)
- Wikia, *The Avengers Movie Wiki,* (2012),
http://theavengersmovie.wikia.com/wiki/The_Tesseract
- Caddy, J., *Beliefs Have an Ancient History and May Reflect our Internal Makeup,*
(2012), http://johncaddy.files.wordpress.com/2012/01/beliefs-have-an-ancient-
history-and-may-reflect-our-internal-makeup1.pdf
- 2KnowMySelf.com, *What is the Subconscious Mind?* (2012),
http://www.2knowmyself.com/Subconscious_mind
- MvLeod, S., *Unconscious Mind,* (2009),
http://www.simplypsychology.org/unconscious-mind.html
- Wikipedia, *Sigmund Freud,* (2012), http://en.wikipedia.org/wiki/Sigmund_Freud
- Wikipedia, *Witch-Hunt,* (2012), http://en.wikipedia.org/wiki/Witch-hunt
- Wikipedia, *Witchcraft Act of 1735,* (2012),
http://en.wikipedia.org/wiki/Witchcraft_Act_of_1735#Witchcraft_Act_1735
- Alexander. S, *The Runes,* (2012), http://www.netplaces.com/wicca-

witchcraft/divination-and-oracles/the-runes.htm
- Wikipedia, *Sylph*, (2012), http://en.wikipedia.org/wiki/Sylph
- Occultopedia, *Sylph*, (2012), http://www.occultopedia.com/s/sylph.htm
- The Manly P. Hall Archive, About, (2012), http://www.manlyphall.org/
- Wikipedia, *Dwarf* (Germanic mythology), (2012),
http://en.wikipedia.org/wiki/Dwarf_(Germanic_mythology)
- Wikipedia, *Elf*, (2012), http://en.wikipedia.org/wiki/Elf
- Wikipedia, *Goblin Origins in folklore*, (2012),
http://en.wikipedia.org/wiki/Goblin#Origins_in_folklore
- Wikipedia, *Hel* (being), (2012), http://en.wikipedia.org/wiki/Hel_(being)
- Jo Edkins, *Tyr and the Wolf Fenrir*, (2009),
http://gwydir.demon.co.uk/jo/nordic/tyr.htm
- Wikia, *Fenrir Greyback*, (2012),
http://harrypotter.wikia.com/wiki/Fenrir_Greybac
- Jung, C., *Memories, Dreams, Reflections, Fontana Press*, Reissue edition, (1995)
- Thunderbolts.info, *Lightning-Scarred Gods and Monsters*, (2005),
http://www.thunderbolts.info/tpod/2005/arch05/050412scarface.htm
- Wikipedia, *Immanuel Velikovsky*, (2012),
http://en.wikipedia.org/wiki/Immanuel_Velikovsky#.22The_Velikovsky_Affair.22
- Wikipedia, *Catastrophism*, (2012), http://en.wikipedia.org/wiki/Catastrophism
- Wikipedia, *Comparative Mythology*, (2012),
http://en.wikipedia.org/wiki/Comparative_mythology
- Wikipedia, *Mythology*, (2012), http://en.wikipedia.org/wiki/Mythology
- Wikipedia, *Flood Myth*, (2012),
http://en.wikipedia.org/wiki/Flood_myth#Mythologies
- eTeacher Group Ltd, The Story of the Flood in Mesopotamian Literature,
(2012), http://blog.eteacherbiblical.com/2008/01/07/the-story-of-the-flood-in-
mesopotamian-literature/
- Wikipedia, Sumerian Creation Myth, (2012),
http://en.wikipedia.org/wiki/Sumerian_creation_myth
- Wikipedia, Gilgamesh Flood Myth, (2012),
http://en.wikipedia.org/wiki/Gilgamesh_flood_myth
- Sarissa.org, Sumerian Deities, (2012), http://sarissa.org/sumer/sumer_g.php
- Diffen, Greek Gods vs Roman Gods, (2012),
http://www.diffen.com/difference/Greek_Gods_vs_Roman_Gods
- Wikipedia, Worlds in Collision, (2012),
http://en.wikipedia.org/wiki/Worlds_in_Collisio
- Ryall. J, Japan's Ancient Underwater 'Pyramid' Mystifies Scholars, (2007),
http://news.nationalgeographic.co.uk/news/2007/09/070919-sunken-city.html

- Kidd. P, Where Do Phobias Come From?, (2012),
http://sciencefocus.com/qa/where-do-phobias-come
- Velikovsky. I, Worlds in Collision, Paradigma Ltd, (2009)
- Alford, A., The Atlantis Secret: A Complete Decoding of Plato's Lost Continent,
Eridu Books, 2001.
- Alford, A., When the Gods Came Down: The Catastrophic Roots of Religion
Revealed, Hodder & Stoughton Ltd, (2000)
- Wikipedia, Magisterium, (2012), http://en.wikipedia.org/wiki/Magisterium
- Irishoriginsofcivilisation.com, Appendix Seventeen, (2012),
http://www.irishoriginsofcivilization.com/appendices/etymology.html
- Wikipedia, Arnaldo Pomodoro, (2012),
http://en.wikipedia.org/wiki/Arnaldo_Pomodoro
- Wikipedia, Sphere Within Sphere, (2012),
http://en.wikipedia.org/wiki/Sphere_Within_Sphere
- Tordoff. H, The Book of Dzyan, (2012),
http://www.esolibris.com/articles/theosophy/book_of_dzyan.php
- Holleran. P, The Secret Doctrine, (2012),
http://www.mountainrunnerdoc.com/page/page/4566172.htm
- Wikipedia, Zecharia Sitchin, (2012),
http://en.wikipedia.org/wiki/Zecharia_Sitchin
- Freer, N., The Annunaki and the Myth of a 12th Planet, (2006),
http://www.redicecreations.com/specialreports/2006/01jan/annunaki.html
- Dalley, S., Myths from Mesopotamia: Creation, The Flood, Gilgamesh, and
Others, Oxford Paperbacks, Revised edition, 2008.
- Wikipedia, Georgia Guidestones, (2012),
http://en.wikipedia.org/wiki/Georgia_Guidestones
- one-heaven.org, Epic of Atrahasis, (2012), http://one-
heaven.org/sacred_texts/book/Epic_of_Atrahasis/c/7.html
- Wikipedia, Enlil, (2012), http://en.wikipedia.org/wiki/Enlil
- Noahs-ark.tv, Epic of Atra-Hasis, (2012), http://www.noahs-ark.tv/noahs-ark-
flood-creation-stories-myths-epic-of-atra-hasis-old-babylonian-akkadian-
cuneiform-flood-creation-tablet-1635bc.htm
- Dictionary.com, Architect, (2012),
http://dictionary.reference.com/browse/architect
- Wikipedia, Middle-Earth, (2012), http://en.wikipedia.org/wiki/Middle-
earth#cite_note-Gerrolt-1
- Patterson. H, Interview with J.R.R. Tolkien, (1971),
http://www.lordotrings.com/interview.asp
- alarguild.org, Subcreation – Writing Middle-Earth, (2012),

Bibliography

http://valarguild.org/varda/Tolkien/encyc/papers/dreamlord/stages/stages_of_ima
gination.htm#24
- Wikipedia, *Mumm-Ra*, (2012), http://en.wikipedia.org/wiki/Mumm-Ra
- Wikipedia, *Nehebkau*, (2012), http://en.wikipedia.org/wiki/Nehebkau
- Wikipedia, *Pineal gland*, (2012), http://en.wikipedia.org/wiki/Pineal_gland
- CompanionBibleCondensed.com, *The Gospel According To Matthew,* (2012),
http://www.companionbiblecondensed.com/NT/Matthew..pdf
- NothingButYoga.com, *6th Chakra*, (2012),
http://www.nothingbutyoga.com/6th-chakra.html
- Wikipedia, *Dimethyltryptamine*, (2012),
http://en.wikipedia.org/wiki/Dimethyltryptamine
- Wikipedia, Psychedelic Experience, (2012)
http://en.wikipedia.org/wiki/Psychedelic_experience
- Wikipedia, *Rick Strassman*, (2012), http://en.wikipedia.org/wiki/Rick_Strassman
- Strassman, R., *DMT: The Spirit Molecule: A Doctor's Revolutionary Research into
the Biology of Near-Death and Mystical Experiences,* Park Street Press, (2001)
- Strassman, R., *Mind-Altering Drugs: The Science of Subjective Experience,*
Oxford University Press, (2005)
- Wikipedia, *REM Stage of Sleep,* (2012),
http://en.wikipedia.org/wiki/REM_stage_of_sleep
- Wikipedia, *V* (2009 TV series), (2012),
http://en.wikipedia.org/wiki/V_(2009_TV_series)
- Wikipedia, *V* (1983 miniseries), (2012),
http://en.wikipedia.org/wiki/V_(1983_miniseries)
- Wikipedia, *J. A. B. van Buitenen,* (2012),
http://en.wikipedia.org/wiki/J._A._B._van_Buitenen
- Buitenen, V., *Tales of Ancient India,* University of Chicago Press, New edition,
(1969)
- Buitenen, J., *The Maitrayaniya Upanisad: A Critical Essay, with Text, Translation
and Commentary,* Mouton, (1962)
- Buitenen, J., *The Mahabharata, Volume 1, Book 1: The Book of the Beginning,*
Chicago, (1973)
- *Buitenen, J., The Mahabharata, Volume 2, Book 2: The Book of Assembly; Book 3:
The Book of the Forest,* Chicago, (1975)
- Buitenen, J., *The Mahabharata, Volume 3, Book 4: The Book of the Virata; Book
5: The Book of the Effort,* Chicago, (1978)
- Buitenen, J. and Fitzgerald, J., The Bhagavadgita in the Mahabharata, Chicago,
(1981)
- Theosophical University Press, *The Secret Doctrine,*

http://www.theosociety.org/pasadena/sd/sd-hp.htm, (2012)
- Budge, E., *The Gods of the Egyptians*, Dover Publishing Inc, 1904 (reprint 1969).
- Doniger, W., *The Rig Veda*, Penguin Classics, New York, (2005)
- Budge, E., *The Egyptian Book of the Dead*, Dover Publishing Inc, (1967)
- Wikipedia, *Snake worship*, (2012), http://en.wikipedia.org/wiki/Snake_worship
- Wikipedia, *Asura*, (2012), http://en.wikipedia.org/wiki/Asura
- Wikipedia, *Rakshasa*, (2012), http://en.wikipedia.org/wiki/Rakshasa
- Wikipedia, *Yaksha*, (2012), http://en.wikipedia.org/wiki/Yaksha
- Wikipedia, *Gandharva*, (2012), http://en.wikipedia.org/wiki/Gandharva
- Wikipedia, *Matali*, (2012), http://en.wikipedia.org/wiki/M%C4%81tal%C4%AB
- Wikipedia, *Indra*, (2012), http://en.wikipedia.org/wiki/Indra
- Wikipedia, *Pandavas*, (2012), http://en.wikipedia.org/wiki/Pandavas
- Wikipedia, *Kuru Kingdom*, (2012), http://en.wikipedia.org/wiki/Kuru_Kingdom
- Garg, G., *Encyclopaedia of the Hindu World: Ar-Az*: 003, South Asia Books, (1992)
- Wikipedia, *Yayati*, (2012), http://en.wikipedia.org/wiki/Yayati
- Wikipedia, *Matsya Puranam*, (2012),
http://en.wikipedia.org/wiki/Matsya_Purana
- Wikipedia, *Hastinapur*, (2012), http://en.wikipedia.org/wiki/Hastinapur
- Wikipedia, *Vyasi*, (2012), http://en.wikipedia.org/wiki/Vyasa
- Wikipedia, *Shiva*, (2012), http://en.wikipedia.org/wiki/Shiva
- Wikipedia, *Trimurti*, (2012), http://en.wikipedia.org/wiki/Trimurti
- Arbour. K, *King Tut's tomb filled with canes*, (2010),
http://www.examiner.com/article/king-tut-s-tomb-filled-with-canes
- Wikipedia, *Sceptre*, (2012), http://en.wikipedia.org/wiki/Sceptre
- Wikipedia, *Code of Hammurabi*, (2012),
http://en.wikipedia.org/wiki/Code_of_Hammurabi
- Fawkes, G. and Allan, R., *Aquat*, (2012),
http://www.kingmixers.com/CLA196/AQHAT.pdf
- Wikipedia, *Snake Goddess*, (2012), http://en.wikipedia.org/wiki/Snake_Goddess
- Wikipedia, *Ghatokacha*, (2012), http://en.wikipedia.org/wiki/Ghatotkacha
- rt.com, *Fukushima Mutant Butterflies Spark Fear of Effect on Humans*, (2012),
http://rt.com/news/fukushima-radiation-butterflies-mutate-672/
- Swoboda, L., *Races of Man*, (2012), http://www.astrologyedmonton.com/article-racesofman.htm
- remnantofgod.com, *The Eighth King*, (2012),
http://www.remnantofgod.org/king8.htm
- Biblos, *Revelation 17:10*, (2011), http://bible.cc/revelation/17-10.htm
- Wikipedia, *Root Race*, (2012),

Bibliography

http://en.wikipedia.org/wiki/Root_race#The_first_root_race
- Farthing, G., Deity, *Cosmos and Man: Outline of Esoteric Science*, Theosophical Publishing House, (1993)
- Gold. C, *Root Races*, (2010), http://campbellmgold.com/archive_esoteric/root_races.pdf
- Wikipedia, *Gondwana*, (2012), http://en.wikipedia.org/wiki/Gondwana
- Mojzesz, N., *The Stanzas of Dzyan*, (2008), http://users.ez2.net/nick29/theosophy/stanzas.htm
- Wikipedia, *Hesiod*, (2012), http://en.wikipedia.org/wiki/Hesiod
- OnlineTeosofiskaKompanietMalmo, *Bamian Buddha Statues and Theosophym*, (2001), http://www.teosofiskakompaniet.net/BamianTeosofiHPB2001.htm
- Afghan-network.net, *Bamiyan*, Afghanistan, (2012), http://www.afghan-network.net/Culture/bamian.html
- Theosociety.org, *The Bamian Statues: Their Mysterious Origin*, (2012), http://www.theosociety.org/pasadena/sunrise/50-00-1/as-hpb.htm
- Wikipedia, *Odyssey*, (2012), http://en.wikipedia.org/wiki/Odyssey
- Wikipedia, *Trojan War*, (2012), http://en.wikipedia.org/wiki/Trojan_War
- Wikipedia, *Troy*, (2012), http://en.wikipedia.org/wiki/Troy
- Scribd, *The Dogon*, (2012), http://www.scribd.com/doc/5007776/Marcel-Griaule-The-Dogon
- Wikipedia, *Dogon people*, (2012), http://en.wikipedia.org/wiki/Dogon_people
- Wikipedia, *Stonehenge*, (2012), http://en.wikipedia.org/wiki/Stonehenge
- Sagan, C. and Shklovskii, I., *Intelligent life in the Universe*, Delta Books, (1966)
- Wikipedia, *Alexander Polyhistor*, (2012), http://en.wikipedia.org/wiki/Alexander_Polyhistor
- Bergrun, N., *Ringmakers of Saturn*, The Pentland Press, First edition, (1986)
- NASA, *Solar System Exploration*, (2012), http://solarsystem.nasa.gov/planets/profile.cfm?Object=Saturn
- Wikipedia, *Saturn*, (2012), http://en.wikipedia.org/wiki/Saturn
- Dictionary.com, *Saturn*, (2012), http://dictionary.reference.com/browse/saturn
- SETI Institute, *Saturn's Ring System*, (2012), http://pds-rings.seti.org/saturn/
- Wikipedia, *John F. Kennedy*, (2012), http://en.wikipedia.org/wiki/John_F._Kennedy
- Hsu, J., *Saturn's Rings Still Puzzle Scientists*, (2009), http://www.msnbc.msn.com/id/32542771/ns/technology_and_science-space/t/saturns-rings-still-puzzle-scientists/#.UJQrDMUxruQ
- Wikipedia, *Cassini-Huygens*, (2012), http://en.wikipedia.org/wiki/Cassini%E2%80%93Huygens
- Wikipedia, *Galileo Galilei*, (2012), http://en.wikipedia.org/wiki/Galileo_Galilei

- Baalke, R., *Historical Background of Saturn's Rings,* (2012),
http://www2.jpl.nasa.gov/saturn/back.html
- Dawes, R., *Transit of Titan's Shadow across the Disk of Saturn, on 15th April
1862,* (2012), http://adsabs.harvard.edu/full/1862MNRAS..22..264D
- HubbleSite, *How Thick are Saturn's Rings?,* (2012),
http://hubblesite.org/reference_desk/faq/answer.php.id=11&cat=solarsystem
- Wikipedia, *William Rutter Dawes,* (2012),
http://en.wikipedia.org/wiki/William_Rutter_Dawes
- Wikipedia, *Moons of Saturn,* (2012),
http://en.wikipedia.org/wiki/Moons_of_Saturn#Tables_of_moons
- Wikipedia, *Space probe,* (2012), http://en.wikipedia.org/wiki/Space_probe
- Wikipedia, *Voyager 1,* (2012), http://en.wikipedia.org/wiki/Voyager_1
- NASA, *Voyager: The Interstellar Mission,* (2012),
http://voyager.jpl.nasa.gov/science/planetary.html
- Atkinson, N., *Voyager 1 Has Outdistanced the Solar Wind,* (2010),
http://www.universetoday.com/81662/voyager-1-has-outdistanced-the-solar-wind/
- Abovetopsecret.com, *Gigantic Alien Craft Photographed By Cassini,* (2007),
http://www.abovetopsecret.com/forum/thread301532/pg1
- Pegasus Research Consortium, *Cosmic Secrets,* (2007),
http://www.thelivingmoon.com/46_mike_singh/03files/Ships_Saturn.html
- Wikipedia, *Quasar,* (2012), http://en.wikipedia.org/wiki/Quasar
- Wikipedia, *Light-year,* (2012), http://en.wikipedia.org/wiki/Light-year
- Wikipedia, *Black Hole* (2012), http://en.wikipedia.org/wiki/Black_hole
- Freudenrich, C., *How Galaxies Work,* (2012),
http://science.howstuffworks.com/dictionary/astronomy-terms/galaxy5.htm
- Wikipedia, *Rings of Saturn,* (2012),
http://en.wikipedia.org/wiki/Rings_of_Saturn#Cassini_Division
- Wikipedia, *Johann Encke,* (2012), http://en.wikipedia.org/wiki/Johann_Encke
- Wikipedia, *James Edward Keeler,* (2012),
http://en.wikipedia.org/wiki/James_Edward_Keeler
- Wortham, J., *Cassini's Cosmic Recordings Double as Sci-Fi Soundtrack,* (2007),
http://www.wired.com/underwire/2007/11/cosmic-recordin/
- *ScienceDaily,* NASA's Cassini Listens To Eerie New 'Sounds' of Space Near
Jupiter, (2001),
http://www.sciencedaily.com/releases/2001/01/010108073050.htm
- Chen, E., *Saturn (Chronos), Eating His Children,* (2011),
http://www.science20.com/alchemist/saturn_chronos_eating_his_children
- Wikipedia, *Saturn Devouring His Son,* (2012),
http://en.wikipedia.org/wiki/Saturn_Devouring_His_Son

Bibliography

– Brinlee, D., *Who is the God of Time?*, (2012),
http://www.askdeb.com/education/greek/chronos/
– Wikipedia, *Tartarus*, (2012), http://en.wikipedia.org/wiki/Tartarus
– Wikipedia, *Tom Van Flandern*, (2012),
http://en.wikipedia.org/wiki/Tom_Van_Flandern
– NASA, *Cassini Images Bizarre Hexagon on Saturn*, (2007),
http://www.jpl.nasa.gov/news/news.php?release=2007-034

What was the original civilization on Earth?

Sumer, ancient China & the Indus Valley – the oldest civilizations on Earth.

what is our reason for existence ?

→ Close your eyes, Take a deep breath + ask yourself
→ how does my intuition answer this question ?

Steganography is the art + science of writing
hidden messages in such a way that only
the sender + intended recipient know
what the message is.

The Apostolic Palace is the official
residence of the Pope in the Vatican City

The extra-Terrestrials seem to be the Elohim of
the Bible

It is in the Third Race that the separation
of sexes occurred.

Pitris. pg. 122

budding - a type of asexual reproduction in
which a new individual or branch develops from
an outgrowth on the body of a plant or certain
lower animals.

→ Our god + the One True God are two different
entities.

204